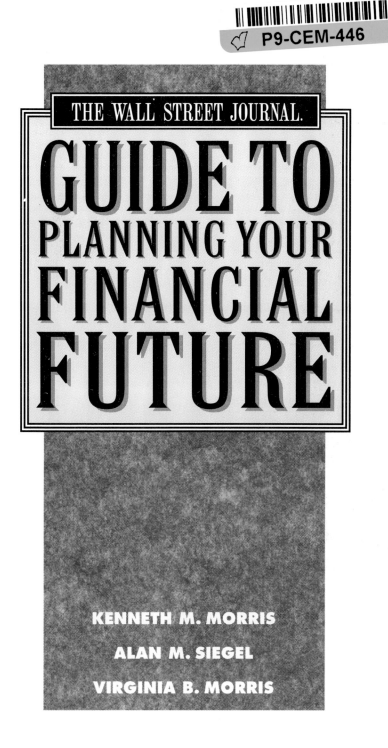

THE WALL STREET JOURNAL.
GUIDE TO
PLANNING YOUR
FINANCIAL
FUTURE

KENNETH M. MORRIS

ALAN M. SIEGEL

VIRGINIA B. MORRIS

LIGHTBULB

PRESS

CREDITS:

Creative Director
Dean Scharf

Design
Dave Wilder

Production
Leslie Daley, Kathleen Dolan,
Chris Hiebert, Kwee Wang

Illustration
Krista K. Glasser, Barnes Tilney

Photography
Andy Shen

Research
Richard Kroll

Film
Quad Right, Inc.

SPECIAL THANKS TO:

Dan Austin, Joan Wolf-Woolley, Doug Sease,
Deborah Lohse, Ellen Schultz, Nancy
Travaglione, Lottie Lindberg and Elizabeth
Yeh, *The Wall Street Journal*, Dow Jones & Co.

Hugh Joyner and John A. Gill, TIAA-CREF

Robert Berger, Carla Fey and Richard Irving,
Social Security

Greg Hess, Christy & Viener

Ira Cohen, Karen Halloran, Bill Lieber, Siegel &
Gale, Inc.

PICTURE CREDITS:

The Bettmann Archive, New York (pages 24, 68, 69, 70)
General Motors Corporation (page 95)
Comstock, New York (pages 40, 58, 59, 60, 82, 84)
FPG, New York (pages 36, 40, 60, 61, 83, 84)
The Image Bank, New York (pages 42, 54, 55, 61, 71, 84)
Reuters/Bettmann, New York (page 71)
UPI/Bettmann, New York (pages 61, 68, 70, 71)

LIGHTBULB
PRESS

*F*rom the time you receive your first paycheck you're making a down payment on your financial future. The money that's withheld for Social Security and Medicare is designed to provide a basic income—and help pay your health care costs—when you're retired.

But there's far more to planning your financial future—and a comfortable retirement—than Social Security. Along the way, there are critical decisions to make, numerous options to choose from, and special rules to know about, as well as plenty of baffling words you need to understand.

For example, what are the real advantages of investing in a 401(k) or another retirement savings plan?

What investments are safest, or most profitable, over the long haul?

When do you start withdrawing money from your retirement plan, and how much do you have to take?

What is a defined contribution plan? A bypass trust? A reverse mortgage? What does intestate mean? And why do you need to know?

In this guide, we've tried to answer these and many other perplexing questions that people face in planning their financial future. Perhaps the biggest question—"When should I start?"—is the easiest to answer: the sooner the better.

While it's never too late to start financial planning, thinking ahead when you're in your 20s and 30s can pay you very large dividends in your 60s and 70s—and probably beyond. The earlier you begin to put money away (even in small amounts), invest it for the long term, and know how to protect it, the more you'll have when you need it, or want it.

Though we realize there are many lifestyle decisions in planning for retirement, we've focused primarily on the financial issues, since they tend to be the most complex, and the least well understood. Yet they often have the greatest impact.

In preparing the guide, we are again deeply indebted to The Wall Street Journal for the resources and expertise they made available to us.

Kenneth M. Morris
Virginia B. Morris
Alan M. Siegel

THE WALL STREET JOURNAL.

GUIDE TO PLANNING YOUR FINANCIAL FUTURE

LOOKING AHEAD

6 The Retirement Marathon
8 Planning for the Future
10 Protecting Your Future
12 Money Matters
14 Making Critical Choices
16 Where to Live?
18 Using Your Equity
20 Making the Move

EMPLOYER PLANS

22 Qualified Retirement Plans
24 Pensions
26 Defined Benefit Plans
28 Defined Contribution Plans
30 Salary Reduction Plans
32 Matching and Switching
34 Self-directed Pension Plans
36 Supplemental Retirement Plans
38 Pension Decisions
40 Pension Choices
42 Pension Annuities
44 Lump Sum Distributions
46 Changing Jobs, Changing Pensions
48 Some Pension Problems

INDIVIDUAL PLANS

50 IRAs: What They Are
52 IRAs: Your Show
54 IRAs: Weighing the Merits
56 IRA Rollovers
58 SEPs
60 Keogh Plans
62 Keoghs
64 IRA Withdrawals
66 Taking Money Out

CONTENTS

SOCIAL SECURITY

68 Social Security
70 Changing for the Better
72 Benefit Ins and Outs
74 Social Security Up Close
76 Got You Covered
78 Figuring What You Get
80 When to Apply
82 Working after Retirement
84 Family Coverage
86 Survivor Benefits
88 Disability Benefits
90 Taxing Benefits

INVESTING

92 Personal Investing Goals
94 The Impact of Inflation
96 A Winning Strategy
98 The Right Moves
100 Diversity
102 Investment Risk
104 Allocating Your Assets
106 Asset Allocation Choices
108 Figuring Yield
110 Finding Return
112 Deferred Annuities
114 Immediate Annuities

ESTATE PLANNING

116 What's Your Estate?
118 What's in a Name?
120 Estate Taxes
122 Wills
124 Cooking Up a Will
126 Who's in a Will?
128 Beneficiaries
130 Acting as Executor
132 A Matter of Trust
134 Revocable Living Trusts
136 Irrevocable Living Trusts
138 Testamentary Taxsavers
140 The Universe of Trusts
142 Gifts
144 And More Gifts

HEALTH CARE

146 Protecting Health and Wealth
148 Examining the Details
150 Are You Covered?
152 HMOs
154 Medicare
156 What Medicare Covers
158 The Medicare Dictionary
160 The System at Work
162 Bridging the Gap
164 Shopping for Protection
166 Putting Medigap to Work
168 Long-term Care Insurance
170 The Limits of Coverage
172 Medicaid

The Retirement Marathon

Planning your financial future is planning for retirement—
and having the money to enjoy it.

In 1900, retirement wasn't a hot topic. Employers didn't offer pensions, there was no Social Security, and the average life expectancy was 50.

But nearly a century later, everything's changed. More than a million people retire every year, at an average age of 63—and they expect to live to be nearly 85. Current estimates even suggest that a million or more people now in their 40s can expect to live to be 100 or more.

READY, SET, GO
The general wisdom is that planning your financial future starts with your first job. That's when you can begin putting money into a tax-deferred Individual Retirement Account (IRA). Even though you'll probably have lots of shorter-term reasons to invest, such as buying a car or a home, you should be thinking early on about long-term goals: your financial security and the security of those you care about. You'll quickly discover that there are lots of ways to invest for the future—including some that have tax-advantages built in.

In Your 20s: Getting Started

You can get a head start on building your financial future if you start early. The two opportunities you don't want to pass up:

- Contributing to a **voluntary tax-deferred retirement plan**

- Setting up an **investment account** with a mutual fund, brokerage or bank.

While you may be paying off college debts or struggling to meet living expenses, the advantages of getting an early start on a long-term investment plan are too good to pass up.

Ideally, you should be investing up to 10% of your income, but half of that is better than nothing. If you're in an employer-sponsored plan that deducts your contribution from your salary, your taxable income will be reduced. That means tax savings—a reward for doing the right thing.

Though some of what you've put aside should be **liquid**, or easy to turn into cash, the best investments are generally stocks or stock mutual funds. The growth they provide usually justifies the risk of possible setbacks in the short term.

In Your 30s & 40s: Hitting Your Stride

Even while you're juggling your income to pay for things that might seem more pressing, like buying a home, supporting a family, or anticipating your children's college expenses, you need to build your long-term investments.

One technique is to split the amount you invest between long- and short-term goals. Even if you put less into long-term plans than you'd like, at least these investments will grow, especially if you're building on a portfolio you started in your 20s. Experts agree that long-term investments should still be in stocks or stock mutual funds, but short-term investments should be more liquid.

Keep in mind that investing for the long term is good for your current financial situation too:

- **You save on taxes by participating in a salary-reduction plan.**

- **You may qualify for a mortgage more easily if you have investment assets.**

- **You can borrow from some retirement investments without incurring taxes and penalties.**

WHAT THE FUTURE HOLDS

The truth is that retirement age is relative, not fixed. Many government workers retire after 20 years of service—sometimes as soon as their early forties. Some people work productively through their 80s, thinking of retirement as something other people do. Many others retire the first day they're eligible. Still others leave work unwillingly, taking early retirement packages they can't refuse.

What you do about retirement may fit one of those patterns, or maybe one you design for yourself. But whether retirement is a long way off, or sneaking up on you faster than you care to imagine, planning for your financial future has three main ingredients:

- **Your financial security**
- **Adequate health care**
- **Benefits for your heirs**

In Your 40s & 50s: The Far Turn

You may be earning more than before, but you may be spending more too. College expenses can wreak havoc on long-term investment goals. So can expensive hobbies, or moving to a bigger house.

On the other hand, if you've established good investing habits—like participating in a salary reduction plan and putting money into stocks and stock mutual funds—your long-term goals should be on track. You may also find that the demands on your current income eventually begin to decrease: the mortgage gets paid off, the children eventually grow up, or you inherit assets from your parents.

That means you can begin to put more money into your long-term portfolio—through your employer's voluntary salary-reduction plans, through mutual fund or brokerage accounts, and through some income-producing investments such as CDs and bonds.

AN EASY FORMULA

One rule of thumb for deciding what investments to make: add a percent sign to your age. You should have no more than that percentage of your money in fixed income investments like bonds or CDs. The rest should be in stocks.

In Your 60s: The Home Stretch

When you start thinking seriously about retirement, you have to be sure you have enough money to live comfortably. If you have a good pension and substantial investments, you'll have the flexibility to retire when you want.

Because you can expect to live 20 or 30 years after you retire, you'll want to continue to invest even as you begin collecting on your retirement plans. One approach is to deposit earnings on certain investments into an account earmarked to make new ones. Another is to time the maturity dates of bonds or other fixed income assets, like CDs, so that you have capital to reinvest if a good opportunity comes along.

Some of the other financial decisions you'll be facing may be dictated by government rules about when and what you must withdraw from your retirement accounts. Others may be driven by your concerns about health care or your desire to leave money to your heirs. At the least, you'll have to consider:

- **Shifting investments to produce more income with fewer risks, in case of a sudden downturn in the stock market**

- **Rolling over retirement payouts to preserve their tax-deferred status**

- **Finding ways to reduce estate taxes and pay for those that are unavoidable.**

Planning for the Future

To live comfortably after you retire, you have to be realistic about how much you'll need to pay the bills.

Good health is wonderful. So is a nice place to live. But what you really need when you retire is money— money to pay your bills, with enough left over to do the things you want. The general rule of thumb is this: you'll need 70% to 80% of what you're spending before you retire, more if you have expensive hobbies or plan to travel extensively. For example,

CURRENT INCOME X 80% = PROJECTED NEED

if your gross income while you're working is $6,000 a month—that's $72,000 a year— you'll probably need $4,800 a month, or about $57,600 a year, after you retire.

UP OR DOWN?

You can be pretty sure some of your living expenses will shrink after you retire, but others are equally certain to go up. Planning your financial future includes anticipating those changes.

WHAT COSTS LESS

- By the time you retire, you'll probably have paid off your mortgage.

- Unless you were older than average when your children were born, you will have finished paying for their educations.

- If you commuted to work, you'll probably spend less on day-to-day travel and restaurant meals. You may need only one car, and will probably spend less on clothes and make fewer visits to the dry cleaner.

WHAT COSTS MORE

- Home maintenance costs and property taxes tend to go up, not down, over time, unless you move to a smaller place or to a state with lower taxes.

- If you're home all the time, your utility bills may increase.

- Home and car insurance are apt to increase.

- Medical expenses, including the cost of insurance, tend to skyrocket—500% or more over pre-retirement costs isn't unheard of. These costs will continue to rise as employers cut back on health care coverage in general, and for retirees in particular. For example, the average retired person spends $500 a year on prescription drugs, which aren't covered under most insurance plans.

INFLATION'S BITE

Inflation is another factor you have to consider when planning your retirement budget. If you were retiring this June, for example, you'd need 80% of what you were spending in May. But next June you'd need more money to pay for the same goods and services.

That's because of **inflation**, the gradual increase in the cost of living. Inflation has averaged 4% in the U.S. since 1926, and while it has been lower in the last few years, it has sometimes been substantially higher—hitting 14% in the early 1980s, for example.

That means if you're planning on a 20-year retirement, you'll need more than double the income in the 20th year than you do in the first, just to stay even. How can you manage that, especially if you're not working any more? The surest way is by earning money on your investments, at a rate that tops the rate of inflation (see page 94).

DOING THE MATH

While it might take a long time to estimate your retirement needs if you were doing the math yourself, you can use one of the software programs available through mutual fund companies and brokerage houses to get a sense of where you stand. Often you can get the packages free for the asking. The Wall Street Journal regularly reviews the programs available and tells you how to obtain them.

The software programs are generally easy to use. All you have to do is plug in the financial information they ask for, along with details about your plans for the future. The program will tell you how much more you'll need to invest to have enough money to retire on. Not surprisingly, you'll also get suggestions for ways to invest through the company that has developed the program.

If a financial planner or bank officer does the analysis for you, you may be charged a fee. But chances are they'll use programs similar to the ones you could use yourself for free.

ADDING IT ALL UP

	STARTING AGE	PERCENT SAVED	SALARY REPLACED
	30	10%	70%
	40	21%	70%
	50	48%	70%
	55	84%	70%

If you start investing 35 years before you're ready to retire, and you save only 10% of what you earn each year, you'll have enough put aside to replace 70% of your salary.

For each year you delay, you'll have to save more of your yearly earnings to build up the same reserves. Most people would have trouble taking that much out of their salary, no matter how important they know it is to save.

SPECIAL CASES

You may have certain special advantages in planning your financial future. Veterans, for example, can apply for mortgages, health care coverage and disability benefits through the Veteran's Administration. They may also qualify for local tax breaks, and get pension credit for their years on active service.

Union members and members of professional and other organizations may qualify for health and life insurance at lower rates than those available to the general population, or for other kinds of reduced-rate goods and services. Sometimes members of the clergy are offered discounts too.

In any case, you should check with any groups you're part of for the long-term financial advantages that may come with your membership. The larger ones may also keep you up to date on tax and other changes that affect your finances directly, through newsletters, journals or other publications.

Protecting Your Future

The best protection for a comfortable future is a strong financial plan.

To safeguard your own financial future and the future of people who matter to you, you need a strategy that builds your assets at the same time that it protects them against the assaults of taxes, inflation, and the general costs of living.

Job-related pensions and retirement savings plans, plus the investments you make throughout your working life, are the basic asset-building materials you need. The sooner you begin hammering them into place, the stronger your position will be. And by writing a will and perhaps creating a trust or two, you can go on protecting the security you've built for your heirs to enjoy.

THREATS TO YOUR FINANCIAL SECURITY

INFLATION
Inflation erodes your buying power because prices always go up. Your income may not keep pace.

HEALTH CARE
The cost of health care has been increasing much faster than inflation in general.

ESTATE TAXES
Estate taxes can gobble up to 55% percent of what you leave to your heirs.

WITHDRAWAL PENALTIES
You have to pay a penalty each time you take too much or too little from your retirement plans.

INCOME TAXES
Income taxes can be your single largest expense, even after you retire.

LOCAL TAXES
Some places are much more expensive to live in because they have higher taxes.

FINDING A BUILDER

There's no single source for the information you need to build your financial future, but you can get parts of what you need from your employer or professional association's retirement adviser, from Social Security, and from your broker, banker, lawyer, accountant or financial planner.

If you use a financial planner, look for one who is paid on a fee-only basis. That means you pay a consulting fee, but the planner does not earn commissions on financial products you buy, or investments you make. When earnings are tied to commissions, you may be pressured—sometimes subtly and sometimes not so subtly—to plan for retirement in ways that enrich the planner. If you don't get a straight answer on how your planner is paid, you're probably better off looking for someone else.

THE MAIN PROTECTIONS

EMPLOYER PENSIONS
Pensions can provide a significant part of your post-retirement income.

RETIREMENT SAVINGS PLANS
Qualified plans let your retirement investments grow tax-deferred.

SOCIAL SECURITY
By contributing while you work, you earn the right to income after you retire.

WISE INVESTMENTS
The difference between just getting by and living comfortably will probably depend on your investments.

MEDICARE
You'll be entitled to basic medical coverage after you retire if you contribute while you work.

HEALTH INSURANCE
You can buy health insurance to help ward off financial catastrophe.

WILLS AND TRUSTS
With advance planning, you can reduce estate taxes and benefit your heirs.

Money Matters

Taking care of business won't take any less time after you retire, though you can save money.

If you think of retirement as a simpler time of life, you may be in for a shock, at least in the paperwork department. That's because things your employer handled—tax withholding and health insurance payments, for example—are now your personal responsibility.

On top of that, you'll probably have to spend more time moving money among accounts to maintain your cash flow once you get your final paycheck. And if you're taking money out of tax-deferred retirement plans, you'll have to be on top of the withdrawal rules. They're different for different accounts.

There's also the added time and expense of making photocopies of medical bills for your records. You'll need them as backup if you want to contest a Medicare decision or claim a tax deduction. But if being retired won't save you time, it may save you some money on different types of taxes.

TAX MATTERS

One of the biggest changes after retirement may be paying estimated income taxes four times a year. Of course, if you've worked for yourself or had a lot of non-salary income, filling out the forms and writing a check to the IRS (and your state tax department) is nothing new. But if you've always had your income taxes withheld from your salary, figuring out what you owe each quarter can be an eye-opener.

You make your first payment on April 15—the same day the previous year's tax return is due—and the others on June 15, September 15, and the following January 15. In most cases, you must prepay either 90% of what you'll actually owe or 100% of what you paid in tax the previous year, in installments that are at least 25% of the total. However, if your taxable income is more than $250,000, you must prepay 110% of last year's total tax.

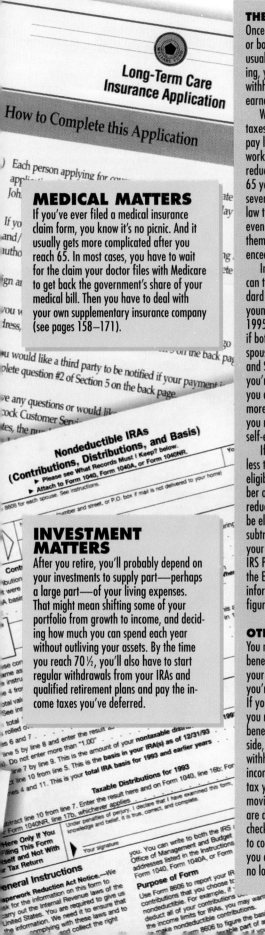

MEDICAL MATTERS

If you've ever filed a medical insurance claim form, you know it's no picnic. And it usually gets more complicated after you reach 65. In most cases, you have to wait for the claim your doctor files with Medicare to get back the government's share of your medical bill. Then you have to deal with your own supplementary insurance company (see pages 158–171).

INVESTMENT MATTERS

After you retire, you'll probably depend on your investments to supply part—perhaps a large part—of your living expenses. That might mean shifting some of your portfolio from growth to income, and deciding how much you can spend each year without outliving your assets. By the time you reach 70½, you'll also have to start regular withdrawals from your IRAs and qualified retirement plans and pay the income taxes you've deferred.

THE SMALLER TAX BITE

Once you retire or reach the age of 65, or both, your tax picture often changes—usually for the better. After you stop working, you won't have Social Security taxes withheld, since pensions aren't considered earned income.

While you'll still owe federal income taxes after you retire, chances are you'll pay less than you did while you were working, especially if your total income is reduced. That's because once you turn 65 you may be able to take advantage of several provisions in the tax law that lower your bill, even though the tax rates themselves aren't influenced by your age.

In the first place, you can take a larger standard deduction than a younger person—in 1995 it is $1,500 more if both you and your spouse are over 65, and $950 more if you're single. And you can make slightly more money than a younger person before you must file a return at all unless you have self-employment income.

If your total income after retirement is less than $83,850 (for 1994), you're also eligible for a deduction based on the number of exemptions you claim, which will reduce your taxable income. And, you may be eligible for a tax credit, which you can subtract directly from the tax that's due if your income falls below a specific amount. IRS Publication 524, Tax Information for the Elderly and the Disabled, provides the information and worksheets you need to figure out where you stand.

OTHER TAX BREAKS

You may not owe tax on your Social Security benefit if your total income (including half your Social Security) is less than $25,000 if you're single, or $34,000 if you're married. If your income is more than that, though, you may owe tax on 50% to 85% of your benefit (see pages 90–91). On the brighter side, you won't have Social Security taxes withheld from your pension or investment income. The state where you live may not tax your pension—or you may consider moving to a state that doesn't. The rules are different in each state, so you'll have to check. One caution, though: some states try to collect income taxes on pension money you earned within their borders, even if you no longer live there.

Making Critical Choices

You'll have the answers you need down the road if you ask the right questions now.

The idea of retiring isn't new. People who grew too old or too ill stopped working and stayed home long before pensions and Social Security. But as people stop working sooner and live longer, the retirement experience takes on a different meaning. Not only can you expect more years of retirement than of adolescence, but they can be a lot more satisfying and rewarding.

Q: What financial decisions do I make?

A: Set your retirement timeline

55

- You can take a one-time $125,000 capital gains exclusion on the sale of your home.
- You can begin withdrawing from 401(k)s, Keoghs, SEP-IRAs and profit-sharing plans without a 10% penalty if you retire, quit or are fired.
- You may be eligible for full pension benefits from some company plans if you have enough years of service.

59½

- You can withdraw money from tax-deferred savings plans (IRAs, Keoghs, SEPs) without paying a 10% penalty.
- You can qualify for forward averaging of a lump-sum pension payout.

60

- You can receive Social Security benefits if you are a widow or widower.

SOME CRITICAL CHOICES

As morbid as sounds, even as you're looking forward to retirement, you need to deal with two critical issues: the medical decisions you want made if you're ill, and what you want to happen to your property after you die. If you don't make your intentions clear, your family and friends face a greater emotional burden and often greater expense than they might otherwise. And you might not approve of the decisions that are made without your direction.

It's not enough just to tell people what you want to happen. State laws often require written proof of your wishes concerning life-prolonging treatment if you're critically ill, just as they require a legal will to transfer your property.

Q: How do I make my health care wishes known?

A: A Living Will

A **living will** is a document that describes the kind of medical treatment you want—and don't want—if you are terminally ill or in a permanent vegetative state (which means you're unconscious, not able to communicate, and unlikely to get better). In writing your living will, you should be as specific as possible about the kinds of drugs and medical procedures you have in mind and the situations under which they should—or should not be—used.

Though all states accept living wills, the laws of each state are a little different, so you want to be sure that the living will you sign

Q: How can someone make decisions for me?

A: Health Care Proxy

A living will makes your wishes known, but it does not always guarantee they will be followed. Someone will still have to authorize your treatment, or make a decision not to continue it. You can appoint a health care agent or surrogate in a signed and witnessed document known as a **health care proxy,** or you can grant a **durable power of attorney for health care** to someone who will make the decisions you would have wanted.

You should also be sure to ask the permission of the person you name, and describe your feelings about your care in detail. Without understanding what you want, it would be very difficult for your surrogate to see that your wishes are carried out. Because there are still unresolved legal questions about the extent of a surrogate's authority, it probably makes sense to get legal advice in preparing these documents.

62
- You may be eligible for full pension benefits from your employer.
- You can receive reduced Social Security benefits.

65
- You can receive full pension benefits from most employers.
- You can get full Social Security benefits if you were born before 1940.
- You qualify for Medicare benefits.

70
- You can receive full Social Security benefits even if you are working full-time.

70½
- You must begin withdrawals from IRAs and other tax-deferred savings plans.

meets local requirements. One area that remains unresolved, for example, is whether a hospital will respect your wish not to receive food and water. Some states require that feeding be continued as long as you are alive. Others allow it to be ended if that's what you've indicated in your living will.

Since professional caregivers generally choose to prolong life when possible, you probably don't need a living will if you agree with that approach. But if you're opposed to extraordinary measures to keep you alive, such as heart-lung machines, intravenous feeding and similar techniques, you should sign a living will and ask two people to witness it. You should also be sure your family and your doctor know that you've signed a living will and where they can find a copy.

You don't need a lawyer to draw up the document, although if you're in the process of preparing a regular will, you can sign both kinds at once, probably for little or no additional charge. Otherwise, you can get a standard form to fill in, or a model to copy. One source is the Choices in Dying, at 200 Varick Street, New York, NY 10014.

THE RIGHT TIME

When's the right time to sign a living will and a health care proxy? If you have strong feelings about the way you want to be cared for if you're ill or injured, you can do it as soon as you reach the age of majority in the state where you live, either 18 or 21. It's easy to think of health care as a problem for the elderly, but the truth is most of the major court cases involving a patient's right to receive a particular type of treatment or her right to die have dealt with young people—often in their late teens or early 20s—who were injured in an accident or became ill unexpectedly.

DRAFTING A WILL

If you want your wishes about the transfer of your property and the care of your dependent children carried out after you die, you must **execute,** or sign, an official will and have it witnessed (see pages 122–125). Young people, and those without dependents or property, may be able to postpone making a will. But anyone else is making a serious mistake by putting it off.

Where to Live?

Is your home your castle, or just a place to hang your hat?

Where will you live when you retire? The majority of Americans—about 75%—stay put, not only in the same community where they've spent their working lives, but often in the same house or apartment where they've been living. Of those who do move, most settle less than 30 miles away. Only a few—about 5%—actually move out of state.

One increasingly popular option, if you can swing it financially, is **sojourning**, or using your primary residence as home base, but shifting to a second home during part of the year. People who enjoy the flexibility and change of scene consider it an ideal way to enjoy the best of two worlds. For others, who've tried but abandoned it, it's rootless and unsettling.

Our Estate

WHICH HOME SWEET HOME

MARKET FORCES

If you own your home outright or have only a small mortgage, you can probably make enough from selling your home to move wherever you want, especially if you're in the market for a smaller place. In fact, most people sell their homes for more than they paid for them unless their neighborhood has gone downhill or the property itself needs a lot of work.

Remember, though, that real estate isn't a liquid investment, and you can't count on how much the property will be worth when you're ready to sell. The housing market is sometimes slow, or depressed, which might mean you can't sell at all or have to settle for a lower price than you counted on. The reverse is also true: if real estate is in a boom period, you'll make more on your house than you expected. But you might also have to pay more for the place you want to move to.

LIVING ABROAD

Every month, Social Security sends around 400,000 checks to U.S. citizens living outside the country. And that doesn't include the people who have their checks deposited in banks at home. There are lots of financial advantages, and probably an equal number of drawbacks, to making the move abroad. Most of them hinge on tax issues, though currency fluctuation, health care and estate planning are also involved.

SHARING YOUR SPACE

If the cost or the work involved in keeping up your home is a problem, one option is to share your living space, either with friends or family members who split the costs, or with tenants who pay rent.

Having people in the house can be a real plus, since they provide companionship as well as help with finances or household chores. There's certainly a tradition behind it. But, before you commit yourself to sharing, you'll want to consider the arrangements carefully, and check restrictions in local zoning laws.

WEIGHING THE FACTORS

You can weigh financial and other factors to help you decide whether to move or to stay put. They include:

- Annual cost of maintenance and upkeep, including mortgage, utilities and taxes
- Physical demands of maintenance and upkeep
- General cost of living, including food, transportation and entertainment
- Availability of quality health care
- Distance from family and friends

SELL BUT STAY

Another way to use the equity in your home is to sell on the condition you can go on living there, an agreement known as a **sale-leaseback**. You can make your agreement with family members, friends, charities or commercial investors at whatever price you agree on (often somewhat less than fair market value of your home), for whatever term you like (often 10–15 years). Setting a fair value is most important if the buyer is a family member, because you don't want the transfer to be considered a taxable gift.

The new owner pays off the cost of the home over the term of the agreement, and you pay rent out of the income you're getting on the sale. To prevent a problem if you want to continue living in your home when the agreement ends, you can buy an annuity to replace the income you'll need to pay the rent.

There are often estate-planning advantages in sale-leasebacks. If you sell to a relative or close friend, you can reduce your estate for tax purposes, and avoid probate (see pages 122–123).

Using Your Equity

Your home has financial as well as emotional value.

If you're reluctant to move after you retire, but find that living in your home costs more than you can afford, you can look for ways to use your **equity**, or share of ownership, as a source of occasional cash, or even of regular income.

REVERSE MORTGAGES

Reverse mortgages are one way people who own their homes may be able to tap the equity they've built up.

With a reverse mortgage, a bank or other lender sets the amount that you, the homeowner, can borrow. But instead of repaying the lender a fixed amount each month until the loan is paid off and you own the home—as you would with a regular mortgage—just the opposite happens: The lender *gives you money* against the equity in your home, either on a fixed schedule over a period of years or as often as you need it. In other words, you gradually give up ownership of your home in return for cash.

The long-term effect is the reverse of a regular mortgage, too. With a regular mortgage, you build up your equity each time you make a payment. But with a reverse mortgage, your equity decreases each time the lender gives you money.

Because a reverse mortgage is a *loan*, just the way a regular mortgage is, the lender charges you interest. Sooner or later the lender will want back not only the full amount of the loan, or principal, but also the interest that has built up on the amount you borrowed.

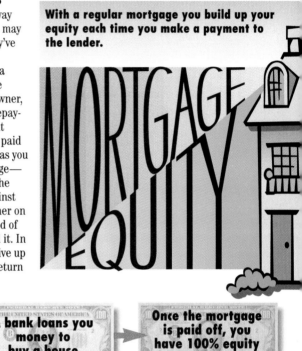

With a regular mortgage you build up your equity each time you make a payment to the lender.

A bank loans you money to buy a house

Once the mortgage is paid off, you have 100% equity in your house

In most agreements, the loan amount plus interest is paid off by your estate after you die, usually by selling your house. In the meantime, however, your equity in the home, including any increase in value over the term of the loan, is transferred to the lender. That means that when the house is eventually sold, the lender, and not your estate, benefits from the increased value.

THE SCORECARD FOR REVERSE MORTGAGES

PLUSSES	MINUSES
Ready source of cash	Reduced equity in your home
No income taxes due on payments because it's a loan, not income	Loan must be repaid
No capital gains tax, though loan amount is based on the current value of your property	No benefit from additional increases in the value of your home
No reduction of Social Security payments, since it's a loan, not income	Possibility of paying high interest rates, and sometimes high closing costs
	Potential for being dispossessed
	Reduced estate to leave your heirs

ARRANGING A DEAL

When you apply for a reverse mortgage, the lender determines how much you can borrow and the interest rate you'll pay. The loan amount is based on three things: the value of your house, your equity in it, and your age. Generally speaking, the older you are, the larger the loan you qualify for.

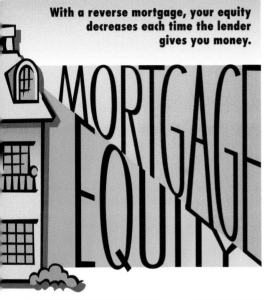

With a reverse mortgage, your equity decreases each time the lender gives you money.

A bank gives you a reverse mortgage based on your equity in the house → **The payments you get reduce your equity to zero by the time the mortgage ends**

BORROWER BEWARE

If you sign an agreement that covers a fixed number of years instead of your lifetime, you could still be alive when the pact ends. With the equity in your house used up, you might not be able to afford to go on living there. The same could happen to your surviving spouse, unless the agreement specifically covers both your lifetimes. One of the advantages of government-insured loans is that repayment is never due while you (or your spouse) is still living in the house. But that doesn't solve the problem of what happens if you are forced to move out.

And if you decide to move after you're agreed to a reverse mortgage, you'll have to pay back all the money you've received, plus interest, closing costs on the loan, and any appreciation in the value in the house. That would probably use up most of what you could sell your house for—and maybe more.

MORTGAGE TYPES

Since there are only a limited number of lenders, and these loans are breaking new ground, the rates have tended to be high—something you should watch in negotiating any agreement.

If you decide to take the mortgage, you'll begin getting your money according to the terms you agree to. These are the different types in order of popularity:

- **Lines of credit, which let you take money from your reverse mortgage account as you need it, usually by writing a check against the available amount**

- **Regular monthly payments, which are the most like a regular mortgage, but in reverse**

- **Lump sum payments, in which you get the total amount of the loan at one time.**

INSURED LOANS

Some reverse mortgages are backed by the Federal Housing Administration (FHA) or the Federal National Mortgage Association (FNMA). Those agencies guarantee that you'll get the full amount of the loan you've agreed to even if the lender gets into financial trouble. However, FHA and FNMA set a cap on the amount you can borrow based on your equity and the housing market you live in. That amount is usually considerably less than the actual value of the house, because the cost of borrowing plus the cost of the insurance must also be covered by the equity.

BREAKING GROUND

The first reverse mortgage dates back to 1961, but the concept hasn't exactly taken the market by storm. In 1989, the federal government began its program of insuring the loans through the FHA, authorizing up to 25,000 of them through September 1995. But whether it's a growth market or not remains to be seen.

Making the Move

Some people have their bags all packed, ready to move the day they retire.

Though the statistics show that most people stay put after they retire, you may think of retirement as the time to move to the mountains, the desert or the beach—or any place away from where you live now. Before you go, you may want to sell your home so you can afford the new life and home you want.

THE COSTS OF SELLING

If you use a real estate agent to sell your house, as most people do, you'll owe a commission, usually 5% to 7% of the sale price. You'll owe your lawyer a fee, too, plus a state transfer tax and your share of the real estate taxes. And you may be responsible for certain closing costs as well, depending on the terms of the sales contract. There's no hard-and-fast rule about who pays for specific expenses like termite inspections or title searches.

There's more flexibility in how much fix-up and repair work you do to make your house attractive to buyers. Some people believe it doesn't pay to put money into the house because the buyers will have their own ideas for improvements. Others argue that buyers respond better to places that look good, and that some new paint and a general fix-up pay for themselves in quicker sales and higher prices.

If there are major problems with the house, though, like a bad roof or an aging furnace, you may have to lower the sales price in negotiating the final contract. You have to gamble on which way you'll come out ahead.

CAPITAL GAINS TAX

If you sell your house for more than you paid for it, you may owe tax on your **capital gains**. You figure capital gains by subtracting the **cost basis** and the expenses of selling from the price you get when you sell your property. The cost basis is the amount you've paid, plus what you've invested in improvements. What remains is your profit, or **gain**, also known as your **adjusted sales price**.

FIGURING COST BASIS

Original purchase price	+	Cost of improvement	=	Cost basis

for example

$ 89,000	Original purchase price	
+ 9,000	Replaced roof	
+ 5,500	Remodeled bedroom	
+ 12,000	Converted attic	
= $ 115,500	**COST BASIS**	

FIGURING PROFIT OR LOSS

Selling price	−	Cost basis	−	Cost of selling	=	Profit

for example

$ 250,000	Selling price
− 115,500	Cost basis
− 600	Title insurance, transfer taxes
− 750	Legal fees
− 15,000	Real estate commission
= $ 118,150	**PROFIT**

Form **2119**

Department of the Treasury
Internal Revenue Service

Your first name and initial. If a joint return, als give s

RICHARD AND

Fill in Your Address
Only If You Are Filing
This Form by Itself
and Not With Your
Tax Return

Present address no, s
331 M
City, town or post office,
GRAND

Part I General Information

1 Date your former main home was so
2 Have you bought or built a new mai
3 Is or was any part of either main hor

Part II Gain on Sale—Do not inclu

4 Selling price of home. Do not include
5 Expense of sale (see instructions)
   Amount realized. Subtract line 5 from
   Adjusted basis of home sold (see instr
   Gain on sale. Subtract line 7 from line

Is line 8 more than zero? — Yes →

— No

If you haven't replaced your home, do yo
• If line 9 is "Yes," stop here, attach this
• If line 9 is "No," you must go to Part III

III One-Time Exclusion of Gain for
the one-time exclusion (see instruc

Who was age 55 or older on the date of sa
id the person who was age 55 or older ow
ast 3 years (except for short absences) of th
the time of sale, who owned the home?
cial security number of spouse at the tim
above. If you were not married at the tim
lusion. Enter the **smaller** of line 8 or $12
n, go to line 15

Adjusted Sales Price, Taxable Gain

e 14 is blank, enter the amount from line 8
ine 15 is zero, stop and attach this form t
ne 15 is more than zero and line 2 is "Yes
ou are reporting this sale on the installmer
thers, stop and **enter the amount from line
up expenses** (see instructions for time lim

17 If line 14 is blank, enter amount from line
18 **Adjusted sales pri**

DEFERRING YOUR TAXES

You can postpone paying tax on your profit if you buy another house that costs more than the one you just sold—provided you meet these conditions:

- **You buy within two years.**
- **The property (in each case) is your primary residence.**
- **You haven't deferred taxes on the sale of another house within the last two years.**

If you pay less—as you might if you buy a smaller house or move out of a high-priced area—you can still postpone taxes if you make enough improvements to boost your cost basis above the amount you got for selling your old house. There are no restrictions on what you do. You just have to make the improvements within two years.

Eventually, of course, your accumulated gains—those you've deferred each time you moved—may come due. But if you leave your house to a new owner in your will, that person doesn't inherit the tax bill.

BEFORE YOU SAY "I DO"

If you're planning to marry, and each of you owns your own home, it pays to do some prenuptial calculation to get the most out of the age 55 exclusion. If either spouse has ever taken the exclusion, you won't be eligible to take it as a couple after you marry. It might not be a problem if you're planning to move into one of the homes. But, if you're each planning to sell and buy a new home together, each of you is entitled to an exclusion before you marry. Just think of it as a wedding present from Uncle Sam.

AND BETTER YET...

If you're 55 or over when you sell, you can take advantage of a once-in-a-lifetime tax **exclusion** of up to $125,000 in profit on the sale of your primary residence.

If you own a second home that has appreciated more in value than your primary one, you might consider shifting your official residence to take advantage of the larger exclusion. It does involve some planning ahead, though. You must have lived in the house full-time for three of the five years before you sell.

Sale of Your Home

- Attach to Form 1040 for year of sale.
- parate instructions. ▶ Please print or type.

OMB No. 1545-0072

1993

Attachment Sequence No. 20

RY GARDNER Last name

STREET no., rural route, or P.O. box no. if mail is not delivered to street address)

Your social security number
123 : 45 : 6789

IP code
E, VT 08765

Spouse's social security number
098 : 76 : 5432

h, day, year) ▶ 1 1 / 10 / 95

out or used for business? If "Yes," see instructions — ☑ Yes ☐ No
nts you deduct as moving expenses. — ☐ Yes ☑ No

property items you sold with your home

4	250,000 —
5	16,350 —
6	233,650 —
7	115,500 —
8	118,150 —

2 is "Yes," you **must** go to Part III or Part IV, whichever applies. If line 2 is go to line 9.

nd attach this form to your return.

do so within the **replacement period** (see instructions)? ☐ Yes ☑ No
our return, and see **Additional Filing Requirements** in the instructions.
V, whichever applies.

Age 55 or Older—By completing this part, you are electing to take you are not electing to take the exclusion, go to Part IV now.

the property as his or her main home for a total of at — ☐ You ☐ Your spouse ☑ Both of you
period before the sale? If "No," go to Part IV now

if you had a different spouse from the — ☐ You ☐ Your spouse
, enter "None". — ☐ Yes ☑ No ☐ Both of you

62,500 if married filing separate return). ▶ 13 NONE

djusted Basis of New Home 14 118,500 —
ise, subtract line 14 from line 8
turn.

ine 16 now. 15 0

d, stop and see the instructions.
chedule D, col. (g). line 1

WHY SAY NO?

While you can take the exclusion anytime after age 55, you may wait, to keep your options open. Then its still available if you decide not to buy again—for example, if you move into a retirement community—or if you decide to buy a smaller, cheaper house. In either case, having the exclusion can save you money.

THE RIGHT FORM

You're required to report the sale of real estate to the IRS, whether you exclude, defer or pay the tax that's due on your gain. You can find out everything you need to know in Publication 523—Selling Your Home. You have to report the sale of your primary residence on Form 2119, and the sale of vacation and rental property on Schedule D.

Qualified Retirement Plans

If you cultivate tax-deferred investments, you'll have a cash crop to live on when you retire.

To produce a healthy supply of cash—and to be sure it's there when you need it—you have to invest for retirement while you're working. You can participate in employer-sponsored retirement plans, invest in retirement savings plans of your own, or both. As long as you're using a plan that meets the government's legal requirements, it counts as a qualified retirement investment.

GREENBACK

QUALIFIED INVESTMENT PLAN

GROWS FAST TAX-RESISTANT

- SOW EARLY AND OFTEN
- CULTIVATE WELL
- DO NOT HARVEST UNTIL MATURE

PRIZE-WINNING PLANS

Many types of plans are qualified, and, in general, they work like this: in return for postponing taxes until you start receiving your retirement income, you give up access to the money that's invested.

If you're contributing to a plan that you set up yourself, as you might do if you're self-employed, you have to be sure your plan complies with the regulations. But if your plan is employer-sponsored, the plan administrator is responsible for following the rules:

ELIGIBILITY

A plan must offer the same options to everyone who is eligible to participate, and the eligibility rules must be applied consistently.

ANNUAL CONTRIBUTION

There are specific limits on the amount you can contribute each year to certain qualified plans.

PAYOUT REGULATIONS

In most cases, you must be 59½ before you start to withdraw from a retirement plan. There is also a limit on the amount you can receive from all your qualified pension plans in any year before owing additional tax.

TYPES OF QUALIFIED PLANS

Both employer-funded plans and employee contribution plans can be qualified. The major difference is the source of the money that's invested—whether your employer puts it in, over and above your salary, or it's taken out of your salary. You may participate in several different plans, either at the same time or at different points in your working life.

Pension plans are funded by your employer, with money that's separate from your salary. Your employer gets to deduct the contribution from corporate income tax.

Retirement savings plans are funded with a portion of your earnings. The amount of your contribution is subtracted from the amount reported as income to the IRS, decreasing your current taxes.

Many employers also contribute to your retirement savings plan, often a percentage of your contribution up to a fixed cap.

A Qualified Advantage

With a qualified retirement plan, you postpone or defer paying taxes on contributions and investment earnings, until you begin withdrawing money. The difference in growth between a tax-deferred and a taxable investment is shown dramatically in the chart below. For example, it can mean that a $100,000 investment becomes $215,892 before taxes after 10 years—instead of $171,000. That's an unqualified advantage.

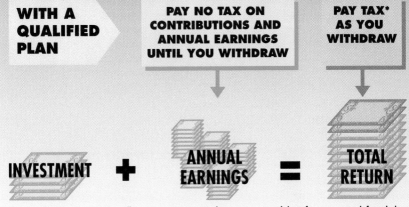

WITH A QUALIFIED PLAN | **PAY NO TAX ON CONTRIBUTIONS AND ANNUAL EARNINGS UNTIL YOU WITHDRAW** | **PAY TAX* AS YOU WITHDRAW**

INVESTMENT + **ANNUAL EARNINGS** = **TOTAL RETURN**

* You will owe taxes at your regular rate as you withdraw from your tax-deferred plan.

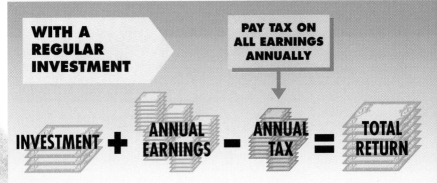

WITH A REGULAR INVESTMENT | **PAY TAX ON ALL EARNINGS ANNUALLY**

INVESTMENT + **ANNUAL EARNINGS** − **ANNUAL TAX** = **TOTAL RETURN**

NONQUALIFIED PLANS

Like qualified retirement plans, certain nonqualified plans let you defer taxes on investment earnings. But with a nonqualified plan, you have to pay taxes on the money before you invest it, which means you have less to invest. But if you aren't eligible for a qualified plan, or if you've invested all the money you can in a given year, you can use a nonqualified plan to save for retirement.

For example, you can invest in variable annuities or certain types of insurance that accumulate tax-deferred. Or maybe you can persuade your employer to provide retirement benefits for you that other employees aren't getting. You won't have to deal with restrictions on how much can be invested or what you can withdraw.

Pensions

You can collect a pension after you retire—if you work for an employer that provides a pension plan.

Pensions evolved from the belief that employers have an obligation to provide for retired employees who've spent a lifetime working for them. Under traditional pensions, called **defined benefit plans,** employers put money into funds that pay retired workers, and sometimes their survivors, a regular income for the rest of their lives. The amount is usually based on what they were earning and how long they worked.

In recent years, many employers have modified their approach to pension plans. Using **defined contribution plans**, employers put money into pension funds without guaranteeing the retirement benefit employees will receive.

The amount you get from a pension can vary enormously, from a small check at the time you retire to a generous percentage of your final salary every year. The payout depends on the kind and level of plan your employer provides, how well it's managed, and how long you participate.

> **Employer contributions to traditional plans average 10%–12% of your salary. But the most generous put only 3%–3½% into the increasingly popular 401(k)s.**

with more than 250 employees—and virtually all government agencies provide pension plans for their employees. Most small companies don't.

In the early 90s, for example, only 8% of all businesses with fewer than 100 employees offered plans, leaving about 26 million people without pensions. Part-time workers are rarely covered by a pension plan, even when they're long-time employees. The same applies to seasonal workers, and to people who work in low-paying retail and service jobs.

Though there are tax incentives for workers without pension plans to establish Individual Retirement Accounts, many don't, either because it doesn't seem important or because they have a hard time putting aside the money they are entitled to invest.

WHO'S COVERED... AND WHO'S NOT

Any business that has employees and anyone who is self-employed can set up a pension plan. Most large companies—

PENSION FINE PRINT

An **integrated plan** is a variation of a pension plan, which can leave you with much less retirement money than you expected. In an integrated plan, your

THE HISTORY OF PENSIONS

The first pensions we know about were paid to aged and disabled Roman soldiers when they could no longer fight for the Empire. In the same tradition, military pensions in the U.S. date back to the American Revolution.

By the early 1800s, government workers in several European countries were supported after they retired. The U.S. government introduced pensions in the 1920s to help support retiring civilian employees. Generous pensions, in fact, are a hallmark of public-sector jobs, compensating civil servants for lower salaries than they could earn in the private sector.

The history of most corporate pensions in the U.S. began in the 1930s, and is linked closely to the aftermath of the depression, the introduction of Social Security, and the influence of labor unions. Where the unions were strong, they fought for employer-funded pensions in contract negotiations. Their successes led to increased benefits for other, non-unionized, workers in those companies.

EVERY WORKER DESERVES A PENSION

Two Kinds of Plans

THE COMPANY PUTS MONEY INTO A PENSION FUND IN YOUR NAME

DEFINED BENEFIT PLAN

" Company A guarantees you a yearly pension equal to 30% of your salary if you've worked for them for at least 25 years before you retire. "

DEFINED CONTRIBUTION PLAN

" Company B agrees to invest an amount equal to 5% of your salary in your retirement plan each year, and offers you a variety of investment options. "

employer counts a portion of what you get from Social Security as part of your defined benefit—and reduces the amount of your pension accordingly. It's perfectly legal, and it must be explained in the material you're given when you enroll in the retirement plan. But many people miss that detail until it's too late.

PENSIONS AND THE LAW

The federal government does not require companies to provide pension plans, but it does offer an incentive: companies can deduct the money they pay into a pension fund from their corporate taxes.

At the same time, to help insure that plans live up to their promises to pay, and to protect tax revenues, the government carefully regulates and monitors them. As a result, many small companies have shied away from participating, and in recent years a number of companies that had traditionally offered plans have ended them.

Some companies have used their pension funds to buy policies with insurers who take over the responsibility of paying retired workers. Others offer bonuses and salary increases instead of retirement account contributions, or give employees a check for the amount accumulated in their pension account.

What these changes mean for the future is that workers will have a much greater long-term responsibility for funding their retirement themselves.

PENSION PLAN LIMITS

The government limits the size of the annual contribution an employer can make to any defined contribution plan. The cap runs from 15% to 25% of salary, depending on the plan. There's also a dollar limit for each type.

Defined benefit plans don't have a contribution limit, but there is a cap on the total amount that an employee can receive from the plan in any single year. That amount is either $90,000, plus a cost of living adjustment, or 100% of a recipient's average salary.

Defined Benefit Plans

Defined benefit pensions are a lot better to look forward to than death and taxes—but they aren't always as certain.

Conventional, employer-funded pension plans, known as **defined benefit plans**, are designed to pay a fixed, pre-established benefit when you retire. If there's a defined benefit plan where you work, you'll probably be included in it if you work full-time. And chances are you won't have many options about how the plan works or how the money is invested. That's the trade-off for the advantages the pension plan provides.

Defined benefit plans generally pay you a regular monthly benefit for your lifetime, sometimes with a final payment to your survivors. In other cases, though, you may be able to choose a lump sum payment when you retire, which you can reinvest (see page 44). With a generous plan, you might expect an annual income equal to between 30% and 50% of your final salary. But there's no law about how much a pension has to promise to pay, and some workers end up getting very little.

CALCULATING YOUR PENSION

The way your employer figures the amount you get is spelled out in the plan itself. In some plans, for example, there is a standard pension for everyone who meets minimum years-in-service requirements. In others, the annual amount you get reflects what you were earning, with better-paid employees getting higher pensions.

The rules are clear, though, so you can calculate ahead of time what your pension will be. Usually the major factors in determining the amount you'll receive include:

- **Your final salary**
- **The time you've been on the job**
- **Your age.**

GETTING ADVICE

Since defined benefit pension plans vary, you need to understand the fine print of any one you're depending on.

Your employer's benefits officer should know the answers to questions like these:

- Is your pension based on your average compensation, your final year's salary, or some other amount?

- Do different length-of-service requirements apply to employees who were hired at different times?

- What's the normal retirement age? What happens to your pension amount if you retire sooner?

- Is there any advantage to working past age 65?

- Is there a COLA?

LONGER IS BETTER

One common formula for finding your pension amount is to multiply the years you've been on the job times a certain percentage, such as 1.5%, and then multiply the result times your final salary.

$$\frac{\text{Years}}{\text{on job}} \times \frac{\text{Final}}{\text{salary}} = \text{Pension}$$
$$\times .015$$

for example

	30	Years
x	.015	
=	.45	
x $	72,000	Final salary
= $	32,400	Annual pension

YEARS ON THE JOB

STAYING PUT

Even if you can also count on pensions from a couple of earlier jobs, you'll probably wind up with less money than if you'd been with the same employer for your entire career. That's one reason some workers prefer the more portable defined contribution plans.

BEING VESTED

Being **vested** means you have the right to collect a pension benefit at a specific age, even if you've left the job before then. Without vesting rights, you forfeit any benefit when you leave, and the money becomes part of the general fund.

If you joined a private company plan after 1988, you are vested under one of two minimum schedules imposed by the Tax Reform Act of 1986. You are either

- **100% vested after five years, or**

- **20% vested after three years and fully vested after seven years.**

With some employers, you are vested more quickly, and in certain cases immediately. Some other plans—like a few for government

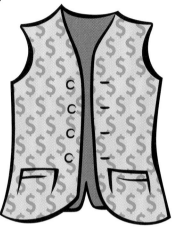

workers and many teachers—still require you to be on the job for ten years or longer before you're vested.

501 HOURS

If you leave your job before you're vested, you usually lose the credits you've built up toward retirement. But there are ways to keep up your ties and your benefits. One is part-time work. In most cases, working 501 hours a year, the equivalent of 12½ weeks, is enough to keep you on the pension books. However, if you end your career working part-time, your pension will probably be quite small—since your final salary usually determines the amount you get.

You won't lose pension credits, either, if you take up to 501 hours of family leave to care for a new baby or a sick family member.

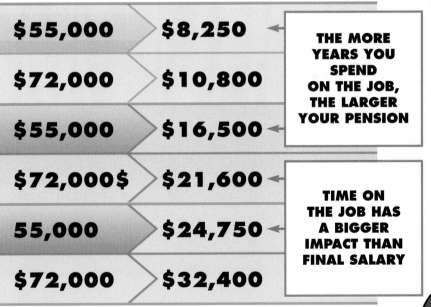

SALARY	PENSION	
$55,000	**$8,250**	← **THE MORE YEARS YOU SPEND ON THE JOB, THE LARGER YOUR PENSION**
$72,000	**$10,800**	
$55,000	**$16,500**	←
$72,000$	**$21,600**	← **TIME ON THE JOB HAS A BIGGER IMPACT THAN FINAL SALARY**
55,000	**$24,750**	←
$72,000	**$32,400**	

WHAT'S IN A COLA

Once you retire and your pension is calculated, the amount is usually fixed. Fewer than 5% of private U.S. pensions come with COLAs, or cost-of-living allowances, that increase the amount of your pension to keep pace with inflation. Some employers voluntarily increase pensions for retired workers from time to time. Government pensions, on the other hand, are generally adjusted annually to make up for increased living costs.

PENSION

Defined Contribution Plans

The potential risks of defined contribution plans are offset by their potential rewards.

The way retirement plans are funded and run is still changing. Since the mid-1970s, the trend has been away from defined benefits pensions, with their guaranteed payments, to **defined contribution pension plans**. In a defined contribution plan, your employer contributes to a pension fund in your name but has no obligation to provide a fixed amount when you retire. The amount of your pension is determined by how much is invested and the way it grows. If the economy is healthy and your pension account does well, you'll be in good shape. But if your account's performance lagged, you could end up with less. There's no way to predict what you'll get until the day you actually retire.

One major advantage of these plans is that they offer employees strong growth potential and a greater sense of control, plus the ability to transfer them to a new employer.

WHO OFFERS THEM?

More and more employers, both private and public, are offering defined contribution plans. In 1980, 70% of all pension plans fit into this category. By 1994, the figure was 84%. Some employers offer them as supplemental savings plans in

Types of Defined Contribution Plans

	Type	Funding	Contribution
	MONEY PURCHASE PLANS	Employer	Employer contributes to plan based on a formula that covers all participating employees
	PROFIT-SHARING PLANS	Employer	Employer contributes percentage of profits; some plans are based on total profits, while others use a sliding scale
	EMPLOYEE STOCK OWNERSHIP PLANS (ESOPS)	Employer	Employer contributes stock or subsidizes employee purchase of stock
	THRIFT OR SAVINGS PLANS	Employer and Employee	Employer matches some or all of the amount an employee defers from pre-tax salary into the plan
	401(K) PLANS	Employee and Employer	Employee contributes pre-tax salary to the plan; employer may, and often does, contribute an amount based on an announced formula
	403(B) PLANS	Employee and Employer	Employee contributes pre-tax salary to the plan; employer may, and often does, contribute an additional amount
	SECTION 457 PLANS	Employee	Employee contributes pre-tax salary to the plan

PACKING YOUR PLAN
Portability is a major attraction of defined contribution plans, along with quicker, or even instant, vesting rights. When you switch jobs, you can often move your accumulated assets to your new employer's plan. That way, you're not starting at pension zero each time you move. If you can't move it, you can often leave your account with your former employer so that it goes on growing until you're ready to retire.

addition to defined benefit plans. Others have replaced their conventional plans with these more flexible ones. And most employers setting up plans for the first time choose to make a defined contribution rather than provide a defined benefit.

It's easy to see why. Defined contribution plans are easier to administer and less subject to government regulation. And they can provide employees with investment choices.

VARIETY SPICES UP THE PENSION STEW

Some employers offer only one type of defined contribution plan, like a profit-sharing or money purchase plan. In most cases, these plans are funded by the employer, with the year's contribution tied to how well the company did.

Other employers let you choose among a variety of plans or participate in more than one. Usually, when you have a choice, you have to contribute before your employer's contribution kicks in.

IT'S YOUR CHOICE

Many defined contribution plans are optional. You get to choose whether or not you want to participate. What you agree to if you do participate is that you'll contribute some of your current salary to fund your pension. On the plus side, you don't owe tax on the amount you put away until you begin to receive benefits. But you will have less take-home pay.

The problem with voluntary plans is that employees who decide not to participate—because they think retirement is too far off or because they're reluctant to cut back on their take-home pay—give up their right to a pension.

Eligibility	Loan Privileges
All eligible company employees	NO
All eligible company employees	YES
Employees of stock-issuing businesses	NO
Federal employees and employees of companies offering plans	YES
All employees of businesses that sponsor plans	YES
Restricted to employees of non-profit, tax-exempt employers	YES
Restricted to state and municipal workers	YES

Salary Reduction Plans

If you want to diversify your retirement fund investments, 401(k)s, 403(b)s, and 457 plans are the right vehicles.

In 1992, more than $1 trillion was invested in **salary reduction plans**—about a sixth of all pension fund money in the U.S. And that share is growing, as more people recognize the advantages of making tax-deferred investments when they have the chance.

The 401(k)s, 403(b)s, and 457s—their catchy names are the sections of the tax code that describe them—are also increasingly popular because they are sometimes the only game in town—or at least the only way many employees can participate in a pension plan.

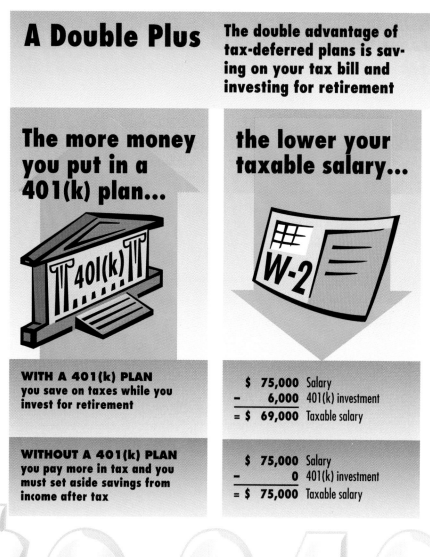

A Double Plus

The double advantage of tax-deferred plans is saving on your tax bill and investing for retirement

The more money you put in a 401(k) plan...

the lower your taxable salary...

WITH A 401(k) PLAN you save on taxes while you invest for retirement

$	75,000	Salary
−	6,000	401(k) investment
= $	69,000	Taxable salary

WITHOUT A 401(k) PLAN you pay more in tax and you must set aside savings from income after tax

$	75,000	Salary
−	0	401(k) investment
= $	75,000	Taxable salary

OUT IN THE COLD

If you contribute the full amount to your 401(k) each year, you're in for a chilly surprise. The ceiling for 1995 has been frozen at 1994 rates—$9,240. When it thaws, it will rise more slowly than in the past. Limiting pension contributions (and increasing your taxable income) is one of the ways the government plans to pay for the costs of the new GATT treaty.

HOW SALARY REDUCTION WORKS

You invest in a salary reduction plan by having a percentage of your salary deposited in your pension account. The amount you deposit is deferred—it does not count as part of your taxable income for that year.

Employers who offer salary reduction (or salary deferral) plans arrange for you to invest your money in different fixed income, equity, or money market accounts. You choose among the options, and pay the costs of investing, such as

WHEN A 403(b) IS NOT A 403(b)

If you work for a nonprofit organization, you may not recognize the name 403(b), even if you're participating in one. Salary reduction plans are frequently known by other names, including TSAs, tax shelters, and savings plans, especially when they're offered as supplements to defined benefit plans.

administrative fees. But you do not have to pay any tax on these funds or their earnings until you withdraw from the account.

at the same time. For example, if you're single, make $75,000, and put 8% of your salary in a 401(k), 403(b), or 457 plan you'll pay $1,860 less in federal income taxes, and you'll have $6,000 growing tax-deferred.

the less tax you pay...

and the faster your investment grows.

$16,920 *Taxes on $69,000 salary

$6,000 earning 8% tax-deferred will grow to $7,560 after 3 years, and $12,960 after 10 years

$18,780 *Taxes on $75,000 salary

Less to invest and no tax-deferred growth

*Tax at 1993 rates.

THE 400 FAMILY

While 401(k)s are the best known of the salary reduction plans, they're just one of a group of defined contribution pension plans available to people who work for different types of organizations. Each of these plans is restricted to a specific group of workers, and each has an annual contribution maximum.

The plans also have different rules on employer contributions, who can partici-pate, and the way the plan is adminis-tered, although they operate under similar government regulations. They may also play different pension roles. 401(k)s, for example, may be the only way for some corporate employees to participate in a pension plan. In contrast, federal, state, and nonprofit salary reduction plans like 403(b)s and 457 plans are often set up to supplement defined benefit pensions.

Matching and Switching

Getting the most from your retirement investment requires some fancy footwork.

Many corporate employers who offer salary reduction plans match, or add to, your contribution, up to a limit. A typical formula is to match 50% of what you put in, up to 6% of your salary. There's also usually a cap on the amount an employer will contribute in each pay period. That means you'll end up with more if you spread out your contributions to qualify for matching instead of having your share taken out in big installments early in the year.

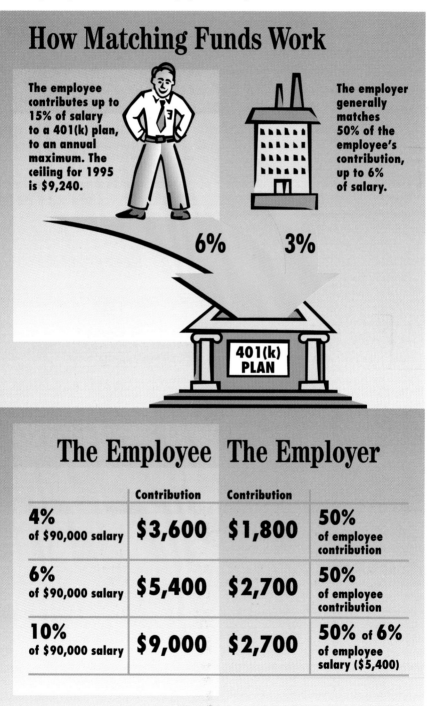

How Matching Funds Work

The employee contributes up to 15% of salary to a 401(k) plan, to an annual maximum. The ceiling for 1995 is $9,240.

The employer generally matches 50% of the employee's contribution, up to 6% of salary.

6%   3%

401(k) PLAN

The Employee The Employer

	Contribution	Contribution	
4% of $90,000 salary	**$3,600**	**$1,800**	**50%** of employee contribution
6% of $90,000 salary	**$5,400**	**$2,700**	**50%** of employee contribution
10% of $90,000 salary	**$9,000**	**$2,700**	**50%** of **6%** of employee salary ($5,400)

MOVING THINGS AROUND

Generally, a salary reduction plan lets you put money in as many of the available options as you choose and move your investment from one option to another. Some plans permit only annual transfers, but others allow them quarterly or even daily. In some cases, though, there are large surrender fees when you switch between different types of investments, or from one fund to another.

The reason for using different options is to keep your investment diversified. Moving assets around works best when you have a strategy for investing your retirement funds, like balancing growth and income. It makes less sense to move between funds if you're constantly trying to guess how the markets will move (called timing the market), or you're reacting in panic to a downturn in the stock or bond markets.

THE 403(B) ADVANTAGE

If you work for a college or university, a school system, or other nonprofit group, you may be able to participate in a 403(b), the most flexible salary reduction plans. Generally you have more investment choices than 401(k) or 457 plans provide, and you may be able to contribute a larger percentage of your salary, to an annual cap of $9,500.

You may also have access to more information and advice about your investment, especially if you participate in the TIAA-CREF plan available to colleges, universities and certain other non-profit educational institutions.

You may also have the right to make a tax-free transfer from any option your employer offers to a mutual fund or annuity of your own choosing as long as you have contributed all the money in the fund yourself, and none of it is matching funds from your employer.

The advantage is that you can move money into high-performance, low-fee funds, although being able to make additional investments once you've transferred money to a new account can be complicated. And while the transfers may be tax-free, they're rarely fee-free. Some 403(b)s impose very steep surrender charges, which can total 7% or more of the assets you're moving, especially on assets in certain fixed income accounts or variable annuities.

PASSING THE $66,000 TEST

In addition to the salary limits for figuring contributions, there are rules that govern what percentage of salary employees can contribute to a defined contribution plan like a 401(k). Basically, the rules tie the contributions of employees who make more than $66,000 to the contributions of employees who make less. Higher paid employees can contribute only 2% more of their salaries than the average percentage contributed by the rest of the employees.

For example, if the average contribution for employees earning less than $66,000 is 3% of their salaries, the most anybody earning more can contribute is 5%. In this case, no employee earning more than the $66,000 cut-off could come close to meeting the dollar limit on contributions to salary reduction plans. Someone making $67,000 could contribute $3,350 (instead of $9,240) and someone making $150,000 could contribute $7,500.

IS THE SWITCH WORTH IT?

Often, the answer is yes, even if you take a big hit on the fees. If the fund or annuity you're switching to has a better track record, or provides greater diversity, than your current investment, the long-term returns may be worth the cost of the transfer. But you do have to compare fees carefully, as they can vary significantly.

New participants in 403(b) plans have many more options than were available in the past, so they may be less likely to get caught in the surrender fee crunch than people who began contributing to their plan before 1990, when the IRS issued a ruling making these transfers easier.

Paying for the Plans

Bigger is cheaper, as this chart shows. 401(k) investors typically pay their account administrators higher fees than corporations and other large employers pay to have their pension funds managed.

TYPE	ASSETS	AVERAGE FEE
BIG PLANS	**$150 MILLION** (12,000 employees)	**0.5%**
401(K) PLANS	**$1.5 MILLION** (115 employees)	**1.4%**

Self-directed Pension Plans

Contributing to your pension plan is only the beginning of the story. Along the way, you're responsible for managing it too.

MUTUAL FUND

One major difference between defined benefit and defined contribution plans is who takes responsibility for how well your pension fund performs. In defined benefit plans, you have no say at all over investment decisions. In fact, you probably have no idea where the money is invested. But if you contribute to a defined contribution plan, like a 401(k) or a 403(b), making decisions about pension funds investments is entirely your responsibility. The choices you make determine the return you'll get when it's time to collect.

GROWING NUMBER OF CHOICES

Fortunately, you can choose where to put your money in a defined contribution plan. Many plans typically provide between four and seven options, including mutual funds, annuities, stock purchases, and savings bonds. Usually, there's at least one stock fund, a balanced fund, a bond fund or fixed income account, and maybe a money market account. And sometimes you can choose from as many as two dozen or more different funds.

PUT MORE STOCK IN STOCK

Although stocks, and stock funds, historically provide better returns than other investments, only 25% of the people participating in defined contribution plans own stock or stock funds, and only 3.7% have half or more of their investment in stock or stock funds.

Stock ownership in defined contribution plans

75% HAVE NO STOCKS

ONLY 3.7% HAVE MORE THAN 50% IN STOCKS → **25% HAVE STOCKS**

FINDING SOLUTIONS

Your freedom to choose the best investments is limited, of course, by the options your employer's plan offers. And your investing decisions have to take into account your age, other sources of income, and your tolerance for risk. But there are questions you can ask to help you decide which of the options you'll choose:

- **What are my investment choices?**
- **What are the objectives of each option, and what are their risks?**
- **How well have the various options been doing over various time periods?**
- **How do the annual expenses compare?**
- **Who pays the investment fees and administrative charges?**
- **Are there commissions or surrender charges?**

GETTING INVESTMENT ADVICE

Some employers provide very little if any investment advice about which options to

COMPANY STOCK

FIXED INCOME INVESTMENT (GIC)

MONEY MARKET FUND

SOME DISAPPOINTING RESULTS

Despite the vast sums that employees have contributed to self-directed pension plans—current estimates make it about $1 trillion a year—financial experts caution that these investments may not produce as much as they should. Three reasons are frequently mentioned:

RISK **Employees are not making the best choices among the options offered**—usually because they don't realize that in choosing what seems safest, they are limiting their return. Close to 60% of 401(k) money, for example, is invested in Guaranteed Investment Contracts (GICs), where long-term return is vulnerable to falling interest rates and rising inflation.

RETURN **The funds offered in many self-directed plans are not always the best performers in their categories**, so their returns don't keep pace with the market. Some of them may have been good choices once, but haven't performed well recently. Or, the bank, brokerage, or mutual fund company that administers the plan may have chosen funds they make more money on.

FEES **The investments are treated as individual accounts** by mutual fund companies, banks, and other financial institutions that manage them, so employees usually don't benefit from the smaller commissions and the reduced fees that large pension funds with investment clout characteristically enjoy. These higher costs come out of the employees' accounts, reducing the investment amount and lowering the return.

choose or how to allocate your money for the best return. They may fear being held liable if their advice doesn't produce good returns, so they shy away from providing advice at all. In addition, self-directed pension funds are generally administered by human resources departments, who are typically not financial managers with expertise in providing investment advice. Whatever the explanation, if you need advice, you may have to get it from other sources.

Supplemental Retirement Plans

A company's basic retirement plan may be only the starting point for some employees.

Since the promise of a secure retirement is a way to recruit and keep valuable employees, companies use **SERP**s, or **Supplemental Executive Retirement Plans**, to help feather certain nest(egg)s. The tighter the restrictions get on regular retirement plans, the more widespread supplemental plans become—despite their limitations for both employers and employees.

HOW SERPS WORK
If you're covered by a supplemental plan, it pays to know how they work for you—and sometimes against you. On the plus side, because SERPs are nonqualified plans provided by your employer, there are no limits on the amount that can be contributed. And since you have no access to the money—you can't get it before you leave or retire—your tax liability is deferred until the money is paid out.

SERPS HAVE DRAWBACKS
First, you might never collect. Supplemental retirements are paid out of a company's general operating budget, not a special pension fund. Your share is an entry in the company's books, but there's no ownership protection, no insurance, and no government watchdog. So if the company goes bankrupt, or if it's sold, there's no guarantee you'll ever get the money you were promised. Some companies, however, buy insurance or set up trusts to protect SERP money.

Supplementing Your Retirement Plans

WHAT COMPANIES CAN CONTRIBUTE

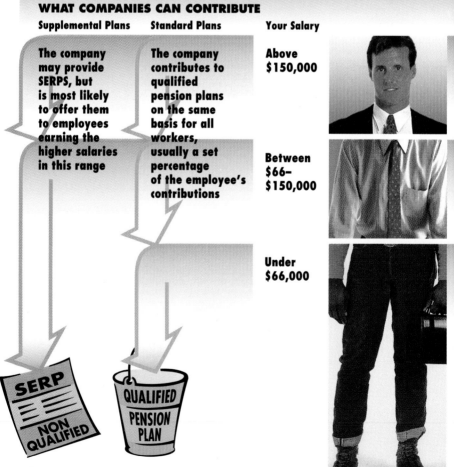

Supplemental Plans	Standard Plans	Your Salary
The company may provide SERPS, but is most likely to offer them to employees earning the higher salaries in this range	The company contributes to qualified pension plans on the same basis for all workers, usually a set percentage of the employee's contributions	Above $150,000
		Between $66–$150,000
		Under $66,000

SERP NON QUALIFIED

QUALIFIED PENSION PLAN

A second potential problem is how your employer values the growth of your investment. If the money is not actually invested anywhere, it isn't providing a real return. If your employer assumes a money market return of around 4%, instead of a well-performing stock fund return, which might be closer to 12%, your account will be worth much less than it would have been. One solution is for your employer to link the return on your supplemental account to the performance of your 401(k) or some other pension fund.

When you do get the SERP money you were promised, you'll owe tax on the amount. That's because you can't roll the payout over into an IRA or a retirement plan at your new job since SERPS aren't qualified plans. If you quit or get fired before you're 59½, you'll owe an early withdrawal penalty on top of the taxes, which would put a big dent in your payout.

NEW RULES/NEW WRINKLES

Until recently, SERPs—sometimes referred to as **top hat plans**—were pretty much limited to highly paid executives.

But in 1994, the top salary on which contributions to qualified pension plans could be figured was lowered from $235,840 to $150,000. As a result, many employers are looking for ways to put more retirement money away for employees who fall into that range and might not have qualified for special treatment before.

EXCESS 401(K)S...

Another way to beef up your retirement accounts is to make excess contributions to your 401(k). That means you can contribute the difference between the salary reduction limit that's permitted in any one year—$9,240 for 1994—and the 15% ceiling on contributions.

For example, if your salary is $125,000, a 15% contribution comes to $18,750. So you can add the $9,510 balance between that amount and the $9,240 you'd already put in. And your employer can make additional contributions too.

Like regular 401(k)s, the investment grows tax-deferred. But there are some catches:

- **Your excess contribution isn't a salary reduction. You put in money you've already paid tax on**

- **Your employer's excess contribution isn't tax-deductible the way regular retirement contributions are. That limits the enthusiasm for matching funds**

- **When you begin withdrawals, or if you want to roll over your 401(k) into an IRA, figuring the tax you owe will be much more complicated.**

AND EXCESS 403(B)S

If you didn't begin contributing to a 403(b) as soon as you were eligible, you have a chance to catch up, an uncommon phenomenon in the world of retirement savings. The usual pattern is to increase the percentage of salary you defer and exceed the normal dollar limit of $9,500 each year for five years. It's an easy way to play catch-up that also saves on your current tax bill.

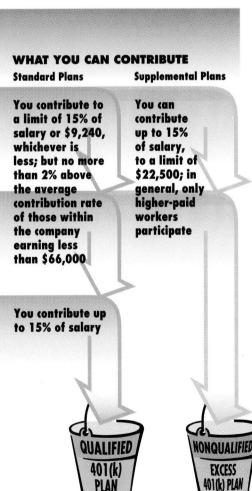

WHAT YOU CAN CONTRIBUTE

Standard Plans	Supplemental Plans
You contribute to a limit of 15% of salary or $9,240, whichever is less; but no more than 2% above the average contribution rate of those within the company earning less than $66,000	You can contribute up to 15% of salary, to a limit of $22,500; in general, only higher-paid workers participate
You contribute up to 15% of salary	

QUALIFIED 401(k) PLAN

NONQUALIFIED EXCESS 401(k) PLAN

Pension Decisions

When you're mapping out the best route to collecting your pension, there'll be several forks in the road.

Once you've decided to retire, you may have to make a decision about how to collect your pension. The choice is usually between a **lump sum** payment and a lifetime **annuity**, or series of equal payments. The most unnerving element in the process is that once you've committed yourself, you can't change your mind.

If you choose the lump sum, you'll also have to decide what to do with the money. One common option is to put it into an IRA rollover, but you might decide to take a cash payment instead.

THE CRITICAL FACTORS

While you don't have to decide until you're actually ready to stop working, making the best choice is critical. The factors you have to consider are your age and health, what you want to provide for your family, and what other sources of income you'll have. In some cases, too, you have to consider your employer's economic health.

For example, if you're in poor health and concerned about providing for your spouse, you might choose a joint and survivor annuity that will continue to pay while either of you is alive. On the other hand, if your spouse is seriously ill, you might choose a single life annuity that will provide a larger amount for you each month than a joint annuity would. Usually this requires your spouse's consent.

HOW TO COLLECT

Individual plans set their own rules for collecting a pension, just as they do for qualifying. You might have to be a certain age, have worked a certain number of years, or a combination of the two.

For example, sometimes you're not eligible to collect a pension until you reach 65, although other plans allow you to begin sooner. The minimum is usually 55—provided you've participated in the plan for at least ten years. If you're younger, you have to wait to collect.

SINGLE LIFE ANNUITY

ANNUITY

GOLDEN YEARS VALLEY

COLLECT PENSION AHEAD

ONE WAY TRAFFIC
—
NO U-TURN

In most cases, though, your pension is paid when you actually retire. You usually can't postpone the payout, although it may be possible to defer part of it.

DEFINED BENEFIT PENSIONS

Most employers who provide defined benefit pensions provide experts to give you advice on the differences between the payout options. Even though the final decision is yours, the advisor should give you a detailed comparison showing how each option would work and the money you can expect to receive. When you choose, you have to consider not only how much you'll collect, but for how long, and what the tax consequences will be.

A CORPORATE FIRST

In 1913, AT&T established the first corporate pension plan in the U.S. It paid retirement benefits to workers aged 60 and above who'd been with the company 20 years or more. It also provided accident and disability insurance to long-time employees.

While 65 is no longer the hard and fast retirement age it once was, many defined benefit retirement plans are still set up as though 65 were still the norm. If you retire earlier, your employer may recalculate the pension you were promised to take into account the added years you'll be collecting instead of working.

If you go on working after 65, federal rules require that your pension keeps on growing until you actually retire and collect on it. That should provide a boost to your income, and perhaps act as an incentive to delay retirement.

JOINT AND SURVIVOR ANNUITY

CASH

IRA ROLL-OVER

DEFINED CONTRIBUTION PENSIONS

If you have a defined contribution pension plan, you probably have to make fewer choices at retirement. While sometimes you can choose an annuity or periodic payments, frequently the assets are sold and you get a lump sum distribution, which you are responsible for investing to provide income during your retirement. If you've participated in a stock purchase plan, you can hold onto the shares and continue to collect dividends, or sell your shares and reinvest the money. Again, it's up to you.

LUMP SUM

$150,000 WITHDRAWAL LIMIT

PAYOUT LIMITS

There's a limit—$150,000 for 1994—on the amount of money you get from all your qualified pension plans in any single year before owing a penalty. If you get more than the limit, you'll owe the IRS up to 15% of the excess amount. If you have only one employer-sponsored pension, you're not apt to go over the limit, as the plan's administrator keeps tabs on its payouts. But if you're collecting from several different qualified retirement plans—perhaps including a Keogh, a SEP, or several IRAs—complying with the limits is your responsibility.

The one exception is for lump sum payments. If you take your money all at once, you can get a $750,000 payout without penalty.

Pension Choices

Understanding the small print helps you balance the pros and cons of payout options.

There's no universal right answer about how to take your pension payout, but when you have to make a decision, it helps to know the advantages—and the disadvantages—of your options.

WHAT THE ISSUES ARE

How comfortable you are with investing money is a major consideration in deciding between a lump sum payout and an annuity. If you've been investing successfully for years, the prospect of building your portfolio and your profits with a lump sum pension payout can be appealing—and realistic. The challenge, of course, is producing enough income during retirement.

But if you don't want to worry about outliving your assets, you may opt for the relative security of an annuity. Knowing that the same amount is coming in on a regular basis makes budgeting—and occasionally splurging—a lot easier.

Taxes are also a major consideration. If you'll still be in a high tax bracket after you retire and you're eligible for **forward averaging** (see page 45), you may make out better paying the taxes you owe up front. On the other hand, if your tax rate will drop after you retire because your pension is providing the bulk of your income, you may owe less by taking an annuity.

TAKING YOUR TIME

The good thing about making pension payout choices is that usually you have plenty of time, as retirement doesn't usually take you by surprise. Defined benefit pensions have been in place long enough so that their managers understand the consequences, good and bad, of the various options. Or, you can get additional advice from your union representative, tax consultant, or lawyer.

A Close Look At Some

Type		What it is
ANNUITY		An annuity is a regular, monthly payment, usually for your lifetime
PERIODIC PAYMENTS	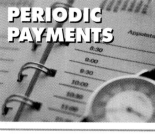	Periodic payments are installment payments of roughly equal amounts paid over a specific period, often 5–15 years
LUMP SUM		A lump sum is a cash payment of the money in your pension fund
IRA ROLLOVER		An IRA rollover is a lump sum payment deposited into a special IRA account. You can either deposit it yourself or ask your employer to do it directly

PENSION MAXIMIZATION

Pension maximization is salesperson's lingo for a single life annuity repackaged to make it seem more attractive to people trying to get the most out of their pension. With **pension max**, you use part of the higher payment under a single life plan to buy a life insurance policy to cover the needs of the surviving spouse. It should come as no surprise that the person selling the policy is usually the one who suggests maximizing. The consensus among those who don't stand to profit from selling the insurance plans is that almost everyone is better off choosing a joint and survivor annuity, especially surviving spouses.

LOCATING THE MISSING

Sometimes pensions get lost in the shuffle—because people forget about them or forget to tell their survivors. Or sometimes a defined benefits plan folds, leaving incomplete records. The Pension Benefit Guaranty Corporation tries to locate the approximately 1,000 people a year who are entitled to pensions but aren't collecting. If you, or someone you know, was part of a plan but has lost touch with the employer, you can contact the Pension Benefit Guaranty Corporation at 1200 K Street NW, Washington, DC 20005. Write to the Administrative Review and Technical Assistance Division.

Important Retirement Choices

Advantages	Drawbacks
● Security of knowing that payments will come in on a regular basis ● Option of spreading the payments out over your spouse's lifetime as well as your own ● Peace of mind in knowing you can't outlive your resources	● Most annuities not indexed for inflation, which means that your fixed annuity will buy less and less as time goes by. Variable annuities are designed to address this issue (see page 112) ● Tax due on the amount you get each year. You may pay at the highest rate if your pension is generous or you have other sources of income ● Some annuities unsafe or underfunded and could fold, leaving you in the lurch
● Assurance of a regular payment at regular intervals ● Relatively large payments because of limited time frame ● Option of rolling some but not all payments into an IRA	● Commitment to payment schedule limits ability to get at lump sum, if needed ● No assurance of lifetime income ● Might leave yourself or spouse without funds after payments end ● Taxes may be due at highest rate ● Inflation can erode purchasing power of payments
● Control over investing and gifting your assets ● Eligible for forward averaging, which reduces taxes, and in some cases for other tax breaks	● Tax due immediately ● Possibility of spending too much too quickly ● Vulnerable to making poor investment decisions ● No assurance of lifetime income—might leave yourself or spouse without funds if assets are exhausted
● Money continues to grow tax-deferred ● Allows you to invest as you want and take money as you need it ● Protection from early withdrawal penalties if you're not yet 59½	● Money not available for immediate use ● May pay more tax over time than you might have paid on the lump sum ● Withdrawal schedule required after you reach age 70½

Pension Annuities

A pension annuity's distinguishing feature, and its greatest charm, is regularity.

A pension annuity pays you a regular retirement income. It can last your lifetime, or your lifetime plus the life of a survivor. But once you choose, it's set.

GAMBLING ON SURVIVAL

If you choose an annuity, you also have to decide whether you want a **single life** (sometimes called **straight life**) or a **joint and survivor option**. In a single life annuity, you get a regular payment every month for your lifetime. Basically, the payment is figured by dividing the amount that has built up in your pension account and what you can expect it to earn over your lifetime by your life expectancy, figured using standard actuarial tables.

If you live longer than statistics predict, you still get your annuity. For example, a woman who retires at 65 can expect to live until she's 85. If she's still collecting her pension when she's 95, the system has worked in her favor. On the other hand, if she dies at 68, the balance in her account reverts—in most cases—to the general pension fund. (There are some exceptions. Certain pension funds make a lump sum payment of the balance of your retirement account to your estate. It's something you should check.)

In a **joint and survivor annuity**, your pension covers your lifetime and the lifetime of your designated survivor—often, but not necessarily, your spouse. The amount of your monthly check is usually less than it would be for a single life annuity. But after you die, your survivor gets a percentage of your pension each month for life. The advantages of the joint and survivor option are clear, especially in cases when your designated survivor is apt to live a long time and doesn't have a separate pension or other income. In fact, the financial benefits that joint and survivor policies provide (for elderly widows in particular) is such good social policy that the law requires companies to provide this option automatically to married employees.

THREE KINDS OF ANNUITY PAYOUTS

The chart below compares an example of a single life payout with the amounts you'd get with a 50% joint and survivor annuity and with a 100% one. The type of annuity you choose determines the size of your monthly payout. As this example shows, a single life annuity pays the most, but a 100% joint and survivor annuity protects your survivor better.

Type of payout	Retiree's monthly payout UNTIL DEATH	Death of retiree	Spouse's monthly payout STARTING AFTER RETIREE'S DEATH
Single life	$4,167		**Nothing**
50% joint and survivor	$3,705		$1,853
100% joint and survivor	$3,335		$3,335

The drawbacks of joint and annuity pensions—the smaller payment and the possibility that your survivor might die before you do—are things you have to weigh before choosing this option. But both you and your spouse must agree—in writing—to waive the joint and survivor option if you select a single life annuity or a lump sum payment.

Period certain annuities provide survivor benefits for a set amount of time after the death of the pension holder. Because the payout period is limited—usually to five or ten years—the amount of the basic payment is higher than a joint and survivor annuity. The best reason for making this choice is to provide short-term support for a younger survivor, a minor child for example. The limited-term payments can be used to pay college tuition or make the down payment on a house, among other things.

Not all 401(k) and profit-sharing plans offer an annuity option. Instead, they will sometimes make periodic payments, over five, ten, or fifteen years. You can roll over periodic payments into an IRA if they're paid out in fewer than ten years. And you can choose to roll over some of the payments and take the others. That gives you much greater flexibility than you get with defined benefit pensions.

PENSION PAYOUTS

Because pension plans are administered by the company—even if you decide how the money is invested—the company may—and often does—determine the way your annuity is calculated without letting you know you have a right to choose the method they use.

There are two ways to figure the minimum payment each year: the period-certain method and the recalculation method. Period certain means you get the same amount every year based on your life expectancy when you retire. Recalculation means the amount is recalculated every year based on your new life expectancy.

If you don't elect the period-certain option, you get the recalculation method by default. That can work to your disadvantage, because it can mean that you must take out money more quickly under certain circumstances and you owe more taxes.

Your employer is not legally required to tell you that you have a choice between the methods, but is required to follow your instructions if you make the choice. Companies choose the recalculation method to insure that they comply with IRS minimum distribution requirements, which say that your pension account must be paid out in roughly equal installments based on your life expectancy.

Lump Sum Distributions

Sometimes you can take your pension in a lump sum and invest it yourself.

Lump sum suggests the comforting image of a mass of money—a bulwark against financial perils. If you invest it right, you can shore up the future by beating inflation, which causes annuities to lose their value. What's more, you don't have to worry about the pension plan going bust or your former employer changing pension policy. But you do need to be concerned about decreasing assets.

HOW LUMP SUM PAYMENTS WORK

When you take a lump sum distribution from a defined benefit plan, your employer figures out how much you would get if the plan paid you an annuity over your projected lifespan, and then calculates how much the pension fund could have earned in interest on that amount during the years of your payout. Your lump sum share is what you would have been entitled to, reduced by a factor of the projected interest earnings known as the discount rate.

If interest rates are high—as they were through much of the 1980s—your lump sum will be less than in a period of low interest. That's because the fund hates to give up any money-producing investment—in this case your share of the pension fund. Once you have the lump sum, the responsibility for investing your pension to make it last through your retirement is yours.

MAKING IT LAST

You should use the discount rate the company uses to calculate your lump sum as a guide to how well you're doing with your investments. If you're earning the discount rate, you ought to do about as well, but if your money is earning less than that, you may come up short.

IT'S YOURS, NOW

You can take a lump sum distribution in cash—or perhaps more precisely by check. Or you can roll over the money into a special Individual Retirement Account (IRA). The only catch is that all the money you roll over must be pretax contributions and their earnings. You can't roll money into an IRA if you've already paid tax on it (as you would have on contributions to company thrift plans or to excess 401(k) accounts).

CASH DISTRIBUTION

ADVANTAGES	DRAWBACKS
● Can use money immediately	● Easy to spend too fast
● May be able to reduce taxes owed	● Taxes due immediately
● No minimum or maximum limits on withdrawal amounts	● Must make initial investment decisions quickly
	● Owe additional taxes on investment gains

FIGURING WHAT YOU EARN

If you invested a lump sum, after paying taxes, in a tax-free investment earning 5%, and an IRA rollover in a tax-deferred one earning 8%, the rollover would provide larger monthly earnings:

WITH IRA ROLLOVER

	$350,000	IRA rollover
x	8%	Earnings
	$ 28,000	A year
– $	4,974	Tax (in 1993)
	$ 23,026	A year
or $	1,918	A month

VS. LUMP SUM AFTER-TAX INVESTMENT

	$263,850	Lump sum after taxes
x	5%	Earnings tax-free
	$ 13,193	A year
or $	1,099	A month

After 20 years, the IRA advantage would be $196,580, even though you'd paid $99,480 in taxes—$13,330 more than you would have paid on a cash distribution.

LUMP SUM

IRA ROLLOVER

ADVANTAGES

- Defer taxes until you withdraw funds
- Make investment decision at own pace
- Investment continues to grow tax-deferred

DRAWBACKS

- May pay more taxes in the long run
- Lose access to large cash sum because of limits on annual withdrawal amounts
- Must begin withdrawals by age 70½

FORWARD AVERAGING

When you take a lump sum distribution, you have to pay the tax that's due on the entire amount. Any way you figure it, the tax will take a big bite out of what you have coming. But if you're at least 59½, you may qualify for **forward averaging**. That means you will owe less, even though you'll still owe it all at once.

When you forward average, you figure the tax as if the lump sum had been paid in equal payments over five years and were your only income in those years. For example, if your lump sum payment were $350,000, forward averaging would let you calculate as if you had received $70,000 in each of five years. You can't take any deductions or exemptions, and you pay at the single taxpayer rate.

A ONE-SHOT DEAL

To qualify for forward averaging, which you can do only once in your life, you have to:

- **Be at least 59½ and in the plan at least 5 years**
- **Stop working for the employer who is paying you the lump sum**
- **Take the entire pension amount as a lump sum directly from your employer.**

In addition, you can't forward average in a year when you're planning to roll over any money from another source into an IRA. If you do, you may lose the tax deferral and have to pay tax on that amount too.

If you were born before 1936, you may be eligible for ten-year forward averaging, or the right to pay tax on your earnings as if they were capital gains taxed at a 20% rate. Either method would reduce your taxes. One thing you can't do is forward average money that's been rolled over into an IRA, even if you take the entire amount.

WHAT IF YOU'RE NOT 59½?

If you get your pension as a lump sum before you reach 59½—because you take the option of retiring, change jobs, are disabled, or are let go—you could face the double hit of taxes and penalties.

If you stop working after age 55, the penalty is automatically waived. The same is true if you can't work. But if you're healthy, younger than 55, and get the money as a lump sum, you'll have to roll over the whole amount into a special IRA or set up a special payment plan to avoid excess taxes and penalties.

You must set up a **segregated,** or special, IRA for your pension payout, otherwise known as your preretirement distribution. You can't add anything to this IRA. But you can roll the amount into a retirement plan at a new job or start withdrawing from it when you retire.

WITH FORWARD AVERAGING

1 Divide your lump sum payout by five to find your taxable annual income.

2 Using the tax tables provided by the IRS, find the tax due. Multiply the annual tax by five to find your total tax bill.

3 Compare that amount with the tax that would have been due on the entire amount.

$ 350,000	Lump sum	$17,230	Tax on 70K*	$ 119,372	Tax on $350,000*
÷ 5		x 5		− 86,150	Averaged tax
$ 70,000	Per year	$86,150	Total due	$ 33,222	**TAX SAVINGS**

*These examples use 1993 tax rates.

Changing Jobs, Changing Pensions

Retirement savings are portable…if you know what you have to move and where to store it

If you change jobs—about 12% of the population does every year—protecting your retirement pension and investments may require some tough choices. Of course, what you can do depends on the type of plan, or plans, you've participated in. Sometimes your employers make all the decisions. But in many cases you'll be responsible for choosing a new home for the money. Even if you're short of cash, the biggest mistake you can make is spending it. You'll need it more after you retire.

CHOOSING WISELY

As a rule, if you're part of a 401(k), a profit-sharing plan, or a stock purchase plan, you'll get a lump sum distribution of the money that's been invested in your name, plus whatever the investment has earned. Then you'll have to decide what to do with the money, before taxes gobble up a big share of it. The chart below summarizes the details of the most frequent options.

Your options and their consequences

OPTION	TAX CONSEQUENCES	PLUSES AND MINUSES
Transfer money directly to IRA	None	Rollover money must go into separate IRA. Preserves right to roll money into future employer's plan. Eligible for forward averaging of lump sum withdrawal after 59½ (see page 45)
Roll distribution into IRA yourself	20% withheld. Total amount must be deposited within 60 days, including the 20%, or subject to tax and 10% penalty if younger than 59½	Gives you short-term access to money, with potential penalties (see page 56)
Begin periodic withdrawals	Tax on distributions, but no early withdrawal penalty	Distributions must continue for five years or until 59½, whichever is longer. Depletes money earmarked for retirement
Leave money in former employer's plan (not always available)	None	Investment continues to grow undisturbed. Later, can be rolled into an IRA or moved to new employer's plan
Take cash as lump sum	Taxed as current income, plus 10% penalty if younger than 59½	May be eligible for forward averaging. Flexibility to use some cash and roll rest into an IRA. Lose ability to roll money into new employer's plan. Risk depleting retirement savings

AVOIDING THE HASSLE

Some pension funds, like TIAA-CREF, the plan for college and university employees, aren't tied to a particular employer. If you move from one institution to another, your pension goes with you. And if you're vested, but change careers, the amount in your plan continues to grow tax-deferred.

Some civil service pensions offer reciprocity: pension contributions you make as a state employee and time spent on the job count if you move to a federal job, or vice versa. A state police officer, for example, who joins the Secret Service begins the new job with a pension credit already on the books.

RESTRICTED RIGHTS

If you're part of a defined benefits plan, your employer usually won't offer a lump sum when you leave, and won't start paying you a pension until you reach the minimum age for early retirement—sometimes 55, but often older. Then you get what accumulated up to the time you left, either in a lump sum or as an annuity.

Thanks to changes in vesting rules, you probably will be entitled to the money your employer has contributed to the plan. But if you change jobs at 40, and can't collect for 15 or 20 years, don't expect the pension to pay a lot. In some cases, your account will have been frozen, so no investment earnings will be credited to your account after you left the job. And inflation will eat away the value of the money you do eventually receive.

HANDLING THE DETAILS

If your pension has included a stock purchase plan, or if your employer has contributed stock to a profit-sharing plan, you can hold onto it since it's in your name, or sell if the price is right. If you hold onto the stock, you can continue to use your former employer as your agent, or you can transfer the stocks into an IRA rollover you open with a brokerage firm. The advantage of a broker can be easier access, and possibly smaller commissions when you do decide to sell.

If you're leaving a 401(k), you may have to turn your investments into cash before you can move them. That could mean a loss in value, if the economy is down.

EARLY RETIREMENT PACKAGES

Sometimes employers offer incentives for retiring early, like adding three to five years to the years you've actually worked, or increasing the percentage of salary your pension will replace. Together, the incentives could mean a significantly bigger pension.

Or your employer may offer you a lump sum payment on top of the pension you would receive if you retired early—like a week's pay for each year you've been on the job.

If you have a choice between a bigger pension or **severance**, a bonus for leaving, multiply the increase in monthly pension you've been offered times your life expectancy, and compare that figure to the amount of the severance offer.

For example, if at age 55 you're offered a $75,000 severance or $500 a month added to your pension, you'd make out better with the pension:

Added pension	x	Life expectancy	=	Value of pension
for example				
$ 500		Added per month		
x 12		Months		
= $ 6,000		Added per year		
x 28.6		Life expectancy		
= $ 171,600		Value of increased pension		
– 75,000		Severance offered		
= $ 96,600		Additional retirement income		

Some Pension Problems

When pension funds are short on cash, their performance doesn't stack up.

When pensions work the way they're supposed to, they help insure the financial security of millions of retired workers. But there can be major headaches for people who are counting on that income if a pension doesn't deliver what it promises.

That can happen if a pension is **underfunded**. Though you can't prevent underfunding, recognizing that it can and does happen will help you make plans for replacing the income if your pension is delayed or reduced.

SHORT ON MONEY

Many private and public pension funds are currently underfunded, some seriously. One reason is that bookkeeping rules have changed. Employers must forecast the future obligations differently than they have in the past, increasing the gap between what they've put away and what they'll owe.

In addition to the impact of the new rules, private plans come up short if:

Underfunded means that a pension is short on the money it needs to meet its projected expenses

30% OF PUBLIC FUNDS ARE SHORT 75% OF WHAT THEY NEED

Fully funded means that a pension has the funding it needs to meet projected expenses

95% OF PRIVATE FUNDS HAVE OVER 75% OF WHAT THEY NEED

- **The plan's investments don't do as well as expected, currently a major factor**

- **The employer doesn't contribute enough**

- **The employer borrows the money to expand or bail out a faltering business and doesn't—or can't—replace it.**

Public pension funds are underfunded because state and local governments are reluctant, in the face of increasing opposition, to raise taxes enough to meet their projected obligations. Some states have also tried to use the contributions they should be making to the pension fund to meet short-term obligations.

THE OTHER SHOE

Underfunding also occurs because there are government limitations on what a company is allowed to contribute to a pension fund if it is fully funded. Just as you're limited to $2,000 in an IRA or $9,240 (for 1994) in a 401(k), a company can't make tax-deductible contributions that raise pension funds much above the full funding level. When the accounting rules changed, some funds went from fully funded to underfunded overnight.

People who look on the bright side of the underfunding issue see it primarily as the consequence of low interest and inflation rates, at least for private pensions. They predict that when the rates increase, underfunding will stop being a problem.

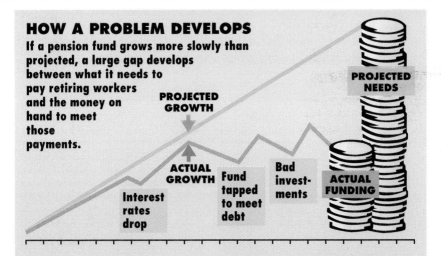

HOW A PROBLEM DEVELOPS

If a pension fund grows more slowly than projected, a large gap develops between what it needs to pay retiring workers and the money on hand to meet those payments.

PROJECTED NEEDS

PROJECTED GROWTH

ACTUAL GROWTH

Fund tapped to meet debt

Bad investments

ACTUAL FUNDING

Interest rates drop

LOOKING FOR A WAY OUT

There are other solutions, too. As more and more people reach retirement age, many private employers are cutting back on pension promises to newer employees, renegotiating existing obligations, increasing the use of defined contribution plans (which can't be underfunded), or ending their defined benefit plans altogether. Health insurance coverage, for example, has been radically reduced or eliminated, even for former employees who have already retired.

ERISA, the Employee Retirement Income Security Act, does protect employees to some extent. If the plan where you work is ended, your employer must provide the money you're entitled to at that point, by buying you an annuity or making a lump sum payment. But neither of those is likely to provide the same level of long-term income a pension would provide.

MAKING NOBODY HAPPY

State and local governments, which have depended on the promise of generous pensions instead of high salaries to make themselves competitive with the private sector in attracting qualified workers, are also looking for ways to reduce their pension obligations.

One solution has been to make the biggest cuts in benefits to people working fewer than ten years, or to require them to work more years to qualify. Other approaches have been to increase the amount workers must contribute themselves to pension plans, to limit cost-of-living increases, and to reduce the use of overtime to boost final year salaries that are the basis for pension payouts. Elected officials, though, must weigh the political cost of public employee anger against the consequences of imposing higher taxes.

Public pension plans are not covered by ERISA, so they can make more radical changes than private plans can, including cutting or delaying benefits.

PENSION GUARANTEES

The Pension Benefit Guaranty Corporation, established in 1974, guarantees pension payments to approximately 40 million workers who are covered by 85,000 defined benefit plans. The PBGC doesn't promise you'll get the full amount you planned on, but it does guarantee that you will get something.

Pension Rights Center
918 16th St. N.W. St. 704
Washington D.C. 20006

CHECKING UP

The Pension Rights Center, 918 16th Street NW, Suite 704, Washington DC 20006 is a resource for answers to your pension questions. For information closer to home, you can ask your employer for a copy of Form 5500, which has to be filed every year with the government, reporting on the plan's investments and its financial health.

IRAs: What They Are

IRAs are retirement plans for individuals—easy to set up, but not always easy to understand.

Individual Retirement Accounts (IRAs) are tax-deferred retirement plans that anyone who earns money can open.

INVESTOR-MANAGED PLANS

You can make all your IRA investment decisions yourself, including the choice of letting your broker decide how to invest your account.

$2,000 MAXIMUM ANNUAL CONTRIBUTION

The most you can contribute to an IRA each year is $2,000. Working spouses can contribute up to $2,000 each into separate accounts.

SPOUSAL ACCOUNTS

If your spouse doesn't work, you can contribute an annual total of $2,250 into separate, spousal IRAs. You can divide the money between the accounts any way you like.

LIMITS ACCESS

What you give up with an IRA is access to your money. In most cases, you'll owe a 10% penalty for taking money out before age 59½, in addition to the taxes that are due.

HAPPY 59½ BIRTHDAY

OPEN AN
IRA
INDIVIDUAL RETIREMENT ACCOUNT

ASK INSIDE FOR INFORMATION

DEFERS TAXES

You don't owe any tax on your earnings until you begin to withdraw from your account. That means your investment grows faster.

MAY REDUCE TAXABLE INCOME

If you're not part of another retirement plan, or if your income falls below certain levels, you can deduct your contribution from your taxable income, reducing your current taxes.

INVESTMENT OPTIONS

You can invest your IRA money almost any way you like, from sedate savings accounts to volatile options on futures. And you can change your investment when you please without paying tax on your gains.

1974 $739 BILLION	1987 $231 BILLION
Before change	After change

TOTAL IRA CONTRIBUTION

THE GOOD OLD DAYS

When IRAs were introduced in 1974, they were much less complex. Anyone who earned money during the year could open an IRA, contribute up to $2,000 and then take the amount of that contribution as a tax deduction. But when the deductibility rules changed, lots of people dropped out.

TO OPEN OR NOT TO OPEN AN IRA— THAT IS THE QUESTION

It's easy to open an IRA by filling out a relatively simple application provided by the financial institution you choose to be the **custodian**, or holder, of your account.

Because IRAs are self-directed, meaning you decide how to invest the money, you're also the one responsible for following the rules.

You must have **earned income**—money you work for—to contribute to an IRA. Any amount you earn qualifies, and you can contribute as much of your earnings as you want, up to $2,000. But you can't contribute more than you earn. For example, if you earn $1,800, that is how much you can put in.

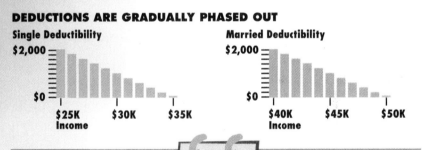

WHO IS ELIGIBLE

And whether you earn $3,500 or $350,000, you can only contribute up to the $2,000 limit.

The one exception is the contribution that's allowed for a spouse who doesn't have a job. You can put away an extra $250 if that's the case in your household, raising your total contribution to $2,250.

If you qualify, you may be able to deduct all or part of your IRA contribution from your taxable income. For example, you can deduct the entire amount if neither you nor your spouse is covered by another retirement plan. Otherwise, as your income gets higher, the amount you can deduct gets

WHAT IS DEDUCTIBLE

smaller, and is eventually phased out altogether.

Contributions are fully deductible for single people earning up to $25,000, and for married couples filing jointly earning up to $40,000. Then, for each $1,000 of added income, you lose $200 in deductibility, to ceilings of $35,000 and $50,000.

DEDUCTIONS ARE GRADUALLY PHASED OUT

Single Deductibility

$2,000 —
$0 —
$25K Income $30K $35K

Married Deductibility

$2,000 —
$0 —
$40K Income $45K $50K

You have until April 15—the day taxes are due—to open an account and make the deposit for the previous tax year. Your account administrator will send you a statement by May 31 telling you how much you contributed for the previous tax year. But it's your job to keep track of your annual contribution. If you put in more than the $2,000 that's allowed, you'll owe a penalty.

WHEN TO CONTRIBUTE

You can contribute $2,000 to your IRA in a lump sum or spread the deposit out over the 15 months. You get the best return on your investment if you put in the whole amount the first day you can, January 2 of the tax year you're making the contribution for. But if you're like most people, you're more apt to make the deposit the last possible day. $10.6 billion found its way into IRAs by April 15, 1993.

January 2

Best day to deposit lump sum

April 15

Last day to deposit lump sum

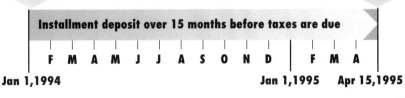

Installment deposit over 15 months before taxes are due

| F M A M J J A S O N D | F M A |

Jan 1,1994   Jan 1,1995   Apr 15,1995

IRAs: Your Show

You call the shots on your IRA, so it helps if your goals are in focus.

You set up your IRA on your own with a bank, mutual fund, or brokerage firm.

You can invest your IRA money in almost anything you can think of from aggressive growth stocks to conservative savings accounts, or from high interest junk bonds to government-insured certificates of deposit. The exceptions are fine art, gems, coins (other than U.S.-minted gold and silver coins) or other collectibles.

One strategy is to use your IRA for investments that return the highest income, since you are deferring the taxes and might as well rake in all you can. Another is to put IRA money into riskier high-growth investments, like stocks or certain mutual funds, early in your career, and gradually switch them to safer investments as you get older.

Among the investments you should avoid are municipal bonds or municipal bond funds, and investments that produce more capital gains than income. Here's why:

- The interest you earn on **municipal bonds** is tax-free, as long as they're outside an IRA. But once you include them in an IRA, their earnings are treated like all other IRA earnings and taxed when you make a withdrawal.

- The **capital gains tax rate** is lower than the rate for the top income tax brackets. If you're in a high tax bracket when you withdraw money from your IRA, you'll lose the benefit of the lower rate on these gains because all IRA earnings are taxed at the same rate.

Experts disagree about putting IRA money into variable annuities. The ayes stress annuities earning potential. The nays argue that since annuities are already tax-deferred, it's overkill.

SAVING ON FEES

Consolidating your accounts can save you money, because you generally pay an account fee of between $10 and $50 to maintain each IRA. The fee's the same whether you have $2,000 or $20,000 in the account. And some funds waive the fee entirely if your account is large enough.

You can let the bank or mutual fund deduct the fee from your account, or you can write a separate, tax-deductible check to cover it. That way, your entire investment can go on growing.

PRODUCER/DIRECTOR
Mr. Investor

HOLLYWOOD

CASTING CALL:
My Financial Future

STARRING ROLES
★ Mutual Fund IRA
★ Bank CD IRA
★ High-risk Stock IRA
Rated "A"

TITLE My Financial Future
PROD/DIR. J. J. INVESTOR
SCENE 1 TAKE 1
"Retirement Income"

KEEPING TRACK OF YOUR IRAS

While you can set up a different IRA every year, keeping track of your accounts can be a nightmare long before you begin figuring your withdrawals (see page 66). That's an argument for using one broker, bank or mutual fund as the custodian. You can have several different types of investments, but your records will be on one statement that provides all the information you need.

Your recordkeeping is also simplified if all of your IRA contributions are deductible. You report the contribution (and the deduction) when you file your tax return. But you must report a nondeductible IRA contribution on Form 8606.

And you must keep those records for as long as you have your IRAs to avoid paying taxes twice on your nondeductible contributions. If the prospect of holding on to 50 years of tax forms is annoying, think how you'll feel if you can't prove that you've already paid taxes on several thousands of dollars of investment—and you have to pay again.

IRA PROTECTION

Many people put their IRAs in bank CDs or savings accounts because the money is insured by the Federal Deposit Insurance Corporation (FDIC). But the old level of protection has been revised—downward.

Accounts that were opened before December 19, 1993, are insured up to $100,000 apiece, no matter how many different ones you have in the same bank. But all accounts opened after that date are insured up to $100,000, *total*. If you have different types of accounts— an IRA, for example, and a Keogh (see page 60), or two separate IRAs—in the same bank, only your first $100,000 is protected. That's all you can collect on if the bank collapses.

But if the insurance is important to you, one solution is to use different banks, limiting your deposit to $100,000 in each one. Of course, the insurance applies only to bank deposits. If you're using a bank as your agent for buying mutual funds or other investments, that investment isn't FDIC insured.

NON-DEDUCTIBLE IRAs

Even if you can't deduct your contribution, you might still decide to open an IRA. What you earn on your investment is still tax-deferred until you begin to withdraw. But funding an IRA with money you have paid taxes on may not provide as big a payoff as some other investment options, especially ones with higher limits on annual investment amounts like 401(k)s, or no limits at all like variable annuities or municipal bonds.

INVENTING IRAS IRAs were created on Labor Day 1974 when President Ford signed the Employee Retirement Income Security Act (ERISA). The story has it that the committee designing the plan to encourage personal savings struggled to find a name with a pronounceable acronym—and borrowed their solution from Ira Cohen, the IRS actuary who was working with them.

IRAs: Weighing the Merits

It's hard not to love an IRA, but look before you leap.

THE PLUSES

IRAs are great investments for many people. If you qualify to deduct the contribution, you'll certainly benefit from setting one up.

$31,000

START CONTRIBUTING AT AGE 18

STOP CONTRIBUTING AT AGE 28

For example, if you contributed $2,000 a year for ten years as soon as you started earning, and then stopped contributing, your $20,000 investment would go on growing, and you'd owe no tax until you were ready to withdraw.

If you earned 8% a year on the investment, you would have $31,291 in the account when you stopped putting money in at the end of ten years.

THE MINUSES

As terrific as IRAs are for some investors, they do have some drawbacks. For one thing, if you take the money out before you reach 59½, in most cases you'll owe a **10% penalty** on the amount you withdraw. For example, if you put $2,000 away each year for five years, earning 6% a year, your $10,000 investment would be worth $11,950. A 10% penalty would be $1,195, leaving you with earnings of $755, or a return of about 1.5% a year.

THE 10% HIT

$	11,950	Value of IRA before early withdrawal
– $	10,000	Total contribution to IRA
– $	1,195	10% penalty
= $	755	Earnings after penalty

You can't borrow from your IRA either, the way you can from pension plans or insurance policies. But you may be able to get at the money in your IRA on a short-term basis—specifically 60 days—if you take money out of one account, use it for whatever you want, and open a new account with the full amount you withdrew before the 60 days are up. But if you miss the deadline, or you don't deposit the full amount, it counts as an early withdrawal and you'll owe the penalty.

Finally, IRAs are not necessarily the best choice for your retirement savings, especially if you can contribute to a pension plan where you work. That's because most voluntary plans, like 401(k)s and 403(b)s, or Keoghs and SEPs for the self-employed, allow you to contribute more.

MIXING DIFFERENT IRAS: A RECIPE FOR TAX TROUBLE

While it's smart to put several years worth of IRA contributions into the same account, both to simplify your record-keeping and increase your earnings, it's not smart to mix deductible and non-deductible contributions in the same account—or, according to some people, to try to use both types. That's because when it comes time to withdraw, figuring the tax you owe can be a problem.

For example, if, by the time you retire, you have put $40,000 in IRAs—$16,000 in deductible contributions and $24,000

A $600,000 IRA provides at least $40,000 a year for 15 years

$600,000

WAIT UNTIL AGE 70½

If you waited until you were 70½ to start withdrawals, your IRA would be worth around $600,000.

in non-deductible contributions—that has produced earnings of $56,000, how do you figure the tax that's due?

TAXES ON LUMP SUM WITHDRAWAL

	$ 96,000	Total value of IRA
−	24,000	Non-deductible contributions
=	$ 72,000	Taxable part of lump sum

If you were single and in the 28% tax bracket, the tax due on the entire $96,000 would be $25,290, based on 1993 tax tables. But you've already paid tax on $24,000. Subtract $24,000 from $96,000, leaving a taxable balance of $72,000 and a tax due of $17,850. That's not so hard.

BUT THERE'S A HITCH—OR TWO

Chances are you aren't going to withdraw your IRA money in a lump sum. That means you have to figure out what percentage of the money that has already been taxed is included in each withdrawal, and compute the tax you owe on the balance. Using the same example, you can figure out the taxable part of a $3,000 withdrawal in two steps, finding the taxable percentage and the taxable amount:

TAXES ON A $3,000 ANNUAL WITHDRAWAL

First:

	$ 24,000	Non-deductible contributions
÷	96,000	Total value of IRA
=	25%	Non-taxable percentage

Then:

	$ 3,000	Total value of withdrawal
÷	.25	Non-deductible percentage
= $	750	Is non-taxable, so you owe tax on $2,250

It won't work to say you're using up the non-deductible portion of your savings first. The IRS says you must treat withdrawals as if they came from all your IRAs proportionally, even if you have always kept the accounts separate and actually withdraw from just one.

That's why so many people stopped putting money into IRAs when the deductibility rules changed. Chances are, if you have both types of accounts, you'll need the help of an accountant or tax professional to figure out the amount you owe.

IRA Rollovers

Rollovers are a hop, skip, and a jump from conventional IRAs.

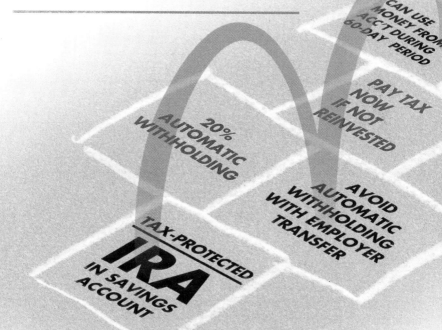

IRA rollovers are like other IRAs in many ways. You pay no tax on your earnings until you take the money out. And there can be penalties if you make withdrawals before age 59½.

The difference is where the money in the IRA comes from. Rollover IRAs are funded with money that's already been put away in a qualified retirement plan, like a pension plan, a 401(k), a Keogh, or another IRA. The rollover lets you move the money without owing any tax.

THERE ARE ROLLOVERS AND THEN THERE ARE ROLLOVERS

The word rollover does double duty when it comes to IRAs. If you close your IRA brokerage account, get the check for the amount you've accumulated, and deposit that amount to open a mutual fund IRA, you're rolling it over. The same is true if you take IRA money out of a savings account and buy a CD. As long as you put the money from the old investment into the new one within 60 days, your IRA is intact.

You could accomplish the same thing by filling out the necessary forms and asking the institutions involved to transfer your IRA directly. You open an IRA rollover, though, with a lump sum payment you get from a pension plan. That might happen when you retire, change jobs, or when a plan is disbanded and the money is paid out.

As always, there are rules

Like IRAs you fund yourself, IRA rollovers are subject to certain regulations. Following the rules postpones taxes and protects you from fees and penalties.

DEPOSIT WITHIN 60 DAYS

First and foremost, the 60-day rule applies. If you put your pension payout into an IRA rollover, you have to deposit the full amount within the official time period—and the clock starts ticking on the date the check is mailed to you.

A bigger problem is that 20% of the payout amount is automatically withheld as tax when you get the payment check. That means if you're going to deposit the full amount, you'll have to tap another source—like your savings—to come up with the 20% that's

TAX-PROTECTED IRA IN BROKER ACCOUNT

60-DAY ROLLOVER TIME LIMIT

WHY USE A ROLLOVER?

If you put your pension payout in an IRA, your investment can keep on growing and you can continue to postpone taxes until you make withdrawals. Then you owe tax at your regular rate.

Once the IRA rollover is set up, you can leave it or, in some cases, transfer it into a new employer's pension plan. You can invest the amount in an IRA rollover any way you wish, just as you can with any IRA.

IRA FEES

IRAs cost little or nothing to set up and aren't expensive to maintain. Banks rarely charge fees at all. Mutual funds and brokerages may charge between

$5 and $50 to open your account and often a similar annual fee, although sometimes they'll waive the charges to attract or keep your business, especially if you have a sizeable sum.

Since some of the fees are fixed, and not based on the size of your IRA, they have a much smaller impact than the fees often imposed on other retirement savings plans. And you can subtract the annual fee as a miscellaneous deduction on your income tax return if you pay the fees by check rather than having them deducted from your account.

But the annual fees don't cover sales charges or commissions on the buying and selling you do within your IRA. Those costs can't be paid separately. They are based on the size of each transaction, and are not tax-deductible. As long as your return, including the cost of the trading fees, is more than the rate of inflation, your investment is growing.

FUTURE CONSIDERATIONS

You can extend the tax-deferred life of your IRA at least five years, and sometimes more, by leaving it to a living beneficiary rather than to your estate. That's because IRA withdrawals are based on life expectancy and an estate hasn't got one. So your account comes to a quick (and bad) end, with a tax bill to settle. It's an easy mistake to avoid.

---

being withheld. You'll get the 20% back—after you pay your taxes for the year, possibly as long as 15 or 16 months later.

Worse yet, if you can't come up with enough to cover the full lump sum payment, the amount that was withheld counts as a withdrawal, even though you never had the money. If you're not 59½ yet, you owe the tax, plus a penalty for early withdrawal.

There is a way to avoid this problem: Have your employer transfer your pension payout to your IRA rollover directly, rather than sending you a check. That way, no tax is withheld. But if you want access to the cash during the 60 days, you're stuck.

KEEP IRAS SEPARATE

When you set up an IRA rollover, sometimes called a conduit IRA, you should keep it separate from any other IRAs you might have. It's especially important if there's a chance you might want to move the money into a new employer's pension plan. If you don't keep the money separate, you won't be able to move it.

DON'T MIX TAXED AND PRE-TAXED IRAS

The only contributions to a pension or retirement fund that can be moved into an IRA rollover are those which weren't taxed. If you've made any after-tax contributions, or if your employer has made supplemental contributions that aren't tax-deductible, that money has to be invested separately. The one advantage of the rule is that it will simplify figuring your tax when you begin to make withdrawals, since everything you take out will be taxable.

PUT AWAY PENSION PAYOUTS

You can put all or part of your lump sum pension payout in an IRA rollover. If the payout is made in a series of partial lump sums over a period of less than ten years, you can put some or all of those payments into an IRA rollover too.

SEPs

Setting up a Simplified Employee Pension isn't exactly a piece of cake, but it can be a sweet addition to your retirement menu.

If you run a small business, a Simplified Employee Pension, or SEP, may offer the most effective way to put money away for retirement. That's because you can shelter a lot more than you can in an IRA and the rules, though they're involved, are a lot less stringent than for other qualified retirement plans, including Keoghs.

Because a SEP is a qualified plan, the amount you contribute each year can be deducted from your earnings, reducing your current taxes. The contribution limits are 15% of what you earn (the salary you pay yourself), with a cap of $22,500.

You can change the amount of your contribution each year, skipping poor years and putting away the maximum in good ones. If you change jobs or end up being covered by another plan, you can roll over a SEP into an IRA without penalty and keep earning money on a tax-deferred basis.

WHAT YOU CAN'T DO WITH SEPS AND SAR-SEPS

There are a few limitations on SEPs that don't apply to other qualified retirement plans:

- **You can't forward average a lump sum distribution (see page 44)**
- **You can't roll over your SEP into a new employer's retirement plan**
- **You can't invest in insurance.**

None of these by itself—or even the three together—are reason to ignore the advantages of a SEP. And, you don't have to file an annual report with the IRS the way you must with a Keogh.

EMPLOYEE PLANS

Since SEPs are actually specialized IRAs, sometimes referred to as SEP-IRAs, they're always set up and controlled by the person who benefits from them, even though they're funded exclusively by an employer.

That makes it easier for employers: they don't have to pay someone to run a pension plan. It's also better if you're

Comparing SEP-IRAs

Small-company employees may have the option of being included in two different types of SEPs to save for retirement. They are

SEP-IRA LIKE A PENSION, THE CONTRIBUTION COMES FROM YOUR EMPLOYER

Employer contributes up to 15% of your salary, to a cap of $22,500

You don't contribute

ALL ELIGIBLE EMPLOYEES MUST BE INCLUDED

an employee: all the money in your SEP account is yours from the minute it's deposited. You don't have to wait to be vested, as you do with some other qualified plans.

SAR-SEPS

SAR-SEPs, also known as salary reduction SEPs, are the equivalent of 401(k)s for small businesses with fewer than 25 eligible employees. Employees can defer salary up to 15%, to a cap of $9,240 for 1994, and employers can provide matching amounts. The total contribution ceiling is $22,500.

EQUALITY'S THE RULE

If you have employees, you have to give them the same kind of SEP benefits you give yourself. For example, if you contribute 10% of your earnings to your SEP, you have to contribute 10% of their earnings to accounts in their names.

and SAR-SEPs

funded differently and have different rules for participating.

SAR-SEP LIKE A 401(K), YOU MAKE THE BASIC CONTRIBUTION

You contribute up to 15% of your salary, to a cap of $9,240 in 1994

Employer may match part of your contribution to a cap of 15% of salary

AT LEAST 50% OF ALL ELIGIBLE EMPLOYEES MUST AGREE TO PARTICIPATE

PUTTING MORE IN

You may be able to build up your pension by using a SAR-SEP to defer part of your earnings into the plan. However, the total annual contribution is limited to 15% of your salary, or $22,500. So if your employer plans to put in the full 15% into a SEP-IRA, that amount would be reduced by what you put in yourself and you'd lose part of your employer's contribution. But if your employer is putting in less than 15%, you might want to make up the difference. You may also make a deductible $2,000 contribution to an IRA if your earnings are within the limit set by the laws (see page 51).

FIGURING YOUR CONTRIBUTION

Figuring the amount you can contribute to a SEP is a bit trickier than it seems. That's because compensation, or earnings, as far as qualified retirement plans are concerned, aren't what you earn, but your earnings minus the amount you contribute to the retirement plan. The effect is to reduce the maximum SEP contribution from 15% to 13.0435%. If you're self-employed, you also have to subtract half the money you paid in self-employment tax.

The IRS provides a workchart for you to use in figuring your contribution. Or, you can get a sense of your potential maximum contribution using this formula:

$$\begin{array}{c} \text{Net earnings} \\ \text{minus 50\%} \\ \text{employment tax} \end{array} \times \begin{array}{c} \text{Contribution} \\ \text{reduction} \\ \text{factor (.115)} \end{array} = \begin{array}{c} \text{Contribution} \\ \text{amount} \end{array}$$

for example

$200,000	Net earnings
− 6,657	50% of employment tax
= 193,343	
× .115	Contribution reduction
= $ 22,234	Contribution amount

TIMING

Another appealing feature of SEPs, whether you're self-employed or the owner of a small business, is the timetable for setting up and contributing to the plan. Like an IRA, you can open a SEP and fund it when your tax return is due, including any extensions.

As with any savings that accumulate tax-deferred, you make more money if you contribute early in the tax year. But self-employed people in particular can't always be sure how much they'll make in any given tax year, or how much they'll be able to put away for the future. Since there are penalties for putting too much into a SEP, waiting until the end of your tax year can make it easier to get the right contribution amount.

EMPLOYEE CONTRIBUTION LIMITS

SAR-SEP	Combination SEP/SAR-SEP
$9,240 per year	15% of earnings up to $22,500 per year; SAR-SEP portion can't exceed $9,240

Keogh Plans

A Keogh lets you invest for retirement while you're busy earning a living.

How to Qualify

If you're self-employed, earn money for work you do in addition to your regular job, or own a small business, you qualify to open a Keogh plan that lets you build up money for retirement by deferring taxes on the investments you make and the earnings they accumulate.

You can contribute a portion of your net earnings from one or more of these categories, but no income from other sources. There's no requirement that these earnings be your only source of income or the Keogh be your only pension plan. In fact, you can be a fulltime employee covered by a defined benefits plan and still contribute to a Keogh if you earn money in a way that qualifies.

To set up a Keogh you must:

Own your own business and file a Schedule C with your tax return

Have a Subchapter S corporation

OPENING A KEOGH

To set up an Keogh, you need to file an IRS-approved plan. Banks and other financial institutions provide standardized plans, but you can have one specially designed by a lawyer or accountant who is a Keogh specialist. The advantage—some would say the necessity—of a specialized plan is the flexibility it provides for managing and investing your plan's assets.

KEOGHS FOR EMPLOYEES

If you have employees, and you have a Keogh plan for yourself, you must provide comparable benefits to the people who qualify to participate. For example, if you contribute 15% of your earnings to the plan, you must contribute 15% for each employee covered by the plan.

The law says you must have a plan administrator—you can take the job

KEOGH or SEP?

If you qualify to set up a Keogh plan, you also qualify for a SEP—though you can't open both for the same earnings. Each has some advantages and some limitations.

For most people, especially those without employees, the debate comes down to two issues—the option to shelter more money through a Keogh versus the simplicity of a SEP. For employers, the ability to set the standards for participation can also be an important factor.

Advantages	Limitations
SEP	
• Simpler and cheaper to set up	• Contribution amount limited to 15% of earnings
• Easier to administer, both internally and for the IRS	• Employers with plan must cover everyone who works for them
• Doesn't commit you to annual contributions	
KEOGH	
• Offers several ways to structure plan	• Can commit you to contributions even in poor years
• Lets you shelter more money, sometimes much more	• Expensive to set up and administer
• Lets you continue to contribute after age 70½	• Complex tax-reporting requirements
• Allows employers to establish criteria for employees to qualify for participation	

THE MAN WITH THE PLAN
Keogh plans are named for Eugene Keogh, a U.S. Representative from Brooklyn, New York, who sponsored the legislation that established the plans. They went into effect in 1962.

| Be self-employed doing something or selling something | Sit on a corporate board of directors | Be a partner in a business that files a Schedule K | Work as a freelancer |

yourself if you want—and dictates how to compute contributions based on your net profit. There's no law that requires you to hire a Keogh specialist to handle your plan—but there probably ought to be.

HOW A KEOGH WORKS

A Keogh works like employer-sponsored pension plans in many ways. But like an IRA it is often set up to benefit just one person—you. Like other qualified plans, a Keogh lets you deduct pension contributions on your tax return and imposes a penalty if you withdraw funds before you're 59½.

When you reach 70½, you're must set up a specific withdrawal schedule. But unlike other plans, whether funded by your employer or yourself, a Keogh lets you go on making qualifying contributions even after you've started taking mandatory withdrawals.

Like a pension plan, a Keogh permits forward averaging for lump sum withdrawals (see page 45), and allows you to borrow against the funds accumulated in your plan, with some restrictions. Neither of those advantages is available with an IRA or a SEP-IRA.

HOLD THE APPLAUSE

Keoghs are a boon to self-employed people who would otherwise have no way to shelter money for the future, and to employees of small businesses that wouldn't otherwise offer a retirement plan. But being involved with a Keogh is complex.

To begin with, there are three different sets of Keogh regulations: one if you're self-employed, one if you own a business, and one if you're an employee of a company with a Keogh plan.

KEOGH CUSTOM TAILORING

CUSTOMIZE—IT MAY PAY

Ask your lawyer or tax professional to recommend someone to set up your Keogh. Be prepared: a customized plan could cost several thousand dollars. But a plan that locks you into contributions you can't meet or options that limit what you can save costs more in the long run.

Once the account is set up—by December 31 of the first year you are going to take a tax deduction for your contribution—you can make annual or periodic additions to it as long as you don't put in more than the amount you're entitled to contribute in any given year. The deadline for depositing funds is the day your tax return is due, including any extensions you may get.

The same investment limitations that apply to IRAs apply to self-directed Keoghs, with an added prohibition on U.S. coins. But if your Keogh is a trust or custodial account, the money can be invested in anything at all—including wine.

Keoghs

Keoghs have several designs, plain and fancy, to appeal to a lot of different tastes.

While Keogh rules are notoriously complicated, the investment opportunities Keoghs provide have made them a staple of retirement planning. One major advantage is that you can choose the Keogh you want, from among several types of defined contribution options or a defined benefit plan. The options mean that a wide range of people, with different sources of self-employment income, can participate.

Defined contribution plans, which are available in three different versions, are classic Keoghs. They work just like corporate defined contribution pension plans. You put money into the plan, and the amount you have at retirement depends chiefly on how well your investments do.

Defined benefit plans guarantee a specific payout but may require large contributions. They are not for everyone. But they can be ideal for people within 15 years or so of retirement who are making lots of money and don't mind the expense of sheltering it this way.

JUST DESSERTS
MAKE YOUR OWN

DIET SPECIAL

CHOOSE YOUR FLAVORS

DOUBLE SCOOPS

PROFIT-SHARING DEFINED CONTRIBUTION PLANS are the least complicated, and the most popular, Keoghs.

They let you decide each year whether to participate and how much to put away

You can contribute up to 15% of your earnings, or $22,500, whichever is less.

MONEY PURCHASE DEFINED CONTRIBUTION PLANS are the most generous and the most rigid plans.

They let you put away up to 25% of your earnings, to a maximum of $30,000.

You must specify the percentage of earnings when you set up the plan, and you must contribute that percentage each year.

The minimum you can choose is 3%; if you don't put in enough, you'll owe a penalty of up to 100% of the amount you owed but didn't contribute.

PAIRED PLANS are the most flexible Keoghs, combining some of the best aspects of profit-sharing and money purchase. They do, however, lock you into an annual contribution even in years when you don't make much money.

You can set a money-purchase percentage low enough to meet comfortably each year—say 10%—and then contribute an additional amount—up to 25% total—through profit-sharing in good years.

WHAT YOU CAN CONTRIBUTE

The amount you can put into a Keogh each year is a fixed percentage of your earnings. Usually there's a cap, which is determined by the way your plan is set up. For 1994, the maximum contribution ranges from 15% to 100% of earnings, with most plans capped at $22,500.

Keogh earnings aren't what you earn, but what's left of your earnings after you subtract the amount you contribute to your Keogh plan. The effect is to reduce the contribution from 15% to 13.042% in profit-sharing Keoghs and from 25% to 20% for money-purchase and paired-plan Keoghs. If you're self-employed you also have to subtract half the money you paid in self-employment tax from your earnings to find the amount your Keogh contribution is based on. IRS Publication 560 explains the details.

KEOGH TRUSTS

If you want to diversify your Keogh investments without having to watch several different plans, you can set up a self-directed Keogh trust, make all your contributions to the trust, and invest the holdings as you choose. While setting up a trust can be costly and time-consuming, it does more than just save paperwork over time. With a trust, you can make more types of investments and shift your asset allocation among investments more easily. Perhaps most important, a trust simplifies the withdrawal process when the time comes to start taking your money out, since unlike IRAs, you must withdraw the correct amount from each Keogh account separately.

KEEPING THE IRS UP TO DATE

Keoghs can be a recordkeeping nightmare. Every three years you have to file a Form 5500-C with the IRS. Other years you must file Form 5500EZ (if you're self-employed) or 5500-R (if you have employees). Even if you have to gather the records yourself, it's probably worth having an accountant or Keogh expert fill out the form for you.

IRS FORM 5500-C

FORM 5500EZ

IRS FORM 5500R

DEFINED BENEFIT PLANS guarantee a specific annual payout after you retire or reach age 65.

To fund the plan so that it produces the payout you choose (and incidentally to save yourself a lot of current tax), you may be able to contribute up to 100% of your annual earnings.

Figuring out what you must pay in each year is extremely complicated. The law requires that an actuary review your plan annually to determine what you have to put in to meet your projected payout; you must submit a copy of that report with your tax return.

ELASTIC PLANS

If you have a Keogh, you can roll a pension payout from another job into it, instead of into an IRA. That lets you take a lump sum distribution and forward average the entire amount at some future date. That flexibility is an advantage when you start withdrawing from your retirement plans.

Or, if your self-employment income dries up and you can't keep up with a Keogh plan, you can call it quits and roll the money over into an IRA. You're out the money you spent to set your plan up, and might have to pay some penalties. But because a Keogh is a qualified retirement plan, you don't have to take a distribution and pay tax on it.

IRA Withdrawals

You have to be old enough to take money out of your IRA, but you don't have to retire first.

The first things you have to know about withdrawing from your self-directed retirement investments are the magic numbers. One is the otherwise unmagical 59½. That's the point at which you can begin to collect without paying a penalty.

Being eligible at 59½ doesn't mean you must start collecting then: you can wait until you actually retire—at 62 or 65 or 68—or until you're ready to add a source of income to your budget.

The only restriction is that you *must* begin withdrawing by the time you're 70½. At that time, you must set up a plan for getting all the money out of your accounts and into your pockets (and the taxes you owe into Uncle Sam's pockets).

WHAT YOU HAVE TO TAKE

The rules on withdrawing from an IRA are specific but not simple. Basically, your withdrawal schedule has to be set up so that if you followed it, you would get all

59½ [60–70] 70½

Since insurance company actuarial tables consider you already 60 when you reach 59½, and still 70 until you're 70½, Congress used those ages to frame the withdrawal period from retirement accounts.

the money out of all your retirement accounts within one of the following:

- **Your lifetime**
- **The joint lifetime of you and your spouse**
- **The joint lifetime of you and any beneficiary you choose**
- **Any period that's shorter than any of the others.**

You get to set the length of the shorter period. Otherwise the length of time is dictated by the life expectancy tables the IRS provides in Publication 590, *Individual Retirement Arrangements.*

THE TAX BITE

Because IRA investments are tax-deferred, you owe income tax on your withdrawals. For tax purposes, it's considered regular income. That means if your combined income for the year puts you into the 28% tax bracket, that's the rate at which your payouts are taxed.

Many people assume they'll be in a lower tax bracket when they retire, so they'll end up paying less tax. Even if that's not the case—and for many people it isn't—the real advantage of retirement savings plans is the rate at which the investments grow, not the rate at which they are taxed.

YOU <u>MUST</u> START IRA WITHDRAWALS

Since an IRA is a retirement account, with the tax-deferral advantage, the IRS doesn't want it to be a way to build the estate you're planning to leave your heirs. So when you reach age 70½, the law says you must start spending what you've saved—whether you need the money or not. One way to stretch the account (but not bend the rules) is to name a much younger person as your IRA beneficiary. When you die, that person may be able to spread payments from the account over a much longer time.

Happy 59½ᵀᴴ Birthday!

YOU <u>CAN</u> START IRA WITHDRAWALS

Once you reach age 59½ you can start taking money out of your IRA in any amount you want, as long as your income from all your retirement plans isn't more than $150,000 a year. You'll owe tax on the amount you withdraw, but you can spend it any way you like.

THE PENALTY QUESTION

If you take money out of your IRAs before you're eligible—usually at 59½—you'll probably owe a 10% early withdrawal penalty on top of the taxes.

The IRS imposes the penalty to encourage you to leave your retirement money alone and to charge you for getting tax-deferred growth on investments you're making for other reasons.

The truth is that most people have no qualms about taking money out of their retirement savings if they need it. There are two views on enforcing the penalties:

One is to change the law so that people who use their retirement money for worthy causes—like education, buying a house, or health care—would be exempt from the penalty, no matter what their age. The other view is that a penalty is valid because it discourages people from spending the money they're going to need when they retire long before they get close to retirement.

There's a question, too, about whether people would participate in a stricter plan. Several polls suggest that the majority would not put money into an IRA if they knew there was no way to touch it until they hit 59½.

When It's Safe to Withdraw

10% PENALTY FOR EARLY WITHDRAWAL	NO PENALTY FOR WITHDRAWALS BETWEEN AGES 59½ TO 70½	50% PENALTY FOR LATE WITHDRAWAL
50	59½ 70½	80

EARLY WITHDRAWAL WITHOUT PENALTY

There is one way to get access to the money in your IRAs before you're 59½ and avoid the penalty. That's to **annuitize** your distribution. It means you establish a withdrawal plan that pays you, each year, a fixed amount of the money in your IRA, based on your life expectancy. The chief restriction is that the plan must cover at least five years or all the years left until you reach 59½, whichever is fewer.

Annuitization does have drawbacks, though. If what you really need is a large amount of money, you probably won't get it this way unless you're close to 59½. And you're using money that was intended for your retirement, so you're depleting, not adding, to your savings.

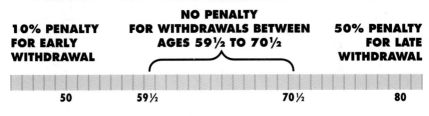

ANNUITIZED WITHDRAWAL FROM AGE 50
$23,000/YR

Fund balance $280,000

Total payout $782,000

Age   50   60   70   80

REGULAR WITHDRAWAL FROM AGE 59½
$45,000/YR

Fund balance $500,000

Total payout $1,080,000

Age   50   60   70   80

Taking Money Out

Investing in an IRA is the easy part. It's getting the mandatory withdrawals right that's tough.

When you're ready to start taking money out of your IRAs, you need a strategy to meet the legal requirements while getting the best return you can.

The more plans you have and the more money you have amassed, the more carefully you need to plan your withdrawals—not so much to avoid overspending, but to avoid the big penalties you'll have to pay for taking out too much or too little in any given year.

HAVING TOO MUCH

Though it seems a curious way to reward planning for the future, you get hit with a penalty if you've put too much away. In 1994, the most you're allowed to withdraw a year from your pension and retirement savings plans combined is $150,000. If you take more than that, you pay 15% of the amount over $150,000 on top of whatever tax is due.

Realistically, to get that large a payout, your retirement investments have to be substantial—probably several million dollars. But someone with a generous pension plus a SEP or Keogh, or someone who begins to put money away early in a successful career and invests it profitably might easily be in that position.

Since the one source of retirement income you can control is what you take out of your IRAs, one solution is to start your withdrawals earlier than 70½. By spreading out the number of years you collect, you can lower each annual amount. But for many people who continue earning through their 60s, and anticipate living well beyond that, withdrawing money they don't need now and might need later has serious drawbacks.

THE OLDER YOU GET, THE LONGER YOU LIVE!

According to IRS life expectancy tables, the longer you live the longer you can expect to live. If you're 70, you can expect to live until you're 86—but at 86, you're looking at 92, and at 92 it's 96.

1 ADD UP YOUR IRAs
Withdrawals are based on the total value of all your accounts.

SETTING THE AMOUNT
You can set the amount of your annual withdrawal for life when you are 70½ by choosing the term-certain method of withdrawal. **Term-certain** withdrawals are calculated, using your current life expectancy (based on your age alone). The amount is fixed, for as long as your withdrawals continue.

You can take the entire withdrawal from just one IRA account, even if you have several. One advantage is that you can avoid withdrawing from accounts that are growing at a faster rate. Another is simplified bookkeeping.

2 FIGURE YOUR WITHDRAWAL AMOUNT
You don't want your account to provide too little money or run out too quickly.

GETTING THE RIGHT NUMBERS
If you have $250,000 in your IRA, and you have a life expectancy of 18 years, you need to withdraw $13,888 a year. You can use the formula below for figuring out the size of the withdrawal you have to make:

$$\frac{\text{Account balance}}{\text{Life expectancy}} = \text{Minimum annual withdrawal}$$

for example

$$\frac{\$250,000}{18} = \$13,888$$

RECALCULATING THE AMOUNT

You can—within certain limits—change the amount you withdraw each year by recalculating your life expectancy annually. The advantage is that you can take smaller payments in the early years, letting your investments grow and reserving more for later years.

There are some drawbacks, though. Once you choose to recalculate, you commit yourself to doing it every year. And if your life expectancy calculation is based on two lives (yours and your spouse's, for example), and one of you dies, the surviving partner would have to increase the annual withdrawals

You can get Publication 590 and other IRS information you need by calling:

1-800-TAX-FORM

enough to meet minimum requirements. That would mean more taxes, and the potential for spending down the money too rapidly.

For example, if you were 72 and your spouse was 70, you'd have a life expectancy of 19.8 years. But if your spouse died, yours would drop to 14.6. If your IRA balance was $100,000, you'd have to withdraw $1,799 more, and pay more tax too.

TABLE II   (Joint Life and Last Survivor Expectancy)*

AGES	68	69	70	71	72	73
69	21.9	21.5	21.1	20.7	20.3	
70	21.5	21.1	20.6	20.2		
71	21.2	20.7	20.2	19.8		
72	20.8	20.3	19.8	19.4		
73	20.5	20.0	19.4	19.1		

JOINT AND LAST SURVIVOR

	$ 100,000	Value of IRA
÷	19.8	Life expectancy
= $	5,050	Annual withdrawal

TABLE I   (Single Life Expectancy)*

AGE	DIVISOR	AGE	DIVI
70	16.0	108	
71	15.3	109	
72	14.6	110	

SINGLE LIFE

	$ 100,000	Value of IRA
÷	14.6	Life expectancy
= $	6,849	Annual withdrawal

* Table I does not provide for IRA

3

AVOID TAX PENALTIES

You'll owe extra tax for withdrawing too much or too little

GETTING THE NUMBERS WRONG

If you miscalculate the amount you must withdraw, and take too little, you'll get socked with a 50% penalty on the additional amount you should have taken and didn't. That's true even if it was an honest mistake—unless you can prove to the IRS that you were completely befuddled.

If you take too much, of course, you pay more tax than you might have otherwise, and you deplete your account faster. But there aren't penalties for that unless you're over the $150,000 annual withdrawal limit.

4

DECIDE ON A SOURCE

IRA WITHDRAWAL
- ☐ Bonds
- ☐ Stocks
- ☐ CD
- ☐ Money Mkt.

FINDING THE CASH

Figuring out how much you must withdraw each year is only the first step. You also have to decide how to get at it. Since wise investment strategy suggests you diversify your retirement accounts into various moneymaking investments, you probably haven't got the right amount sitting around in a money market fund or savings account.

You could sell stocks, but what if the market is down? You might have to pay a penalty to take money out of a CD. A better option is to open a mutual fund or bank money market account to collect dividend and interest payments from various investments.

Social Security

Social Security is an American institution—now. But it was controversial at the start.

Social Security is a safety net, designed to provide a financial foundation for retired and disabled workers and their families. People without other sources of income get by entirely on their Social Security benefits. But for many Americans, the monthly payment supplies just a part of their retirement budget.

Before Social Security, veterans—disabled ones in particular—got pensions. And in the early 20th century, payments to civilian government workers and to needy widows and orphans expanded the notion that social welfare was a government responsibility. But public opinion was widely split, not only on providing benefits, but on who deserved support.

RELIEF FOR DEPRESSION

President Roosevelt introduced the **Social Security Act** in 1935 as part of his New Deal, a controversial recovery plan designed to cope with the devastating aftermath of the Great Depression and its particularly chilling effect on the financial situation of the elderly and the unemployed.

Today, benefits for retired and disabled workers and their survivors have evolved into the most elaborate and most popular social program in the U.S. Unemployment compensation is also firmly in place. But the other two elements of Roosevelt's original program—public assistance, or welfare, and universal health care insurance—remain controversial.

A COMPULSORY PLAN

Since other countries had tried voluntary retirement income plans without success, Congress decided that everybody who was going to be eligible for benefits had to participate by contributing part of their earnings. To simplify the collection process, they originated the idea of **withholding** and passed the Federal Insurance Contribution Act (FICA) which:

- **Authorized employers to deduct workers' contribution amounts directly from their salaries**

- **Made employers responsible for forwarding the FICA taxes to the Internal Revenue Service (IRS).**

WHERE IT BEGAN

Americans didn't invent the idea of Social Security, although there was a precedent in the pensions paid to Union veterans of the Civil War. In the 1889, **Chancellor Otto von Bismarck** made old age insurance compulsory in Germany, requiring that working people, their employers, and the government all contribute to a program that would provide financial support after retirement. Retired worker programs were widespread in Europe by the 1920s.

EMPLOYER CONTRIBUTIONS

The Social Security system wouldn't have enough money to operate if it ran on employee contributions alone, no matter how big a bite your share seems to take out of your paycheck. So employers are required to pay taxes on the wages they pay their workers—equal to the amount the employee pays. That's true no matter how few or how many employees there are.

If you're self-employed, you pay both shares, or twice the amount you would pay if you worked for someone else. You deduct half of your total payment (the equivalent of the employer's share) on your income taxes, and also when you calculate how much you can contribute to a SEP-IRA or Keogh retirement plan (see pages 58-61).

ALMOST ALL INCLUSIVE

Originally, Social Security included only commercial and industrial employees, but over the years it's been expanded to cover more than 90% of the work force. Several groups of workers don't participate, including some state and local government employees and railroad workers (who have their own retirement plans), and some members of the clergy who don't participate for religious reasons.

People who don't work aren't part of the system either, although they may qualify for benefits as the spouse, child or survivor of someone who has participated in the system.

DOING THE JOB

Social Security insures the financial security of a large—and growing—segment of the population. More than 92% of all households that include someone over 65 get benefits. It provides the main source of income for 63% of the households receiving retirement benefits. And it has achieved one of its primary goals, dramatically reducing poverty rates among people over 65. Without their Social Security income, more than half of the elderly population would be poor according to government standards. But because of the benefits, only 14% fall into that category.

A WIDE NET

There are very few people eligible for Social Security benefits who aren't collecting them. If you move frequently or don't have a permanent address, there's sometimes a delay in getting your payment. But you can collect Social Security almost anywhere in the world—except in jail.

The one group of people who may not be collecting, but should be, are those over 70 who are still working full time. Social Security rules let you collect your full benefit no matter how many hours you work or how much you earn once you reach 70. It doesn't make sense to delay collecting either, because the basic benefit you're entitled to then is the highest it will be.

Percent of benefits awarded in 1993

Retired workers	**62%**
Disabled workers	**17%**
Spouses and children	**12%**
Survivors of deceased workers	**9%**

Changing for the Better

A big part of the system's strength has been its flexibility.

Signing the legislation was only the first step in creating the enormous institution that Social Security has become. Today, it's a comprehensive program that administers retirement, survivor and disability benefits, plus a Supplemental Security Program (SSI) for low income elderly and disabled people.

Growing Pains

The system has been changing, almost since the day it began. Things that once seemed impossible, like getting coverage if you were self-employed, or having to pay taxes on your benefits, are now the norm.

1939 In 1939, supplemental benefits for spouses and children were added to the payment a retired worker received. Payments began in 1940.

1951 In 1951, coverage was extended to include self-employed workers, as well as others who had not been eligible before, including farmers, domestic workers and entrepreneurs.

We've got your number

Identifying the people putting money into the Social Security system—and expecting to get money back—posed another challenge. Names and addresses wouldn't work: people change their names, and they move. How could the government be sure they had the right Charles Smith or Maria Rodriguez? Or that River Road was in Grandview, Ohio, not Grand View, New York?

The solution was assigning everyone a nine-digit number that would last a lifetime, through name changes, job changes, and new addresses. And the system could identify 999,999,999 people without ever having to use the same number twice.

The first three digits indicate the state where you applied for a card. The number changes as more cards are issued in that state.

The second group of digits doesn't have a particular meaning—though they are a related state code.

The last four digits are assigned in numerical order, for example 7091, 7092, 7093, and so on. One exception: twins, triplets, or other multiple siblings don't get numbers in order.

SOCIAL SECURITY

591-55-4170
THIS NUMBER HAS BEEN ESTABLISHED FOR
LEE LIANG WAN

SIGNATURE

MEDICAL

846347785
CERTIFICATE NO:
LEE LIANG
NAME
563 V 4402
CATEGORY
CBP $10 COPA
$10 COPAY DIAG
You must call NYC VE

Plan Number N67795
ID Number 591-55-4170
Payor Number 01227 0046
To Verify Coverage 800-244-6695
Claim Center
THE PRINCIPAL FINANCIAL GROUP
REGIONAL CLAIM CENTER
SIGNATURE 9
335 STORPE AVENUE, SUITE 2020
WALLIN CT 06962

Financial Group

EXPLODING USES

Once, you needed a Social Security number to open a Social Security account and keep track of your contributions. Now, you need one for almost anything you want to do:

- Get a job
- File income-tax returns
- Enroll as a student
- Open a bank, brokerage or mutual fund account
- Get a passport or a driver's license
- Ask for an insurance payment
- Apply for a loan
- Request your credit rating

1957 In 1957, members of the armed forces were covered.

1966 In 1966, the tax was increased to pay for Medicare insurance benefits

1972 In 1972, benefit increases were linked, or indexed, to inflation, to increase as the cost of living increased.

1983 In 1983, the age at which people qualify for full retirement benefits was increased. By 2009, you'll have to be 66 and by 2027, you'll have to be 67.

1984 In 1984, federal workers and employees of non-profit organizations had to be covered by Social Security.

BY THE NUMBERS

The IRS requires everyone to have a Social Security number by the time they're a year old if they're going to be claimed as a dependent on a tax return. In fact, in many states, babies are given a number when their births are registered.

Your number—one of the 365 million that's been assigned so far—can be changed, usually if your records have been confused with someone else's who has the same name and birthdate, or if someone has used your number illegally.

CHANGING YOUR NAME

If you change your name when you get married or divorced, or if you change it legally for any other reason, you can file form SS-5 and have the change made on your Social Security account. You'll have to provide your marriage license, divorce decree, or other legal proof. Your Social Security number doesn't change, though, and your credits are intact.

THREE TYPES OF CARDS

While we talk about Social Security cards as if they were all alike, there are actually three types. The basic cards go to citizens and people living permanently in the U.S.

You need the card—or at least the number—to get a job, collect benefits, and, increasingly, as a universal ID number.

People who are in the country legally, but for a limited time, may get Social Security cards to open bank accounts, for example, or enroll in college. Their cards are stamped *Not Eligible For Employment,* and they're not eligible for benefits. In 1992, a third card was added, stamped *Valid For Work Only With INS* (Immigration and Naturalization Service) *Authorization.* Those cards permit legal immigrants to get jobs and qualify for benefits.

Legally, it's up to a potential employer to be sure that anyone who's hired to work is eligible—and checking for a valid Social Security card is the primary method.

JUST THE BEGINNING

Ida Fuller, of Ludlow, VT, got a check for $22.54 in January, 1940—the first monthly benefit that Social Security paid. But that was only the beginning. Fuller lived to be 99, and the $20 she paid in withholding tax was repaid a thousand times in the three decades she collected.

Benefit Ins and Outs

One of every six Americans—about 42 million people— gets Social Security benefits.

YOUR MONEY GOING IN:

6.2% OF 135 MILLION PAYCHECKS FOR SOCIAL SECURITY

1.45% FOR MEDICARE

(PLUS EQUAL AMOUNT FROM EMPLOYER = 15.3%)

The 6.2% that's withheld is used to make current Social Security payments and to build the reserve that will be needed to meet future needs. It's deposited into two Social Security Trust Funds, one for retirement benefits and the other for disability payments. The 1.45% withheld for Medicare also goes into trust funds set up to pay for medical care.

RETIREMENT TRUST FUND

The core of the Social Security program is a guaranteed monthly income designed to insure a basic level of financial support for retired or disabled people, their families, and their survivors. It's funded by money withheld from your paycheck, and the paychecks of 135 million other working Americans.

SETTING YOUR CONTRIBUTION

The amount you owe for retirement, survivor, and disability insurance is 6.2% of your earned income (including salary, tips, commissions and bonuses) up to a specific limit that's adjusted each year to reflect increases in the cost of living. For 1994, the income limit was $60,600, in comparison to $57,600 for 1993, and $35,700 for 1983.

If you earn less than the limit, 6.2% of your gross, or pre-tax, earnings is withheld from each paycheck throughout the year. If you earn more, the deduction disappears when you've paid the full amount, $3,757.20 (6.2% of $60, 600) for 1994.

Your income from pensions, investments (including annuities), capital gains, sick pay, unemployment insurance or alimony isn't considered **earned**, so it escapes the long arm of withholding.

WHERE'S THE LIMIT

There's an annual cap for retirement contributions, but none for Medicare.	6.2% deduction stops when cap is reached	1.45% deduction never stops
Salary	for example **SS deduction**	for example **Medicare deduction**
$ 20,000	$ 1,240	$ 290
$ 40,000	$ 2,480	$ 580
$60,600	**$ 3,757 CAP**	$ 878
$ 80,000	$ 3,757	$1,160

MEDICARE COSTS MORE

There's more, though. Since 1966, an additional 1.45% has been withheld to fund Medicare benefits for people over 65. And since 1994, there's been no cap on your Medicare obligation, which means that 1.45% of whatever you earn is withheld throughout the year.

WITHHOLDING TOO MUCH

If you have more than one job, or if you work on your own in addition to holding a job, you may have too much Social Security withheld. For example,

- If you earned $65,000 in 1994 at your regular job, $3,757.20, the maximum amount, was withheld.

- If you earned another $15,000 working nights and weekends, your employer withheld $930 (or 6.2% of $15,000).

- That made your total withholding $4,687.20, or $930 too much.

WHAT'S INCOME—TO THE SSA

What counts	What doesn't count
Wages	Pension income
Tips	Capital gains
Commissions	Sick pay
Self-employment	Unemployment
	Alimony
	Investment income (including annuities)

Both employers must withhold at the regular rate, as if each of them were your only employer—even if they know you're working two jobs. The same thing happens if you're self-employed. You owe Social Security tax on what you earn even if you have the maximum withheld at another job.

But, you won't end up overpaying. The excess is credited toward the income tax you owe when you pay your taxes. But you'll be out the money in the meantime.

The only exception occurs when you have too much withheld by one employer, which can happen if you get back pay or a bonus. Then it's your employer's job to repay the extra withholding directly to you.

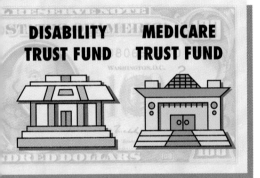

DISABILITY TRUST FUND

MEDICARE TRUST FUND

MONEY GOING OUT:

$1 BILLION A DAY, TO 42 MILLION PEOPLE

TREASURY BONDS

The money in the various trust funds is invested in U.S. Treasury bonds, safely earning interest, while the government uses it to keep its operations running. So far, the system has worked, and current obligations are regularly met. In fact, about $1.5 billion a week goes into the reserve funds.

BENEFIT PAYMENTS

Social Security pays out nearly $1 billion dollars a day. The average retirement payment is $670 a month. The average disability check is $640.

More than 42 million people received benefits in 1993, nearly 30 million retired workers and their dependents, 7.4 million survivors, and 5.3 million disabled workers and their families. Among the beneficiaries, 42% were men and 58% were women.

WHAT THE FUTURE HOLDS

Nobody can say for sure what will happen to Social Security in the 21st century. But its history has been evolutionary from the start, and that's likely to continue. Changes that caused major uproars when they were enacted—like taxing retirement benefits—have become the norm. The only thing that seems impossible is abandoning the system altogether.

We do know that the people collecting benefits will eventually outnumber the people putting money into the system. That may mean that wealthy retired people will get less than they expected, or nothing at all. Or all benefits may be taxed. Or cost-of-living increases might be smaller.

Social Security Up Close

Representatives at your local Social Security office provide advice and assistance face-to-face.

Much of the time, you deal with the Social Security Administration from a distance, using the phone or mail to get information, open an account, or even apply for benefits. But sooner or later, you'll probably visit your local Social Security office, one of 1,300 in the country. The offices can be quite different physically, but they're all equipped to handle the same things, helping you to join the system or take advantage of the benefits it provides. In particular, they can provide up-to-date estimates of what your benefits would be if you chose different options, like retiring early, or getting benefits as a survivor instead of based on your own work history.

> **Over 10 million new numbers are issued annually, making the total more than 350 million**

> **A computer-processed application takes about 30 minutes—instead of 30 to 40 days**

OPENING A SOCIAL SECURITY ACCOUNT

If you got a Social Security number when you were young, your account is open even if you've never worked. But if you don't have a number, you don't have an account. Getting one is relatively simple, though. You fill out form SS-5 which you can get at your local Social Security office and submit it along with evidence to prove your age, identity, and citizenship. You need your birth certificate (or a hospital record or baptismal certificate if you don't have one), plus one other piece of identification, like a passport, driver's license, or school record. The SS-5 application includes a list of the documents Social Security will accept. Parents opening accounts for their children must also prove their own identity and parenthood or guardianship.

If you're over 18, you must appear in person to open your account. If you're younger, you can do the whole thing by mail, but you may not want to. You have to provide Social Security with original copies of your birth certificate and other documents, and you probably don't want to risk having them lost or misplaced.

Don't worry if the nearest office is too far for you to travel to. Social Security representatives visit contact stations in rural areas on a regular schedule. And, if you're unable to get to the office because you're too ill or infirm, and can't get your case resolved over the telephone, they will come to your home.

IDENTIFYING YOURSELF

U.S. citizens born in hospitals within the country's boundaries usually have no trouble providing a birth certificate. But if you were born outside the U.S., you may have to produce extra identification, even if your parents are U.S. citizens.

If you're a naturalized citizen you'll need your citizenship papers as well as a birth record. And if you're not a citizen, you'll need either a birth certificate or passport and documents from the Immigration and Naturalization Service.

USING A REPRESENTATIVE

Most people deal with Social Security directly, but it is legal to pay someone to represent you in filing claims, appealing decisions, or any other business. However, you must file form SSA-1696-U4 and name your representative. And that person must get written approval from Social Security to charge you a fee. The usual limit is 25% of past-due benefits paid, plus out-of-pocket expenses.

Approximately 170 million workers are fully insured for retirement and disability benefits

More than 4 million new benefits awards were made in 1994—more than half to retired workers

SUPPLEMENTAL SECURITY INCOME

If you don't qualify for Social Security, or if your benefits are very small, you may be eligible for Supplemental Security Income (SSI). Unlike other Social Security benefits, these are paid with funds from the regular government budget, not with payroll taxes.

The basic monthly payment is $434 for one person and $652 for a couple, but if you live in certain states—like New York, California, or others with a high cost of living—you may get an additional amount each month.

To be eligible, you can't have more than $2,000 in assets if you're single and $3,000 if you're a couple. That doesn't include your home or car, but it does include savings and

To qualify for SSI you must be a U.S. citizen and fit one of these categories:

- 65 or older
- Blind
- Disabled

other investments. Your income also must be below a specific level, although the amount varies depending on whether or not you work and the state where you live.

The Social Security Administration runs the program and is the best source for information about the benefits it provides.

Got You Covered

It pays to be one of the Social Security crowd.

You have to qualify for Social Security benefits, but it's not hard to do. If you work for a total of ten years—even if you do it a few months at a time, and never earn more than the minimum amount—you'll be entitled to Social Security benefits when you retire. You qualify for Medicare the same way.

People who've worked early in their lives and then left the work force, like women raising families, can return to work after a long break and still accumulate enough credits to qualify for the various programs. Though the dollar amount of a late qualifier's benefit is usually smaller than someone's who has worked all along, the security of knowing you have coverage is the same.

Checking the Details

Your Earnings and Benefits statement reports:

The **maximum earnings** that were subject to Social Security tax each year.

Your **earnings that were taxed** for Social Security each year since you started working.

The **monthly benefit you'd receive** if you started collecting at 62, at your full retirement age, or if you waited until you were 70 to collect.

YOUR EARNINGS RECORD

Years	Maximum Yearly Earnings Subject to Social Security Tax	Your Social Security Taxed Earnings	Estimated Taxes You Paid: Retirement Survivors & Disability Insurance	Estimated Taxes You Paid: Medicare Hospital Insurance*
1982	$32,400	$32,400	$1,749	$ 421
1983	35,700	35,700	1,927	464
1984	37,800	37,800	2,041	491
1985	39,600	39,600	2,257	534
1986	42,000	32,498	1,852	471
1987	43,800	43,800	2,496	635
1988	45,000	45,000	2,727	65?
1989	48,000	34,670	2,101	502
1990	51,300		Not Yet Posted	
1991	53,400	0		

Retirement

If you retire at 62, your monthly benefit in today's dollars will be about . . . . $ 975

The earliest age at which you can receive an unreduced retirement benefit is 65 and 10 months. We call this your full retirement age. If you wait until that age to receive benefits, your monthly benefit in today's dollars will be about . . . . $ 1,325

If you wait until you are 70 to receive benefits, your monthly benefit in today's dollars will be about . . . . $ 1,790

SOCIAL SECURITY
40 CREDITS
QUALIFIED

PUTTING IN YOUR TIME

Social Security is based on a system of **credits** you earn while you're working. To receive retirement benefits, you need to accumulate 40 credits if you were born after 1928 (and fewer if you were born before that). In 1994, you earned one credit for each $620 you made. But you earn only four credits a year, no matter how much you make. For example, a college student who earns $2,500 painting houses during the summer

1994 INCOME	CREDITS EARNED
$ 0	0
$ 620	1
$ 2,480	4

accumulates four credits. So does a bond trader who earns 100 times that amount.

TRACKING YOUR RECORD

The Social Security Administration (SSA) will let you know where you stand on the number of credits you have and how much you've paid into the system. They'll even estimate the kind of benefits you can expect. All you have to do is ask for a Personal Earnings and Benefit Estimate Statement. You fill out Form SSA-7004-SM (which you can get by calling 1-800-772-1213 or visiting your local office), and send it in.

In fact, the SSA encourages people to check their records regularly—every three years or so—to be sure that the details are right. If they're wrong—and they sometimes are—you can submit copies of your W-2 withholding statements and your tax returns to get them corrected. The more quickly you realize there's a problem, the easier it will be to resolve.

Your Medicare Qualified Government Earnings

$ 0
0
0
0

The **tax you paid each year**, divided to show the amount for retirement, survivor and disability insurance, and the amount for Medicare.

If you started working for the **federal government** before 1984, and aren't covered by Social Security, the form will show you the tax you paid for Medicare coverage.

Survivors

Here is an estimate of the benefits your family could receive if you had enough credits to be insured, they qualified for benefits, and you died this year:

Your child could receive a monthly benefit of about.. **$ 805**

If your child and your surviving spouse who is caring for your child both qualify, they could each receive a monthly benefit of about..................... **$ 805**

When your surviving spouse reaches full retirement age, he or she could receive a monthly benefit of about... **$ 1,075**

The **amount your survivors would be paid** if you died during the year the estimate was made.

The **disability benefit you and your family would get** every month if you were not able to work.

Disability

If you were disabled, had enough credits, and met the other requirements for disability benefits, here is an estimate of the benefits you could receive right now:

Your monthly benefit would be about........... **$ 1,060**

You and your eligible family members could receive up to a monthly total of about................ **$ 1,590**

These estimates may be ......
compensation ......

The minimum dollar amount per credit is increased every year to reflect changes in the cost of living, just as the maximum income on which you pay Social Security taxes is. But once you hit forty credits, you're set. Working longer may mean your benefit is larger, but you don't need more credits.

RAPID INCREASES

The amount of your salary that gets taxed for Social Security has increased dramatically in recent years. In its first 35 years, the SSA raised the ceiling only five times, from $3,000 in 1937 to $7,800 in 1972. Since then, when the amount that's taxable was indexed to inflation, it has gone up every year, with the biggest jump between 1980 and 1981, from $25,900 to $29,700, a whopping $3,800, or 14.7%, increase.

$60,600

$7,800

$3,000

TAXABLE CEILING

1937   **1972**   **1994**

Figuring What You Get

Figuring out how much you'll get is a lot harder than qualifying.

Chances are you'll take the SSA's word for the size of your benefit. Figuring it out is complicated, because your career-long earnings must be adjusted to their approximate current value to determine the wage base on which your benefit is figured. The $5,000 you made in 1963, for instance, isn't averaged in as $5,000.

WHAT COUNTS

Unlike most pensions, which are based on what you're earning at the end of your career (see page 26), Social Security counts what you've earned during most of your working life, specifically five years fewer than the number of credits you need to qualify. So, if you were born after 1928 and need 40 credits to be eligible for benefits, your 35 highest paying years are the ones that count in figuring what you will receive.

Like other pensions, though, the more you've earned, the more you get. If you've paid the maximum tax each year and wait until you reach full retirement age to start collecting, you'll get the largest benefit Social Security gives.

UNDERSTANDING THE FORMULA

The SSA figures your benefit, or **primary insurance amount (PIA)**, like this:

What the SSA does	For example
First, they index your earnings up to age 60 to their approximate current value. (Earnings after 60 are counted as they are.)	Average earnings in 1992 were five times greater than 1964, so the $10,000 you earned then is multiplied by five and adjusted to $50,000. The adjustment factor is smaller for more recent years.
Next, they total your earnings for your highest 35 years (or fewer if you were born before 1928) and divide by 420 (the months in 35 years) to find your **average indexed monthly earnings (AIME)**.	If your adjusted earnings were $50,000 a year for 30 years, you'd multiply the two and divide by 420—since all 35 years count even if you weren't working: $1,500,000 ÷ 420 = $3,571
Finally, they compute your basic benefit rate by figuring 90% of the first $370, 32% of the next $1,860, and 15% of the balance and adding the results. The dollar amounts, or **bend points**, for each bracket are adjusted every year.	With an AIME of $3,571, your basic rule retirement benefit rate, or PIA, would be $1,129.25 (rounded to the next lower dime)

90% of $370   = $ 333
32% of $1,860 = $ 595.20
15% of $1,341 = $ 201.15
_____
                $ 1,129.35 PIA

2 INCOME ADJUSTING UNIT
Your annual income is adjusted for inflation so it can be counted at its current value

1 FICA FEEDER
You feed the Social Security machine every year you work

WHAT YOU CAN EXPECT

Although the dollar amount of your benefit reflects your average earnings, the percentage of earnings your benefit will replace goes down as your earned income goes up. That's in keeping with Social Security's mission of providing a basic level of financial support.

You can use the chart to the right to find an **estimate** of the dollar benefit you would get, based on your age and salary. If you were 65 in 1993 and had steady earnings of $30,000 a year, you'd receive a benefit of $998, or about 40% of your salary. You can project the percentage of your income that will be replaced using the following formula:

$$\frac{\text{Monthly benefit} \times 12}{\text{Annual wage}} = \text{\% annual income}$$

for example

$$\frac{\$998 \times 12}{\$30,000} = \frac{\$11,976}{\$30,000} = 39.9\%$$

In comparison, you'd get almost 45% salary replacement if you earned $20,000, and not quite 16% if you earned $85,000.

Of course, the younger you are, the less accurate the benefit projections may be because it's difficult to predict what will happen to the economy.

EXAMPLES OF BENEFITS ESTIMATES

Average Earnings	Current Age		
	45	55	65
20K	777	777	752
30K	1,044	1,043	998
40K	1,177	1,157	1,076
50K	1,301	1,244	1,127
60,600 +	1,400	1,302	1,147

THE INFLATION ISSUE

Unlike most pensions, Social Security benefits are adjusted for inflation. As well as increasing the amount of earnings subject to tax and the amount you have to earn to qualify for credits, the SSA also recalculates the amount you get every year, using a percentage of your basic benefit amount. The new amount is never less than the year before, though the rate of increase varies to reflect changes in the cost of living.

These cost of living adjustments, or **COLAs**, begin when you're 62. If you wait until you reach full retirement age to start collecting, those COLAs are added to the base amount on which your benefit is figured. The larger benefit payments you will receive can be an incentive to wait to apply for your benefits.

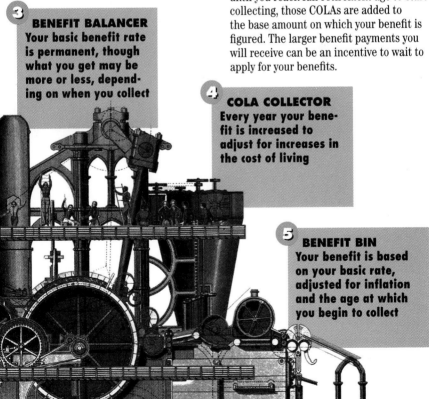

3 BENEFIT BALANCER
Your basic benefit rate is permanent, though what you get may be more or less, depending on when you collect

4 COLA COLLECTOR
Every year your benefit is increased to adjust for increases in the cost of living

5 BENEFIT BIN
Your benefit is based on your basic rate, adjusted for inflation and the age at which you begin to collect

When to Apply

When you're ready to collect, you have to ask for your money.

Your Social Security benefit won't automatically appear in your mailbox the day you're eligible. You'll have to ask the SSA to start paying, and you'll have to provide evidence that you qualify. The same material you used to open your account can be used here, too: birth or baptismal certificates, passports, naturalization papers, or other official documents. You may also need a copy of your most recent W-2 form or tax return. Your local Social Security office can answer the questions you have, or you can call 800-772-1213. The SSA advises you not to delay your application because you don't have the right documentation, or aren't sure what you need. Once you start the process, they'll help you get hold of the information.

Changes in Social Security Retirement-Age Provisions

Year of Birth	Attainment of Age 62	Starting Age for Full Benefits (Year/Months)	Credit for Each Year of Delayed Retirement	Age-62 Benefit as % of PIA
1938	2000	65/2	6.5%	79.2%
1939	2001	65/4	7.0%	78.3%
1940	2002	65/6	7.0%	77.5%
1941	2003	65/8	7.5%	76.7%
1942	2004	65/10	7.5%	75.8%
1943-54	2005-16	66/0	8.0%	75.0%
1955	2017	66/2	8.0%	74.2%
1956	2018	66/4	8.0%	73.3%
1957	2019	66/6	8.0%	72.5%
1958	2020	66/8	8.0%	71.7%
1959	2021	66/10	8.0%	70.8%
1960+	2022+	67/0	8.0%	70.0%

SPREADING THE WEALTH

You can start collecting Social Security as early as 62 or as late as 70. The earlier you begin, the smaller the annual amount you get. And the later you start, the larger your payments. The underlying principle the SSA has adopted in providing these options is trying to equalize the lifetime value of the benefits.

If you must be older than 65 to receive full benefits, you can still start collecting at 62, but the percentage of full payment gradually drops from 80% to 70%. Just the opposite is true if you wait until 70. Your benefit is larger, but chances are you will collect for fewer years.

The general feeling is that you should be collecting as soon as you're eligible. It will take between 12 and 17 years—until you're nearly 80—for the larger amount you would have gotten at full retirement age to add up to more money.

Of course, if you have the option of continuing to work, the added income during those extra years will probably be more than the Social Security payments you would have received. And if your salary increases, the base amount of your benefit will increase as well.

A LONGER ROW TO HOE

In 1983, the SSA increased the age for getting full benefits. If you were born before 1938, you still qualify for full benefits at age 65. But anyone born in 1938 has to be 65 and two months, anyone born in 1939 has to be 65 and four months, and so on. As this chart shows, full retirement age inches up to 66 for people born between 1943 and 1954 and to 67 for anyone born after 1960.

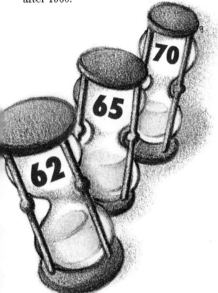

PATIENCE HAS ITS REWARDS

People who wait to begin collecting because they are still working, get a bonus. If they were born before 1938, they get between 3% and 4% a year added on to their basic benefit for each year they wait between age 65 and age 70. But people born after 1943, who have to be age 66 to get full benefits, will get an extra 8% a year more than their primary insurance amount (PIA), or full benefit. There's no point, though, in waiting past 70, because the amount you're eligible for won't increase any more.

RECEIVING THE MONEY

Once you're ready to collect, you can choose how you want to get the money. The SSA will mail you a check—which should arrive on the third of every month—or they'll deposit it directly in your checking or savings account. Many people—about 40%—opt for direct deposit. It's safer, quicker, and usually more convenient than getting a check. It's also cheaper for the government.

To use the direct deposit option, all you need is something that shows your bank and

APPLYING FOR BENEFITS

The SSA suggests that you discuss applying for Social Security benefits with one of their representatives in the year before you actually plan to retire. Since there are several options for timing retirement and the start of your benefits, they can help you figure out the choice that will work best for you. You have three basic choices:

- **Retiring early, any time after age 62**
- **Retiring at full retirement age, which has historically been 65**
- **Postponing retirement past 65**

FOR INFORMATION CALL
1-800-777-1213

THE OTHER ISSUES

Chances are there are several factors behind choosing the age at which you apply for retirement benefits. Your health, your plans for the future, or an incentive your employer offers for leaving your job early can make a difference. So can the type of job you have and whether or not you plan to go on working.

On the other hand, once you start collecting Social Security there are limits on the amount you can earn before you start losing some of your benefit. For many people, who need or want to go on working, postponing taking the benefits makes sense. But, once you retire, you should apply right away. If you don't need the money for living expenses, you can invest it and earn more.

DIRECT DEPOSIT

IN THE MAIL

account number, like a checkbook, a passbook or a bank statement.

People who have moved into retirement or nursing homes, or who aren't managing their own finances, can have their money deposited in a custodial account. That way, the benefit can be used directly for their care.

Working after Retirement

There's no law against working after you retire—but there are limits on what you can earn.

To insure Social Security's integrity as a source of basic financial support after retirement, there are limits on what you can earn while collecting your payments. The basic exception is for people over 70: they can earn as much as they want and still get the full amount they're entitled to.

You can also collect your full benefit if you receive special payments after you retire that you actually earned beforehand. Typical examples include accumulated vacation pay, sales commissions, and deferred salary. The same rule applies to some self-employment income. According to Social Security, some people entitled to receive benefits postpone them unnecessarily because of payments like these.

LETTING SOCIAL SECURITY KNOW

If you're working, you're required to let the Social Security Administration know. You have to estimate your earnings using a special form called **Annual Report of Earnings**. The Social Security Administration reduces the number of monthly checks you get in the following year, based on that earnings estimates.

If you earn less than you estimated, you'll get a check to cover what you're owed. But if you earn more, you have to pay back the difference between what you got and what you were entitled to, either in a lump sum or installments. When your taxes are due in April, you submit form SSA-777 and a copy of your tax return to the Social Security Administration to verify your earnings.

The worst-case situation is failing to report that you're working and then going over the limit. You'll have to pay a penalty as well as send back any overpayment you got.

THE LIMITS

If you're receiving Social Security, there's a fixed amount you can earn each year without losing some of your benefit. As a rule, the cap goes up each year to reflect increases in the cost of living, and is keyed to the average earnings of all employees in the country.

The amount also changes, depending on how old you are. In 1994, you could earn $8,040 if you were between 62 and 64, and up to $11,160 if you were between 65 and 69, and still get full benefits.

THE CONSEQUENCES

The consequences of earning more than the limit is fewer checks from Social Security. Between the ages of 62 and 64, you lose $1 for every $2 over the limit; between 65 and 69, you lose $1 for every $3 over the limit.

However, the limits apply only to earned income, not pensions, annuities, investment earnings, or any government benefits.

If you were 62–64, and receiving about $800 a month, you'd get your first check in June. If you were 65–69, you'd get your first check in March. At the end of the year, based on you actual earnings, SSA might owe you money, or vice versa.

DOES IT PAY TO WORK

It's a judgment call, if the amount you earn is going to reduce your benefit significantly. In general, though, if your earnings are low enough to allow you to get any benefit while you're working, you make out better taking what you're entitled to. For example, suppose you're 63, get a monthly benefit of $793 a month ($9,516 a year) and earn $15,000 a year. You'd still get more than 60% of your benefit. Here's how:

Social Security says if you work over 45 hours a week, you're <u>not</u> retired.

Social Security says if you work less than 15 hours a week, you're <u>retired</u>.

YOUR AGE	MAXIMUM EARNINGS FOR FULL BENEFITS
62-64	$ 8,040
65-69	$ 11,160

IF YOUR INCOME IS $15,000

	62-64	65-69
Amount over limit	$ 6,960	$ 3,840
	÷ 2	÷ 3
Withheld by SS for year	$ 3,480	$ 1,280

	$ 15,000	Earnings
−	8,040	Earnings limit
	$ 6,960	Excess earning
÷	2	Reduced by ½
	$ 3,480	Benefit reduction
÷	9,516	Original benefit
	36.6%	Reduction

CHANGING YOUR MIND

It is true that once you begin receiving your Social Security payments you're locked into the base amount. But you can change your mind about getting the payments, pay back the total amount you've received and start over again— at a higher base—later on.

For example, if you retire and begin to receive benefits when you're 62 but are offered a position that's too good to turn down, you can stop your Social Security payments. As long as you repay any benefits you got, you can start again with a clean slate when you're ready to call it quits for good. Whatever you've earned in the period when you returned to work can increase the amount you're eligible to receive.

SPECIAL RULES

If you retire in the middle of the year, you might have already exceeded the annual earnings limit. So in the year you retire, special rules apply. You can get the full benefit you're entitled to in any month that you're actually retired, no matter what you earned earlier in the year.

But once the Social Security payments start, you can't earn more than $670 a month if you're less than 65, or $930 if you're between 65 and 70. If you go over those limits in any month, you lose the entire benefit for that month. But the next month you start over.

WHAT RETIRED MEANS

When your income is from self-employment, defining retirement is a little tricky. The SSA uses the number of hours you spend working during a week as the measuring stick. If you work fewer than 15 hours, you're considered retired. If you work more than 45 hours, you're definitely not. And then there's the gray area in between, when the quality of the work you do, as well as the time you spend doing it, has to be considered.

The rules are complex. The SSA invites people in that situation to get in touch with them for specific information about the way their benefits are calculated.

Family Coverage

Social Security benefits are a family affair, as long as one person qualifies for coverage.

When you qualify for Social Security retirement benefits, you get them for as long as you live. What's more, your spouse and certain dependents, including your young or disabled children can collect as well, both while you're collecting and after your death.

WHOSE BENEFIT ANYWAY?

If you and your spouse each qualify for benefits, you each collect on your own account when you retire. Not only does it give you more flexibility about when to retire, but it might add up to a larger benefit, especially if your earnings were about the same.

But if the total you get individually adds up to less than you would receive if one of you collected as a dependent spouse, Social Security makes up the difference, as this example shows.

for example		
	Individual Benefits Only	Spousal Benefits from one Account
You	$1,128	$1,128
Your Spouse	415	564
Total Benefit	$1,543	$1,692

Social Security would make up the $149 difference, so your benefit would be $1,692.

SWITCHING GEARS

The choice between getting your own or your spousal benefits is one of those rare situations in retirement planning where you can change your mind. Your initial decision doesn't lock you in, even after you've begun receiving benefits.

If you'd get a larger payment by switching, usually from what you get on your own to what you'd get as your spouse's survivor, all you have to do is request the change and be able to prove your marital status and age.

When you switch, your new benefit is reduced by the amount you've already received in your own name. The SSA will tell you what the new amount is, so you can decide whether switching pays.

THE GENERAL RULES

Who Is Eligible

SPOUSE
- Your spouse must be at least 62 to collect, unless he or she is caring for your child who's younger than 16, or disabled and receiving Social Security benefits

CHILDREN

DISABLED CHILDREN

BENEFIT LIMITS

There is a limit to what Social Security will pay to your family—usually between 150% and 188% of your benefit. Here's how the limit works:

Suppose your benefit is $1,000 a month and you and your spouse have three children under 16 when you retire. With no limits, your family would get a total of $3,000 (your $1,000 plus $500 for each of the others). With the limits in place, the most your family would get would be $1,880. But it's

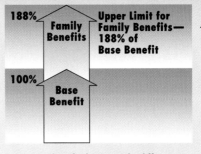

never your benefit that's cut. The difference comes out of what your dependents receive.

FORMER FAMILIES

If you're divorced, you are eligible for Social Security retirement benefits based on your former spouse's earnings. You're entitled to the same benefits you would have received—50% at 65 and 37.5% at 62—if you'd stayed married. You may also be able to start collecting at 62 even if your ex-spouse is still working, provided you have been divorced for at least two years, and the worker is 62.

The SSA imposes these conditions to collect on a divorced spouse's earnings:

you were married for at least ten years, you aren't remarried, and you're not eligible for an equal or larger benefit, based on your own or someone else's earnings.

YOU'RE ALL COVERED

If your ex-spouse is getting Social Security benefits based on your record, it doesn't reduce the amount you and your current family, if you've remarried, are entitled to. And there are no limits to the number of former spouses you're entitled to support, as long as you've been married to each of them the required length of time.

When you apply for benefits for your dependents, you'll have to prove your relationship and how old they are. You'll also have to keep this rule in mind: your spouse and other dependents aren't eligible for benefits until you start collecting yours. For example, a 66-year-old husband can't collect spousal benefits if his wife is still working.

When They Are Eligible

- Spouses who begin collecting at 65, or those who are taking care of minor or disabled children are entitled to 50% of your benefit amount
- If your spouse starts to collect between 62 and 65, though, and there are no eligible children, the benefit is reduced a small percentage each month, to a floor of 37.5% at 62
- A spouse who isn't 62 by the time your last child turns 16 loses eligibility

- Children are eligible for family benefits when you retire if they're under 18 (or under 19 if they're still in high-school full-time); as your children reach 18, they lose their eligibility

- Children are eligible if they're disabled, as long as the disability occurred before they were 22

How Much the Benefit Will Be

- Spouses are eligible for 50% of your full retirement benefit at age 65, reduced slightly for each month before that, to a floor of 37.5% at 62

- Children are eligible for 50% of your full retirement benefit

Survivor Benefits

The Social Security you leave behind is a legacy your survivors can be sure they'll receive.

While Social Security is designed to provide basic financial security after you retire, an equally important role is providing an income for your survivors no matter what age you are when you die. Your widow or widower, your young or disabled children, parents who were dependent on you, and, in certain circumstances, your divorced former spouse are entitled to survivor benefits.

QUALIFYING FOR BENEFITS

To provide benefits for your survivors, you must accumulate enough credits while you're working. You qualify either by having the full number required for your age, or by being currently insured, having earned at least six credits in the three years before your death.

Your age determines the number of credits you need to be fully qualified. It's one for every year between the year you turn 21 and the year before you die or turn 61, whichever comes first. For example, if you were born in 1942, and died in 1995, you'd need 31 credits. (Subtract 1963, the year you turned 21, from 1994, the year before you died: 1994-1963=31). When you turn 61, in 2003, you'll need 40 credits.

HOW MANY CREDITS YOU NEED

The year before your death
− The year you turn 21
―――――――――――――――――――――
= Credits needed for survivor benefits

for example

2003 The year before your death
− 1963 The year you turn 21
―――――――――――――――――――――
= 40 Credits needed for survivor benefits

APPLYING FOR BENEFITS

If you're a survivor who's eligible for Social Security benefits, you should apply immediately. You'll need a copy of the insured person's death certificate, and evidence of your age, relationship, and marital situation.

Your deceased spouse or parent is not entitled to a Social Security benefit for the month he or she dies. When the payment is made, on the third of the next month, you should return it to the SSA.

DEATH BENEFIT

If you have the credits you need to provide benefits for your survivors, Social Security also makes a one-time payment of $255 to your spouse or minor children at the time of your death. Although there are no rules about what the money must be used for, it's often described as a funeral benefit.

WHAT ABOUT REMARRIAGE?

If you're getting survivor benefits, you won't lose them if you remarry after you're 60, or 50 if you're disabled. But if you're eligible for a larger benefit based on your new spouse's earnings record, that takes

THE GENERAL RULES

Who is Eligible

WIDOWS AND WIDOWERS
- At age 60, or 50 if disabled
- Married at least 9 months
- Not remarried before age 60, or 50 if disabled
- Taking care of children under 16, or disabled children who are receiving Social Security benefits

CHILDREN
- Unmarried
- Under 18 (or 19 if full-time high school students)
- Disabled before age 22

PARENTS
- Dependent on covered worker for more than half their support
- Age 62 or more

FORMER SPOUSES
- At age 60, 50 if disabled
- Married to covered worker for at least 10 years
- Unmarried at time of application
- Taking care of children under 16, or disabled children receiving Social Security benefits (no length of marriage rule)

precedence. It isn't a question of loyalty or affection so much as one of economics. With Social Security, the smart decision is the one that pays the most.

If you remarry when your children are younger than 18, they will continue to receive benefits until they are too old to be eligible. Their status as survivors is not affected by your marriage.

BENEFITS AFTER RETIREMENT

If your spouse is receiving retirement benefits when he or she dies, you're entitled as a survivor to 100% of your spouse's Social Security payment. For example, if

NON-TRADITIONAL FAMILIES

So far, Social Security has not extended coverage to non-traditional family relationships. You must be legally married or a blood relative to qualify as a survivor. But the history of Social Security demonstrates that it has changed with the times, providing benefits for divorced people, for example, when divorce became a fact of life. So a change in the definition of family membership is possible, if not immediately likely.

the basic benefit was $1,200 and you were getting an additional $600, you're eligible for $1,200 as a surviving spouse.

At your spouse's death, you can switch from collecting on your own account to collecting as a survivor if it means you're eligible for a larger benefit. The SSA will calculate the amount for you.

The chart below gives you an overview of who's eligible for survivor benefits and how much they're entitled to. Since there are many exceptions to the general rules, your situation may be different. The SSA can explain where you stand.

What the Benefits Are

Other Provisions

- 100% of covered worker's basic benefit for coverage beginning at 65, about 83% at 62 and about 72% at 60
- About 72% for disabled spouses who begin collecting between 50 and 59
- 75% of basic benefit while caring for minor or disabled children

- Surviving spouses earning more than the limit Social Security allows are eligible for benefits, though deductions are imposed; Children under 18 still eligible
- Surviving spouses who remarry after 60 (or 50 if disabled) may still collect

---

- 75% of parent's basic benefit

- Children over 18 (or 19 in certain cases) are no longer eligible even if full-time college students
- Disabled children continue to be eligible

- 82.5% for one parent; 75% each for two parents

- 100% of covered worker's basic benefit for coverage beginning at 65, about 83% at 62, and about 72% at 60
- About 72% for disabled spouses who begin collecting between 50 and 59
- 75% of basic benefit while caring for minor or disabled children

- Former spouses earning more than the limit Social Security allows are not eligible for benefits, though children under 18 continue to be eligible
- Former spouses who remarry after 60 (or 50 if disabled) may still collect

---

There's a monthly limit on the total amount a family receives, though, just as there is with retirement benefits (see page 85).

Disability Benefits

Disability insurance is the most complicated Social Security program.

Controversy swirls around the disability insurance program. Some people argue that it's too expensive because it's too generous. Others insist that people who ought to be receiving benefits are left out in the cold.

The SSA streamlined the program in 1994, to speed up decisions on applications and simplify appeals. Whether those changes will help solve the funding problems isn't clear. The disability trust fund is currently in serious financial trouble, projected to run out of money in 1995.

SOCIAL SECURITY ADMINISTRATION
DISABILITY DETERMINATION SERVICE

Applicant Checklist

☐ **All medical records**

☐ **Insurance history**

☐ **Tax returns**

☐ **Employment records, past 15 years**

☐ **Proof of age**

DEFINING A DISABILITY

The SSA calls its definition of disability "fairly strict." No benefits are paid unless you're unable to earn more than $500 a month, or you're so sick that you're expected to die. Just because you're considered disabled by your employer doesn't mean you're eligible for Social Security benefits. The same is true if your doctor says you can't work. The decision rests with the **Disability Determination Service** in the state where you live.

SOCIAL SECURITY PAYS OUT ABOUT $36 BILLION

or the GNP of Norway

IN DISABILITY BENEFITS TO 5.2 MILLION PEOPLE

or the population of Belgium each year. In 1994, the backlog approached a million cases, almost twice the number for 1992.

Despite the restrictions and the red tape, disability applications and awards, are increasing and the average age of the disability recipients is declining. In 1993, more than 1 million disabled workers and their dependents qualified for new awards.

APPLYING FOR BENEFITS

The more quickly you apply for disability benefits, the better. It takes longer to process a disability claim—about 155 days in 1994—than a claim for retirement or survivor benefits. Plus you have to supply detailed medical and work records. The SSA wants to know, for example, where you worked for the 15 years before you were disabled.

If your claim is approved—and only about half are the first time around—payments can begin in the sixth full month after you were disabled. For example, if you have a stroke in June, you would be eligible for benefits in December and the payment would arrive on January 3. Disability claims for children, or for people eligible for SSI benefits, have no waiting period.

WAIT TILL YOUR NAME IS CALLED

BEING ELIGIBLE

You are eligible for disability benefits if you have earned enough credits while you're working.

You need one credit for every year after you turn 21, to a maximum of 40 at age 62, just as you do for survivor benefits. But to qualify for disability coverage, you must earn 20 of those credits in the ten years immediately before you are disabled.

If you're disabled but don't have enough Social Security credits, you might qualify for Supplemental Security Income (SSI) if you have a small income and few assets.

FIGURING YOUR BENEFIT

Social Security estimates the disability benefit you'd be eligible for when you ask for an Earnings and Benefits statement (see page 76). The amount is based on:

- **Your age at the time you're disabled**
- **Your earnings record.**

Once your basic benefit is set, it doesn't change no matter how many years you're eligible to collect. You do get cost of living adjustments though (see page 79). Social Security doesn't recognize a partial disability, or make partial payments. If you qualify, you get the amount you're entitled to until you recover or improve enough to go back to work.

If you're eligible for other benefits, like Workers' Compensation, you may get less from Social Security (or the other way around). That's because all your disability payments together can't add up to more than 80% of your average recent earnings. But after 24 months of disability benefits, you are eligible for Medicare.

THE APPEALS PROCESS

If the SSA rules you're not eligible for disability benefits, you can appeal the decision. Historically, the administrative law judges working for the SSA have reversed 60% of the rejected applications. If the ruling goes against you internally, and you believe you have a case, you can take it to a Federal District Court.

You May Be Disabled if You Have:

- **Sight loss**
- **Chronic arthritis**
- **Loss of limbs**
- **AIDS or HIV infection**
- **Multiple personality**
- **Schizophrenia**
- **Kidney failure**
- **Mental retardation**
- **Heart Disease**
- **Emphysema**
- **Stroke**
- **Cancer**
- **Chronic Obesity**
- **Paralysis**

or other conditions.

But Only if the SSA Says You Are.

A LONG HISTORY

The original disability pensions in the U.S. date back to 1636, when the Massachusetts Bay Colony began supporting its injured soldiers. More than 300 years later, in 1957, Social Security instituted a disability program for workers over 50 and extended it three years later to include everyone who qualified. By 1993, disability payments accounted for about 9% of all Social Security benefits.

Taxing Benefits

The tax on benefits makes economic sense, but it's not very popular with the 20% who pay it.

The law on taxing benefits is fairly simple: if your total income for the year hits a certain level, you owe income taxes on 50% of your Social Security benefit. And if your income hits an even higher level, you owe taxes on 85% of your benefit.

Since your Social Security contribution, or payroll tax, is deducted from your salary before income taxes are taken out, paying taxes on your benefit is like paying taxes on your IRA or other retirement plan. But since contributing is mandatory, it seems like a double hit when you have to pay income tax on your benefit.

WHAT IS THIS BENEFIT ANYWAY

The underlying question is, should everybody who pays Social Security taxes get retirement benefits? Or should the benefits go only to people who need them to live on?

Because everyone who works must contribute to the system, the idea of using a means test to decide who gets benefits has been rejected—at least so far.

Using a means test, only people whose income falls below a certain level would qualify for benefits. If you're in good financial shape, the argument goes,

The 50 (or 85) Percent Solution

ALL IN THE NUMBERS

You can figure out whether you'll have to pay income taxes on part of your Social Security benefit by using this workchart.

Compare the total on line 6 with the income limits for your filing status in the chart to the right. If the total is less, you don't owe taxes on any of your Social Security benefits.

		for example:
1	Income from Box 5 of SSA 1099 (if you got more than one SSA-1099 include the combined total)	$ 21,600
2	Divide by amount in line 1 by 2	÷ 2
3	Half of Social Security	= $ 10,800
4	Income from pensions, wages, dividends, taxable interest and other sources	+ $ 24,000
5	Income from tax-exempt interest and other non-taxable income	+ $ 4,000
6	Add lines 3–5	= $ 38,800

STARTING A TREND OR TWO

When women made up a smaller segment of the work force, they briefly enjoyed a special privilege: collecting their Society Security benefit earlier. From 1956 to 1961, women, but not men, had the option of retiring with benefits at age 62. By 1961, men were given the same option, and the trend toward earlier retirement was on a roll. Only 2% of those eligible took advantage of the offer in 1956, but by 1994 it was nearly 70%.

Men, on average, still qualify for larger individual retirement awards, but the proportion of women among retired-worker beneficiaries has quadrupled since 1940, and the proportion of women qualifying only as dependents has declined almost 33%.

why do you need the benefits? But if you're not going to get anything back, why should you put anything in? And doesn't using money that everyone must contribute to support only some of the people change the nature of the whole Social Security program? The current solution has been to tax some of the benefits of some of the people, but it hasn't answered the pressing questions.

COUNTING YOUR INCOME

In figuring whether you owe tax on your benefits, you add everything you receive—including tax-exempt interest on municipal bonds and certain other income that you don't normally have to include in your taxable income, like money you earn outside the U.S., but not annuity income:

- Salary
- Pensions
- Taxable investments
- Tax-exempt investments from municipal bonds
- Overseas earnings
- Gambling, lottery winnings
- Tips
- Royalties, rents
- IRA withdrawals

If the total is higher, you include a percentage of your benefit—either 50% or 85%—as part of your taxable income on your tax return. In cases where your income is only slightly greater than the limit, you pay tax on less than the full 50% or 85%. The IRS provides a worksheet you can use to figure out exactly how much you must add to your taxable income.

If you pay estimated taxes, you'll have to include enough to cover what you'll owe on your Social Security benefits.

FILING STATUS	INCOME LEVEL	
SINGLE	$25,000	$34,000
MARRIED, LIVING APART WITH SEPARATE RETURNS	$25,000	$34,000
MARRIED	$32,000	$44,000
MARRIED, WITH SEPARATE RETURNS	ANY INCOME	ANY INCOME

50% OF YOUR BENEFIT WILL BE TAXED

85% OF YOUR BENEFIT WILL BE TAXED

OTHER OPTIONS

If your income falls close to or within the limits that would subject part of the benefit to taxation, you may be able to plan ahead so that some years you're subjected to tax and other years you're not. For example, by timing the date that U.S. Treasury Bills mature, or postponing selling some stock, you might be able to bunch income in one year—and pay the tax—while keeping it under the limits in another.

A WORKING SPOUSE

When you apply for retirement benefits based on your work record, your right to collect is unrelated to whether or not your spouse is working. When you reach retirement age you can collect. But when it comes to figuring whether or not part of your Social Security benefit will be taxed, your spouse's income makes a big difference.

For example, if a man retires at 65 and is entitled to a benefit of $1,128 a month, that's what he gets even if his wife is earning $65,000. But at tax time, their joint income will be way over the level that requires them to pay tax on 85% of his Social Security benefit.

Unless they're married but permanently living apart, there's no way to avoid the tax by filing separate returns. As the chart shows, married couples filing separately pay tax on half their Social Security benefit no matter what their income—just to eliminate this tax-saving option.

When a spouse is eligible for benefits and earning only enough to push the joint income over the limit, it might pay to calculate tax liability both ways, to figure out if it makes more sense financially for both to retire because their taxes will be significantly less.

Personal Investing Goals

Chances are, living the life you want after you retire will depend on your investment income.

In many ways, investing for retirement is just like investing for any other reason. You use your **principal,** or the money you have, to earn more money, which you can use to pay your bills, buy something you want, or make a new investment. But when you're investing for long-term financial security, there's no fixed moment when you need the money. Instead, it's a continuous process.

That means you always have to think about doing three things:

- **Making your investment grow**
- **Producing income**
- **Preserving your principal**

FIRST THINGS FIRST

If you're putting money into an employer-sponsored pension plan, an IRA, a SEP, or a Keogh, you're already investing for retirement in one of the most productive ways you can. That contribution may be most, or even all, of what you feel you can put away. Yet, the truth is, being able to afford the kind of retirement you want will depend—in most cases—on the personal investments you make in addition to the money you put in qualified plans. If you don't start until retirement is within sight, it's tough to invest enough to produce the income you'll need.

WHAT YOU CAN'T KNOW CAN HURT YOU

You can't actually know how much you'll need when you retire, or what the state of the economy will be then. You can get a sense if you can project your salary increases, the rate of inflation, and how much you'll be paying in local taxes 10, 20, or 30 years in the future. But there's a strong element of guesswork in any projection. The only thing you can tell for certain is that if you don't invest, you won't have what you need.

THE GROWTH STAGE

Growth is the first order of business, and investments grow in many ways.

- You can beef up your principal on a regular basis by contributing a percentage of your income to your investment pool. Putting $2,000 into an IRA every year is an example (see page 50).

- You can reinvest your investment earnings rather than spend them, either by using an official plan offered by a mutual fund or stock reinvestment program, or by putting all your interest and dividend payments into a special investment account.

- You can invest your money in places where it is most likely to grow in value, typically in **equity** products like stocks and stock mutual funds.

- You can **diversify,** or put your money into a variety of investments, to take advantage of ups and downs in the stock market and the interest rate.

COMING UP SHORT

Most experts agree that you need 80% of your pre-retirement income after you retire if you want to maintain a similar style of living. Social Security benfits and, in some cases, an employer-sponsored pension, will supply some of what you need.

For example, if you're earning $75,000 when you retire, your financial picture might look like this.

$	75,000	Pre-retirement Income
x	.80	
= $	60,000	Past retirement need
−	15,600	Social Security benefits
−	22,500	Pension benefits
= $	21,900	**YEARLY INCOME SHORTFALL**

MAKING UP THE DIFFERENCE

You might go on working part-time, if jobs are available—though that may not be your idea of retirement. The other option—short of winning the lottery—is a regular income from the investments you've built up over the years. The more carefully you've planned those investments, the more likely it is that you can count on them to produce the earnings you'll need. Here are three examples of ways you might do it.

1

$	7,500	$100,000 Treasury Bonds paying 7.5%
+	7,500	$150,000 IRA paid in 20 payments
+	6,930	$77,000 in stock mutual fund paying 9%
= $	21,930	**INCOME FROM INVESTING**

2

$	10,000	$200,000 SEP-IRA paid in 20 installments
+	3,000	$75,000 in stock yielding 4%
+	10,000	Maturing certificate of deposit
= $	23,000	**INCOME FROM INVESTING**

3

$	4,200	Rental on real estate holdings
+	4,500	Liquidating 5% of a $90,000 stock portfolio
+	13,750	$275,000 Keogh plan withdrawn over 20 years
= $	22,450	**INCOME FROM INVESTING**

THE INCOME STAGE

Income-producing investments are especially important when you need the money to live on, typically after you retire. For example, the interest on a bond or the dividends from a stock help cover day-to-day expenses. Since those payments are made regularly, usually quarterly or semi-annually, you can plan on them. You can also time certain investments, like certificates of deposit or certain bonds, to mature on a specific schedule, to replenish your cash reserve or meet anticipated expenses.

Income from your investments also produces a regular source of new investment money. Or, you can plan to spend a certain amount and reinvest the rest.

THE PRESERVATION STAGE

If you're living on the income your investments provide, you've got a vested interest in making sure they don't shrink in value or, worse yet, disappear altogether. Curiously, the best preservation technique is to concentrate on growth—slower, safer growth than you were looking for when you first began to build your nest egg, but growth nonetheless. Money buried in the backyard, or earning minimal interest in a savings account, doesn't keep its value. In fact, because of inflation, it shrinks. That's one of the biggest threats to your financial security.

The Impact of Inflation

Inflation eats away at the value of a dollar, so it buys less each year.

Inflation is a constant, steady erosion of money's value. The amount of erosion varies—in some years the rate of inflation is higher than in others. But the effect of inflation never changes: the cost of living keeps going up, so you need more money just to stay even.

INFLATION PROTECTION

You can't stop inflation, but you can protect yourself against it by investing for growth. Generally speaking, that means putting at least some of your money into stocks and stock mutual funds. Since 1926, **equity** investments have returned an average of 10% a year, while the inflation rate in the same period averaged around 4%.

The rule of thumb is that you need to earn more than the current inflation rate on your combined investments to keep ahead of the game. That's because your **real rate of growth** is what remains after subtracting the inflation rate from your rate of return. For example, if inflation is running at 3%, your goal is 4% or better: a 4% return minus 3% inflation equals a 1% real return. CDs, money market accounts, and other cash investments rarely, if ever, pay more than inflation and

The higher the real rate of return you're earning on your combined investments, the better your defense against the effects of inflation.

often pay less. That's why you need to invest your money in other ways.

The standard pension fund mix of 60% invested in stocks, 30% in bonds, and 10% in cash has consistently earned 4% more than the inflation rate over the years, which is one of the reasons that companies have been able to meet their pension obligations. As a rule, if the bulk of your investments isn't in stocks or stock mutual funds, you'll probably find yourself earning less than the inflation rate.

INFLATION HAPPENS

Though unexpected changes in the world politics, like a war or an oil embargo, can cause a sudden leap in prices, inflation isn't random or arbitrary. It's cyclical, closely linked to the country's overall economy.

When things are booming, inflation is higher. When employment decreases and the economy slows down, inflation drops. And its natural cycle can be influenced, if not always controlled, by changes in the interest rate.

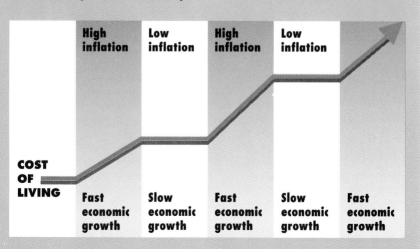

	High inflation	Low inflation	High inflation	Low inflation	
COST OF LIVING	Fast economic growth	Slow economic growth	Fast economic growth	Slow economic growth	Fast economic growth

A LOOK AT THE EVER-DIMINISHING BUYING POWER OF THE DOLLAR OVER THE LAST GENERATION

1963   1994

CUP OF COFFEE
$.10 $.75

LUXURY CAR
$2,800 $36,000

PAIR OF SNEAKERS
$4.95 $89.95

STAMP
$.05 $.29

NEWSPAPER
$.40 $.75

NYC SUBWAY FARE
$.15 $1.25

QUART OF MILK
$.27 $.79

GALLON OF GAS
$.30 $1.39

MOVIE TICKET
$1.00 $7.50

THE RULE OF 72

If it makes you feel better to know how fast your money is losing its value, you can use the rule of 72. Just divide 72 by the current inflation rate to find the number of years it will take prices to double. For example, if the rate is 3%, prices will double in 24 years: the movie ticket that costs $7.50 in 1994 will cost $15 in 2018. (One bright spot, though: if you've retired by 2018, you'll probably be eligible for a senior citizen discount.)

To figure the impact of higher inflation rates on your cost of living, you can use the same rule. If inflation were running at 10%, that movie ticket would double in just over seven years. And if it got to 15%, it would take less than five years.

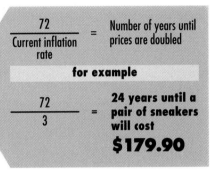

$$\frac{72}{\text{Current inflation rate}} = \text{Number of years until prices are doubled}$$

for example

$$\frac{72}{3} = \text{24 years until a pair of sneakers will cost}$$
$179.90

Inflation also erodes what money is worth. If the rate stays a relatively modest 3%, the $100 you have today will be worth only $50 in 12 years and absolutely nothing in 24. Since many people live at least 24 years after they retire, you can see why inflation is a matter for concern.

WHAT GOES UP

Inflation creates serious problems for people living on fixed incomes, such as pensions, annuity payments, or interest on bonds. A fixed income means that the dollar amount of the payment is set from the beginning and does not change. A $10,000 bond paying 7% will give you $700 a year for as long as you hold it. That means your buying power will decline.

The flip side of inflation's negative effect is that bonds, CDs, and bank accounts pay higher interest during periods of high inflation, providing a healthy current return even though the real return will still be too low to produce growth.

Many retired people saw their interest income decline dramatically during the early 90s because interest rates plummeted during a period of minimal inflation. When CDs that were paying 8% or more matured, new ones were paying only 3%, a huge decline for people depending on interest earnings to pay their bills.

A Winning Strategy

You've got a better chance at the winning shot in the investment game if you've figured out a strategy.

Random buying—a few stocks here, a bond there—rarely produces enough return to provide the extra income you'll need for retirement. Jumping into what's hot works the same way, since usually by the time you hear an investment is hot, it's started to cool off.

THE HEART OF THE MATTER

It's not that there's a single right way for making money with your investments. There are several ways that often work well, and that you can adapt to suit your needs and your resources. To be a successful investor, you need a sense of what you want to accomplish—a goal—and a plan, or strategy, for getting there.

THE MONEY YOU HAVE TO INVEST

IMPATIENT— OUT OF MARKET TOO SOON

RANDOM BUYING

Whatever strategy you adopt in investing for retirement, the same three rules apply:

START EARLY

STICK WITH IT

SALT AWAY AS MUCH AS YOU CAN

BORROWING FOR NOW

If you need cash before you retire, it makes more sense to borrow against your investments than to sell them or withdraw part of the money. It doesn't work with everything—you can't borrow against a mutual fund, for instance. But you can borrow against brokerage accounts, some pension or retirement plans, and insurance policies.

By borrowing, you avoid the taxes that might be due and any penalties you would have to pay for early withdrawal. While you do have to pay the amount back, borrowing can solve a short-term problem without diverting your long-term strategy.

DRAWING ON PRINCIPAL

While preserving principal is critical while you're investing for retirement, there's nothing wrong with using some of the principal—say 5% a year—*after* you retire. But, you need a plan for tapping your resources, similar to a withdrawal schedule for your IRA or Keogh, and a sense of which investments to liquidate.

A maturing CD, for example, can become a source of current income. When it comes due, you can deposit the principal in a money market mutual fund or savings account to draw on as you needed cash. That might be smarter than withdrawing money from an investment that's doing well, like a stock fund, or selling real estate when prices are low.

A PLAN, NOT A STRAITJACKET

As an investor, you need to be flexible. Economic trends change, so you have to modify your plan from time to time. You'll come up short, for example, if you keep lots of money in Certificates of Deposit (CDs) if the interest they offer is only as good as the return on a money market account. Just because CDs are a smart investment at one time doesn't mean they always are. Or, for that matter, that they won't be a wise choice again.

When you're investing for retirement, it usually makes sense to shift your strategy as you get closer to actually leaving the workforce—from concentrating primarily on growth to thinking about producing income. In your 30s and 40s, you can take more chances with your investments, since you'll still have time to make up for mistakes. But a big loss in your 60s can be hard to recover from.

THE MONEY YOU NEED TO RETIRE

CHASING HOT STOCK TOO LATE

INFLEXIBLE STRATEGY

USING WHAT YOU EARN

If you withdraw from your nest egg at the same annual rate at which it's growing, it will stay the same size. Or, you can gradually reduce the amount to zero by withdrawing at more than the growth rate.

The money you start with	Amount you can withdraw monthly for the number of years below, reducing your nest egg to zero			
	10 years	15 years	20 years	30 years
$50,000	$580	$448	$386	$332
$100,000	$1,160	$896	$772	$668
$150,000	$1,740	$1,340	$1,160	$999
$200,000	$2,320	$1,790	$1,550	$1,330
$250,000	$2,900	$2,240	$1,930	$1,660
$300,000	$3,480	$2,690	$2,320	$1,990
$350,000	$4,060	$3,138	$2,706	$2,322

Based on 7% interest, compounded monthly

The Right Moves

To earn more with your investments, consider what they cost as well as what they pay.

By using some basic techniques of effective buying, you can build a strong portfolio that minimizes taxes, controls investment expenses, and protects against market ups and downs. Here are three ways to help get you there.

DOLLAR COST AVERAGING
The old adage that the smartest way to make money is to buy at the lowest price and sell at the highest is easier to say than it is to accomplish. If you could do that regularly, funding your retirement—or anything else—would be no problem.

A less dramatic but more reliable strategy is to make regular investments in specific mutual funds, for example $100 every month, or $300 each quarter. It's much less painful to spread your investment over a year rather than to come up with $1,200 all at once. And, over time you can build a substantial investment.

Using this approach, called **dollar cost averaging**, you can even out the cost of your investment Since the prices of mutual funds fluctuate, sometimes you'll buy at a higher price, sometimes at a lower one. When the price is low, your $100 buys more. When it's high, it buys less. But you're never paying more than the current worth. Better yet, you don't risk making a major investment just before a major drop in price.

To use dollar cost averaging for stock purchases, you can enroll in a company-sponsored reinvestment plan that lets you make additional purchases. Many larger companies offer this option. Or you can put a regular amount each month in a special investment account.

If you have no trouble sticking to a buying schedule, you can write the checks yourself. Or, if it's more convenient, you can arrange for automatic deductions from your account. The advantage of the former is more flexibility, letting you change the amount or skip an occasional month.

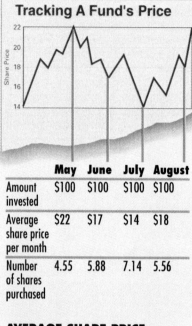

Tracking A Fund's Price

	May	June	July	August
Amount invested	$100	$100	$100	$100
Average share price per month	$22	$17	$14	$18
Number of shares purchased	4.55	5.88	7.14	5.56

AVERAGE SHARE PRICE

$$\frac{\text{Average price per month}}{\text{Number of months}} = \text{Average share price}$$

for example

$$\frac{(\$22 + 17 + 14 + 18)}{4} = \$17.75$$

AVERAGE SHARE COST

$$\frac{\text{Total amount invested}}{\text{Total shares purchased}} = \text{Average share cost}$$

for example

$$\frac{\$400}{4.55 + 5.88 + 7.14 + 5.56} = \$17.29$$

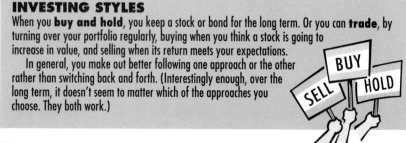

INVESTING STYLES
When you **buy and hold**, you keep a stock or bond for the long term. Or you can **trade**, by turning over your portfolio regularly, buying when you think a stock is going to increase in value, and selling when its return meets your expectations.

In general, you make out better following one approach or the other rather than switching back and forth. (Interestingly enough, over the long term, it doesn't seem to matter which of the approaches you choose. They both work.)

BUY
SELL
HOLD

AVOIDING THE TAX MAN

Of the two great myths about retirement—that your living expenses will drop dramatically and that you'll owe less income tax—the second is probably the bigger misconception. There's not much you can do to influence the tax rate. But some investing strategies can foil—or at least postpone—the inevitable amount due the IRS.

If you're in one of the higher federal tax brackets and live in a high-tax state, one solution is to do some of your investing in tax-exempt municipal bonds. None of the interest is taxed (though **capital gains,** or any profit you make when you sell, will be). While tax-exempt investments usually pay less interest than taxable investments, you can use the following steps to figure out what you need to earn on a taxable investment to equal the income on a tax-exempt one.

1 Subtract your current **federal tax bracket** from 100. For example if you're in the 36% bracket, you get 64.

$$100 - 36 = 64$$

2 Divide the yield on the tax-exempt investment by the number you get in step 1. The answer is the taxable yield you need on a taxable investment to equal the tax-exempt yield.

$$\frac{\text{Tax-exempt yield}}{100 - \text{your tax rate}} = \text{Equivalent taxable yield}$$

If you are in the 36% tax bracket, you'd need a taxable yield of 9.4% to earn as much as a tax-exempt investment paying 6%.

for example

$$\frac{6}{64} = .09375$$

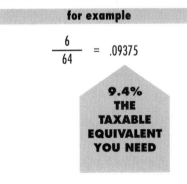

9.4% THE TAXABLE EQUIVALENT YOU NEED

BUILDING A LADDER

If you're buying bonds or CDs, you can use a technique known as **laddering**. When you ladder, you choose investments with different maturity dates, and split your total investment more or less equally among the different bonds.

As each bond comes due, you have the principal to reinvest. When one bond matures, you buy a new one. If interest rates have dropped, say from 8% to 6% on medium-term bonds, only that part of your total bond investment has to be reinvested at the lower rate. By the time the next bond matures, rates could be up again.

Laddering, in other words, is a way to keep your investments fluid and at the same time protect yourself against having to invest all your money at once if rates are low. Laddered investments can also be used as a regular source of income. As they come due, you can put the money into more liquid accounts to use for living expenses. By planning those cash infusions, you can avoid having to sell off other investments that would continue to produce income, like stocks, longer-term bonds, or mutual funds.

HOW LADDERING WORKS

Purchase three treasury bonds with varying terms to split up your principal.
When each bond matures, re-invest the principal in another bond.

- If interest rates rise, you're able to take advantage of high-yielding investments.

- If interest rates drop, you'll have to reinvest only one-third of your total principal at lower rates.

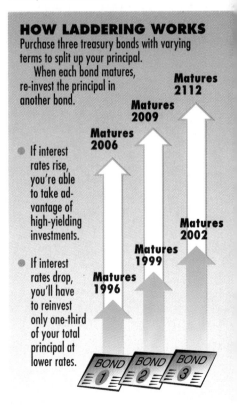

Matures 2112

Matures 2009

Matures 2006

Matures 2002

Matures 1999

Matures 1996

BOND 1 BOND 2 BOND 3

Diversity

If variety is the spice of life, diversity is the heart and soul of investing.

While some of your investments are living up to expectations, others may be in the dumps. If you want your **portfolio,** or list of investment holdings, to produce the income you'll need after you retire, you have to **diversify**, or spread your investment money around.

That's because any time all of your money is concentrated in one place, your financial security depends on the strength of that investment. And no matter how sound an investment may be, there will be times when its price falls or its interest payments don't keep up with inflation.

For example, if your life savings are in CDs paying 3% while inflation is running at 4%, you're facing a loss of buying power. Or if you own hundreds of shares in a company that loses money, cuts its dividend, and drops in the stock market, you'll be short dividend income and even part of your original investment if you sell your shares.

THE FIRST STEPS

Diversifying your investments is no easy matter. For starters, you need enough money to make a variety of investments. And, you have to judge each one not only on its own merits, but in relation to the rest of your portfolio.

If you put long-term investment money into **fixed income investments** like corporate or municipal bonds, you should also make **equity investments** like stocks or stock mutual funds. If some of your short-term investments are Certificates of Deposits (CDs), the rest could be money market funds or U.S. Treasury bills.

THE SECOND STAGE

Diversification also means spreading your investment dollar within a specific type of investment. For example, your stock portfolio is not diversified if you own shares in just one or two companies, or in companies all involved in the same sector of the economy, like health care or utility companies. Nor are your fixed income

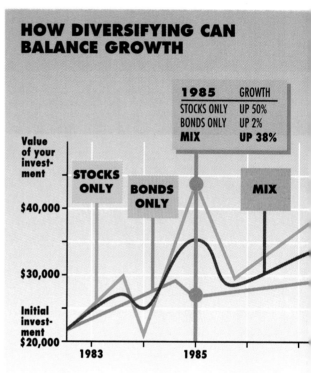

HOW DIVERSIFYING CAN BALANCE GROWTH

1985	GROWTH
STOCKS ONLY	UP 50%
BONDS ONLY	UP 2%
MIX	**UP 38%**

Value of your investment

STOCKS ONLY

BONDS ONLY

MIX

$40,000

$30,000

Initial investment $20,000

1983   1985

investments diversified if you own only municipal bonds issued by the state in which you live. If you invest in eight mutual funds, but they all track small growth companies, you're not diversified either.

Increasingly, real diversification calls for international investments. Because the world economies are linked by round-the-clock trading and stimulated by the opening of new markets, many investors—and their professional advisors—believe that putting money into overseas markets is a good way to balance investments at home. Generally, mutual funds provide the simplest ways to invest internationally, since the funds handle all of the currency and taxation issues that go along with buying and selling abroad.

THE VALUE OF MUTUAL FUNDS

One of the reasons mutual funds keep cropping up in discussions of diversity is that they are, by definition, diversified. Each fund owns hundreds of different stocks, bonds, or whatever it specializes in. That way, if some of the holdings aren't performing well, they are offset by others that are doing better. In fact, some funds balance stocks and bonds to provide diversification in different categories of investment as well as within each of those categories.

Because a fund has so much money to invest, it can achieve a breadth of diversity that no individual can. And because a fund buys and sells in such volume, the cost of diversifying is minimized as well.

ONE MORE THING TO REMEMBER

Diversity is essential for retirement investments. It's especially important if a stock purchase plan is part of your pension plan, because your long-term payout will depend on how well that stock does. You'll probably want to balance your dependence on the company's financial health with different investments in your own accounts, including your 401(k) or similar plan.

Diversity is especially important if your company's stock is **cyclical**, that is, a stock strongly influenced by economic conditions. Airline stocks, for example, tend to be depressed in a slow economy because people travel less. If that's the case, you may not want to put too much money into other stocks that behave the same way.

To extend the idea one step further, you may want to think twice about building a portfolio full of stocks and bonds in companies that are in the same business your employer is in. If the pharmaceutical business declines, for example, and all you own are drug company stocks, you'll really need an aspirin.

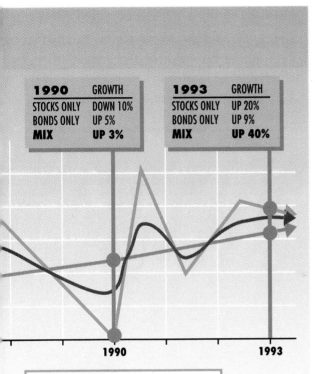

1990	GROWTH		1993	GROWTH
STOCKS ONLY	DOWN 10%		STOCKS ONLY	UP 20%
BONDS ONLY	UP 5%		BONDS ONLY	UP 9%
MIX	**UP 3%**		**MIX**	**UP 40%**

1990   1993

ASK YOURSELF

Achieving diversity isn't a one-shot deal. In analyzing your portfolio, ask the following questions to measure where you are and what's next:

 What resources have I committed to buying stocks, bonds, mutual funds, real estate, and other money-producing investments?

 What are those investments worth in relation to each other? How about in comparison to last year? Five years ago? Ten years ago?

 What investments have I made lately? Are they all basically the same?

4 What am I going to buy next? Why?

DIVERSITY FOR THE LONG HAUL

Diversifying isn't the same as buying randomly. If anything, it's the opposite, because it means buying according to your strategic plan to get the right mix of growth and income in your investments. But there's nothing wrong with achieving diversity gradually. If you decide to expand your equity holdings because the stock market seems poised for steady growth, you can do it and think about beefing up your bond portfolio in the months or years ahead. Taking one from column A doesn't mean you have to add one from column B at the same time.

Investment Risk

There's no such thing as a totally safe investment, but you can choose the level of risk you're comfortable with.

When you invest, you always take a certain amount of risk. At the very worst, you could lose all the money you commit and owe more on top of that. That can be the case with futures contracts, low-rated bonds, and other speculative ventures. Or, your **return on investment**—what you get back for what you put in—could be so small it doesn't really count as an investment at all. At the very best, you could invest a small amount in a growth company and make a fortune. And between those extremes you have enormous investing choice.

Before you invest, you have to know what the potential risks are as well as your own level of tolerance. For example, if a falling stock market makes you lose sleep or, worse yet, sell in a panic, stocks are probably not the investment for you. On the other hand, investing too conservatively poses the real risk of not earning enough to beat inflation.

RISK RATIOS

You can estimate the degree of risk in certain kinds of investments, like stocks or stock mutual funds, by balancing how much you think the investment is likely to increase in value against how far it could fall from its current price. For example, if a stock selling for $40 dollars could increase in value to $70, but could fall to $30, its **risk ratio** is a healthy 3:1 (or $30 up, $10 down). But if the same stock were more likely to stop at $50 and vulnerable to dropping to $10, the ratio would be reversed, to 1:3 ($10 up, $30 down). So the investment would be much risker.

KEEPING YOUR EYES CLOSED

The worst mistake you can make as an investor is to ignore or minimize the risks you're taking, or to assume that nothing is going to happen. By recognizing that very risky investments, like futures, can cost you even more money than you originally put in, you might decide not to try your hand at them. At the same time, you have to be aware of the risk involved in parking your money in one place.

You also have to be alert to investment advisors who swear that anything is risk-free. It's probably fair to say that the more they promise, the greater the risk they're asking you to take.

THE INVESTMENT PYRAMID

Risk is the result of **volatility**—how much and how quickly the value of an investment changes—and **uncertainty**.

HIGH RISK

- **Futures, options, and other derivatives**
- **Speculative stocks and mutual funds**
- **Low-rated bonds**
- **Mining, precious metals**

MODERATE RISK

- Growth stocks
- Small company stocks
- Medium-rated corporate, municipal, and zero-coupon bonds
- Mutual funds
- Rental real estate

LIMITED RISK

- Blue chip stocks
- High-rated corporate, municipal, and zero-coupon bonds
- Conservative mutual funds
- U.S. Treasury bonds and notes

LOW RISK

- Savings accounts
- Money market accounts and money market funds
- CDs
- U.S. Treasury bills
- Fixed annuities

THE SECURITY OF INSURANCE

One of the reasons people feel comfortable about putting money into bank products—like CDs, money market accounts, and regular savings—is that their investments are insured through the Federal Deposit Insurance Corporation. If the bank folds, the money is safe.

Unfortunately, it's not that simple. If a bank is bought out by another bank—a growing phenomenon as large regional banks expand—the money will be safe, but the rates depositors had been earning might not be. Banks that acquire others are under no obligation to pay the same CD rates, for example, that the bank they bought paid.

> ### HIGHEST GAINS OR LOSSES
> You can win big, but lose bigger, with risky investments.

More important though, is the amount of coverage the FDIC provides. In the past, each differently registered account in a bank was insured up to $100,000. If you had $100,000 in a jointly held CD, a similar amount in your IRA, and another $25,000 in your own name in a money market account, the total amount was insured. That's not true anymore. Now you're insured to a limit of $100,000 per bank no matter how many accounts you have. You can spread out investments among three, or five, or however many banks you want to increase the amount of coverage. But the per-bank limits remain.

THE RISK OF HIGH YIELDS

One cardinal rule for successful investing is to know what you're doing. When the economy is down, and interest earnings decline, you might be tempted to seek an investment that produces the same high returns you've gotten used to. The risk is buying lower quality investments (which pay more to attract buyers), or investments you don't know anything about.

> ### LOWEST GAINS OR LOSSES
> $10,000 in a savings account at rates below inflation will be safe but will lose value over time.

Derivative products like collateralized mortgage obligations (CMOs), for example, are often hard to understand and riskier than they seem, despite the promise of a high yield and the comfort of a familiar sounding word: mortgage.

PLAYING IT TOO SAFE

You won't lose your shirt with low-risk investments. But you might not earn enough from them to buy a new shirt when your old one wears out. Trying to avoid risk by investing in only the safest products is a mistake, especially if your retirement is a long way off. If that's your current approach, though, you're not alone. A huge number of Americans—approximately 75%—have most of their retirement money in investments that aren't beating inflation.

The solution is to diversify your risk, just as you diversify the types of investments you make.

OTHER KINDS OF RISK

Beyond the risks of the investments themselves—for example, a new company that fails or an established company that suffers severe losses—there are other risks you can't predict or control but must be prepared for:

MARKET RISK

depends on the state of the economy as a whole. If the stock market tumbles, your stock investment will decline in value even if the company whose stock you own is making money.

CURRENCY FLUCTUATION

is increasingly a factor in investment risk, as more people put money into international markets, especially in mutual funds. As the dollar rises in value, for example, the value of overseas investments declines—and vice versa.

INFLATION RISK

affects the value of fixed rate investments like bonds and CDs. If you buy when inflation and interest rates are low, the value of your investments declines as inflation rises because the interest rate isn't adjusted to keep pace.

POLITICAL TURMOIL

is a risk because the economies of different nations are closely intertwined. Threats to the oil supply, for example, disrupted the economy in the late 70s and could again.

Allocating Your Assets

The recipe for making the most of your investments calls for measuring your ingredients carefully.

Finding the right investment mix, one that balances risk and reward and achieves diversity, means carefully deciding what you're going to buy. The decision is based partly on your age, partly on your goals, and partly on the overall economy. But since these factors are all fluid, allocating your assets is really a continuing process.

Who Has the Best Blend?

Performance of asset-allocation blends recommended by 12 brokerage houses in periods ended March 31, 1994. Houses are ranked by 12-month performance. Also shown is the mix each house now recommends. Figures do not include transaction costs.

	PERFORMANCE			RECOMMENDED BLEND		
BROKERAGE HOUSE	**THREE MONTHS**	**ONE YEAR**	**FIVE YEARS**	**STOCKS**	**BONDS**	**CASH**
Lehman Brothers	-2.8%	2.7%	73.3%	50%	35%	15%
A.G. Edwards	-3.3	2.6	65.1	60	40	0
Smith Barney	-2.8	2.4	70.5	50	25	25
Merrill Lynch	-2.9	2.3	69.1	60	25	15
PaineWebber	-3.4	2.3	69.1	58	40	2
Prudential	-3.1	2.2	74.0	65	15	20
Kidder Peabody	-3.5	2.0	73.0	60	20	20
Raymond James[1]	-2.9	1.9	63.2	60	15	20
AVERAGE	-3.0	2.3	69.3	58.2	26.3	15.2
COMPARISON YARDSTICKS						
Fixed blend[2]	-3.0	2.2	68.9			
Stocks	-3.8	1.4	76.8			
Bonds	-2.9	3.0	64.5			
Cash	0.7	3.2	32.9			

[1]Recommends 5% in real estate
[2]Constant mix of 55% stocks, 35% bonds, 10% cash.
NA = Not applicable (not in study for full period)

Sources: Company documents, Wilshire Associates, Carpenter Analytical Services

KEEPING RECORDS

One complication of a diversified portfolio is keeping track of your investments. If simplicity were your primary goal, you could just keep everything in one savings account. You'd never have to wonder about what your investment was worth or where your money was—although you would have to worry about what you were going to live on as inflation eroded the value of your account.

A hands-off approach that does work is to use one financial institution— a brokerage or a bank—as an administrator for all your investments. They'll send you a consolidated statement each month, detailing your assets and the value of your portfolio. The only extra recordkeeping will be confirmations of what you buy and sell so that you can figure your profit or loss for income tax purposes.

If you're like many investors, with a diversity of accounts as well as a diversified portfolio, you'll need to set aside space and time to keep track of your investments. What you really want to know is how well each one is doing and what share of your portfolio it makes up.

FORM 1099
FORM K-1
BROKERAGE STATEMENT

ALLOCATION MODELS

Asset allocation plans, or models, tend to focus, for the most part, on securities—stocks, bonds, and mutual funds—and cash or its equivalents—investments which can be easily liquidated, like CDs and U.S. Treasury bills.

No single model produces the best results in all economic climates, so brokerage houses and other financial institutions suggest different models at different times. And their models tend to differ from each other as well, as this chart from The Wall Street Journal illustrates. Several brokerages are recomending 60% or more in stocks, while Lehman Brothers, the year's best performer, proposes 50% in stocks.

The same allocation also produces different results over different time spans. Prudential's 65-15-20 allocation produced mid-range results over one year, but the strongest over five years.

Asset allocation models are important for the personal investments you make outside a qualified retirement plan as well as for the money you have in a 401(k) or 403(b) plan. You should develop a sense of how much of your total nest egg should be allocated to each category, and then buy and sell to keep that approximate balance. Your financial advisor will customize a general model to suit your situation, basing it on your age, family situation, and financial status

Experts maintain that asset allocation accounts for 80% of the results you get as an investor. That means having money in stocks when stocks are strong, in bonds when they're hot, and in cash when it's time to wait for a change. The only problem is figuring out when that is!

AVERAGE INVESTMENT RETURNS

10.3% FOR STOCKS

5% FOR BONDS

3.7% FOR CASH

WHAT A DIFFERENCE AN ALLOCATION MAKES

Asset allocation can make a real difference in portfolio performance, as these hypothetical examples show.

Here's what you would earn if you allocated a $100,000 portfolio three different ways and figured an annual return using the average return on each investment type—10.3% for stocks, 5% for bonds, and 3.7% for cash between 1926 and 1993.

60% stock 30% bond 10% cash	OR	30% stock 60% bond 10% cash	OR	10% stock 30% bond 60% cash
$8,050 earnings		**$6,460 earnings**		**$4,730 earnings**

HELP FROM THE COMPUTER

There are a growing number of computer programs to help you analyze your investments and keep track of how they're performing. Some of the programs produced by software companies are comprehensive tools that incorporate advice with background information and work charts. Mutual fund companies and brokerages are other software sources. You can get reviews of what's available for the type of equipment you have, plus critiques of how effective they are, and how complicated to use, regularly in The Wall Street Journal.

INVESTMENT TRACKING SOFTWARE

Asset Allocation Choices

You don't have to reinvent the wheel to plan your asset allocation. It's already been done.

Fortunately, there are a limited number of ways to split up your assets. If you're a cautious investor, you'll stress bonds and cash. And the more aggressive you are—about investing anyway—the more you'll put into stocks. You might even decide that a small percentage of your assets belong in higher-risk investments, like futures or gold mines.

CASH IN THE BANK

A cash investment is money you can get your hands on in a hurry—like a money market fund—without risking a big loss in value. For example, while putting your money in a regular savings account has serious limitations as an investment strategy, the logic behind a cash reserve makes a lot of sense. If all your assets are tied up in stocks and long-term bonds, and you need to **liquidate** (turn them to cash quickly), you may take a loss if the market is down. Or, you might miss a great opportunity for new investing.

TAKING STOCK

In an asset allocation model, stocks represent growth. While some stocks pay dividends that provide a regular income, stocks are essential to long-term investment planning because historically they

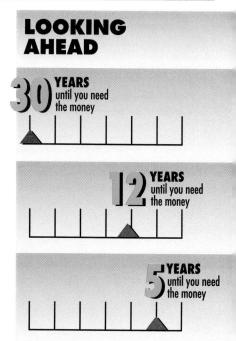

LOOKING AHEAD

30 YEARS until you need the money

12 YEARS until you need the money

5 YEARS until you need the money

increase in value. While it's possible to lose a lot of money in the stock market, in any one year, the longer you stay in the market, the more apt you are to come out ahead.

Financial experts may recommend that you have as much as 80% of your total portfolio in stocks (or stock mutual funds) while you're in your 20s and 30s. That means every time you invest $1,000, $800 of it would go into stocks or stock mutual funds. However, as you get older, say in your 50s and 60s, the percentage of stocks in your portfolio is usually scaled back to 60% or sometimes less. Generally the greater the risk a particular stock carries, the more suitable it is for younger investors.

STASHING THE CASH

Option	Advantages
Bank money market account	● Instant access ● Better interest than savings account ● May reduce cost of checking account ● Check-writing privileges ● FDIC insured
Money market mutual fund	● Easy access; possible overnight electronic transfer ● Interest usually higher than bank money market account ● Check-writing privileges
CDs	● Money available (with early withdrawal penalty possible) ● Interest rate slightly higher than money market accounts ● Due dates can be staggered for convenience ● Bank CDs FDIC insured
U.S. Treasury Bills	● Short-term investments (13 to 26 weeks) ● Enough interest to protect against inflation ● Can be sold any time, though at a potential loss ● Extremely safe

**SHIFTING GEARS
FOR SHIFTING GOALS**
As retirement gets closer you might want to shift your assets from growth toward income.

STOCKS	BONDS	CASH
80% Aggresive growth fund Small company stocks Growth stocks	**15%** Long-term bonds High-yield municipal bond fund	**5%** Money market account
60% International equity fund Blue chip stocks	**30%** Zero coupon bonds Intermediate bonds	**10%** Money market account CD
40% Blue chip stocks S&P 500 index fund	**40%** U.S. Treasury notes Municipal bonds	**20%** CD Money market account Treasury bills

THE BOND'S THE THING

Bonds have traditionally been seen as income-producing investments. You buy a bond, hold it to maturity and receive a regular interest payment every six months or year. Then, you get the principal back when the bond matures. As an added plus, bonds issued by the U.S. government, by most state and local governments, and by top-notch corporations are virtually safe from **default,** or failure to pay what's due. That means bonds appeal to investors—often those nearing retirement—who are looking for steady income and don't want to risk losing their investment.

Most experts advise all investors to include bonds—or bond mutual funds—in their portfolios because they balance movement in the stock market. When interest rates are high, for example, the stock market isn't usually as strong as it is when rates are lower. That means that the steady return on a bond could offset falling stock prices. Further, there's an active market in bond trading that you can use to turn a profit. Buying a bond for less than **par**, or face value, and selling it for more than par can result in a substantial profit.

OTHER FIXED INCOME

Corporate and government bonds are the best known, but not the only fixed income investments. Mortgage-based investments like relatively conservative **Ginnie Maes,** sold by the Government National Mortgage Association, as well as the riskier **CMOs,** or Collateralized Mortgage Obligations, which derive from a package of mortgages, repay your investment with interest. But what you get back often depends more on the state of the economy than it does with corporate or government bonds. For example, if interest rates drop and lots of people refinance their mortgages, investments based on mortgages reflect the amounts being paid back and the rates at which the new loans are made.

Certain annuities and some life insurance policies also provide regular, or fixed, income, usually after you retire. Unlike bonds, with their established maturity dates, the return is paid out either over your lifetime, or for a period you and the issuer agree on.

Figuring Yield

One way to measure how well your investments are doing is to look at what they're paying.

Choosing the right mix of investments is only half the battle. To know if you're succeeding—that is, if your investments are really performing well—you need to know how to measure the **yield** and the **return** your investments provide.

NEW YORK EXCHANGE BONDS

	Bonds	Cur Yld	Vol	Close	Net Chg.		Bonds	Cur Yld	Vol	Close	Net Chg.
Net Chg.	Coastl 11⅛98	10.9	35	102⅜ + ⅝			IntTch 9⅜96	9.7	20	96⅜ − 1⅞	
	Coeur 6⅜04	...	1	93½ − 1½			JCP 6⅜03	7.3	10	87½	...
− ¼	viColuG 9s94f	...	65	118	− ¼		KaufB 9⅜03	10.3	106	90⅝ + ½	
− ¼	viColuG 8¾s95f	...	25	116¼	− ⅛		Kolmrg 8¾09	cv	26	89	...
− ⅝	viColuG 9⅛s95f	...	36	118⅜	− ⅝		Kroger 9s99	8.9	18	100¾ + ⅛	
− ⅜	viColuG 8⅜s96f	...	100	116⅝	...		Kroger 6⅜99	cv	2	133 − 1	
− ½	viColuG 8¼s96f	...	60	116⅜	− ⅛		LaErg 7s13	cv	103	102⅜ + ⅜	
+ ⅛	viColuG 7½s97M f	...	50	112	...		LehmnBr 10¾496	10.3	5	104⅛ − ⅞	
	viColuG 7½s97O f	...	3	112⅝	...		LoneStr 10s03	10.4	26	96¼ − 1	
...	viColuG 7½s98f	...	50	111¾	− ¼		LglsLt 9⅝s24	10.3	15	93⅛ − ½	
− ¼	viColuG 10⅛s95f	...	3	119⅝ + ½			LglsLt 9¾21	10.4	10	93¾	...
− ¾	viColuG 10¼s99f	...	5	122⅛	...		LglsLt 7.3s99	7.9	25	92⅞ − ¾	
− ⅜	viColuG 10¼11f	...	1000	128	...		LglsLt 8.9s19	10.5	21	84⅞ − ½	
− 1¼	viColuG 10½12f	...	1200	127	...		LslsLt 9s22	10.6	90	85 − ½	
− ¼	CmwE 7⅝s03F	8.3	5	91¾ + 1⅜			LglsLt 7½07	9.2	20	81¾ − 1¼	
...	CmwE 8⅛s07J	8.8	5	92 + 1			LglsLt 8.2s23	10.4	14	79 − 1	
	CmwE 8⅛07	8.6	4				LglsLt 8⅝s04	9.0	3	95⅝ − ⅝	

LOOKING FOR YIELD

You find yield by dividing what you receive in interest or dividends on an investment by the amount you spent for it.

for example

$	200	Annual interest
÷	2,000	Invested
=	10%	YIELD

Yield is sometimes confused with the interest rate an investment pays because the rate is also stated as a percentage of investment.

While yield depends on the rate, it is often a different number. That's because the yield represents what someone paying the current price of the bond, rather than its stated, or par, value, receives on the investment. When the price is more than par, the yield is lower than the interest rate, and when the price is less, the rate is higher.

For example, the Lehman Brothers bond paying 10.75% interest is

COMPOUNDING YIELD

The yield on CDs depends on the frequency with which the interest is **compounded**, or paid. A CD with a simple interest rate of 5%, added once a year, yields 5%, or $50 on a $1,000 investment. But if the rate is compounded, meaning it's added to your balance daily, weekly or monthly, the yield will be higher. The more frequently it's compounded, the greater the yield. For example, a rate of 5% compounded daily would yield 5¼%, or $52.50 on $1,000.

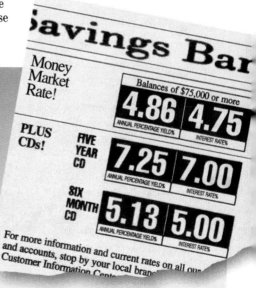

Savings Bar

Money Market Rate!

PLUS CDs!

FIVE YEAR CD

SIX MONTH CD

Balances of $75,000 or more

4.86	4.75
ANNUAL PERCENTAGE YIELD%	INTEREST RATE%
7.25	7.00
ANNUAL PERCENTAGE YIELD%	INTEREST RATE%
5.13	5.00
ANNUAL PERCENTAGE YIELD%	INTEREST RATE%

For more information and current rates on all our and accounts, stop by your local branch. Customer Information Center.

ANOTHER VIEW OF BONDS

Bonds lead a double life in the current investment world. In their traditional role as income producers, they're the backbone of conservative investment portfolios: for little risk and less bother, you get a steady return. More recently, however, bond prices and their yields have fluctuated in response to changing economic conditions. A strong **secondary**

market, where bonds are bought and sold, has flourished, and many investors buy bonds to trade. That means the old rule of buying low—in bond language **at a discount**—and selling high—**at a premium**—also applies. However, the commissions on bond trading can be high. To trade bonds, you also need substantial amounts of money to make the small price differences pay off, as well as a greater tolerance for risk than is generally associated with buying bonds.

Bonds	Cur Yld	Vol	Close	Net Chg.
OhBIT 7½11	8.3	2	90⅛	− 1⅞
OhBIT 7⅞13	8.5	75	92⅜	− ⅝
OldRep 5¾02	cv	10	98⅞	− ⅝
Oryx 7½14	cv	75	76	...
OwnIll 10¼99	10.2	99	100¾	− ¼
OwIll 11s03	10.5	110	104¾	− ⅛
OwnIll 10½02	10.4	73	101	− ¼
OwnIll 10s02	10.0	194	99¾	...
PhilEl 6⅛97	6.4	50	96⅛	+ ⅛
PhilEl 7¾23	9.1	18	85¼	− 1¼
PhilEl 7⅞23	8.7	10	82	− 1
PhilEl 5⅞01	6.5	25	86¼	− ¼
PacTT 7.8s07	8.3	151	93¾	− ½
PacTT 7¼08	8.1	13	89⅜	− ⅝
PacTT 7⅝09	8.4	1	90⅝	...
PacBell 7¼02	7.6	62	95¼	...
PacBell 7¼26	8.6			

Bonds	Cur Yld			
Safwy 9⅞07	9.5			
SallM zr14				
SvcMer 9s04	10			
SvcMer 8¾01	9			
Showboat 9¼408	1			
Snyder 7s01				
SoCnBel 8¼17				
SoCnBel 8½29				
SouBell 5s97				
SouBell 4¾98				
SouBell				
Sou				

currently yielding only 10.3% because the price is $1,041.25 (104⅛), or $41.25 (4⅛) above par. In contrast, the Philadelphia Electric bond paying 7.75% interest is currently yielding 9.1% because the bond is selling for $852.50 (85¼), or $147.50 below par.

In cases where you're not earning interest on an investment, the current market value is used to figure its yield. Property that you bought for $10,000 yields 5% if you can sell it for $12,000 the same year. If two years goes by before you sell, the yield is 2.5%. And unlike the interest that's been added to your CD, the yield on non-interest-bearing investments is not realized until you actually sell them. By next year, you might only get $9,500 for the property, and have a negative yield.

STOP AT THE YIELD

It makes sense to find the best yield you can when there's a basis for comparison, like the interest rates on different investments in relation to their liquidity. Unless you're dealing with large sums of money, however, the difference of a quarter percent makes very little difference in your yield, especially on short-term investments like most CDs.

If the larger yield is not at a local bank, or is at a weaker one, the inconvenience and potential risk may not be worth the few dollars difference. For example, if your $25,000 CD is yielding 5% in your local bank and 5.25% in a bank you know nothing about half a continent away, the $62.50 difference in earnings may not be worth making the switch.

Blindly seeking yield has other drawbacks. The promise of a higher yield on a riskier investment that you don't really know much about, like a high-yield bond, may not justify switching from a safer and more familiar U. S. Treasury or agency bond. When interest rates are low, as they were in the early 90s, this strategy seems appealing. But most experts caution against putting money into investments that you don't understand or that your broker can't explain to your satisfaction.

Timing is also an issue. When interest rates are low, it may not pay to tie up your money in a longer-term CD, for example, that yields only a percentage point or two more than short-term ones. If rates go up, as they invariably do, you risk being locked into a lower yield or facing a loss if you liquidate. One solution may be a CD with an adjustable interest rate, which will increase at least once if rates in general go up.

Finding Return

The real test of success for any investment is what you get back for what you put in.

When you invest for growth, **total return**, or the amount your investment increases in value *plus* the interest or dividends it has paid, is the best measure of how well it has performed:

Dividends + $\dfrac{\text{Gain in}}{\text{value}}$ = Total return

for example

If you spent $6,000 for stock that's now worth $8,000, and you received $360 in dividends,

$360 + $2,000 = **$2,360**
TOTAL RETURN

You can use the total return to figure the percent return, which you can compare with the return on other investments:

$\dfrac{\text{Total}}{\text{return}}$ ÷ $\dfrac{\text{Price of}}{\text{investment}}$ = Percent return

for example

$2,360 ÷ $6,000 = **39.3%**
PERCENT RETURN

If you bought and sold the stocks within one year, your percent return would be the full 39%. But if it took three years, for example, the annual percent return would be 13%.

COMPARISON PROBLEMS

While it's relatively easy to compare the return on similar investments, such as two mutual funds that buy small company stock, it's much harder to compare your return on different kinds of investments. Here are some of the factors that make comparisons difficult:

Time
The length of time you hold different investments varies, making it hard to assess gain or loss in value for a fixed period. So does the timing of your buys and sells. Buying just before a market dip, for instance, can skew your results downward.

RETURN ON STOCK INVESTMENTS
If you bought 200 shares of Long Island Lighting stock at its low of 15 and sold it a year later at its high of 25¾, your total return would be $2,506, or 84%:

	$	5,150	Selling price
-		3,000	Purchase price
= $		2,150	Return on transaction
+		356	Dividends at $1.78/share
= $		2,506	**TOTAL RETURN** (before investment costs)

2,506 ÷ 3,000 = .0835 = **84%**

NEW YORK

| 52 Weeks | | | | | Yld | | Vol | |
Hi	Lo	Stock	Sym	Div	%	PE	100s	H
n 19⅝	14¼	LoneStar	LCE		...	...	127	19
n 9½	6	LoneStar wt			...	...	95	8
25¾	15	LILCo	LIL	1.78	10.2	9	3463	7
27½	21⅞	LILCo pfA		1.99	8.6	...	135	23
72	49	LILCo pfB						

Amount of investment
If you add money to a mutual fund, buy 100 additional shares of a stock, or sell half your shares in a stock to take a profit, figuring your return can become complicated. On the other hand, making money, not ease in figuring return, is the primary purpose of investing.

Method of figuring return
The performance of an investment can be **averaged** or **compounded**, and the method can make a big difference in the return. To figure average return, you add the return for each of the years in your sample and divide by the total number of years. But in figuring a compound return, you have to weigh the impact of each year's return on the total. For example, a return totalling 27% over three years would be 9% a year if the return were **averaged**, or **annualized**, no matter what each annual return

MUTUAL FUND QUOTATIONS

Total Return – TD	39 wks	5 yrs	R
-3.9	−4.8	NS	..
-1.0	−2.2	+10.0	C
-7.6	+4.4	NS	..
-4.0	−4.6	NS	..
NA	NA	NA	..
-1.3	−2.8	+7.9	E
-0.3	+0.2	+6.4	D
-4.4	−5.6	+6.2	D
-1.6	+0.8	NS	..
-0.6	−1.2	+9.0	E
-0.2	−1.8	+9.7	D
-5.7	−6.5	NS	..
-6.8			

	Inv. Obj.	NAV	Offer Price	NAV Chg.	– Total Return – YTD	39 wks	5 yrs	R
Telecom	WOR	17.69	18.57	+0.03	+3.0	+2.1	NS	..
TeleB	WOR	17.55	17.55	+0.03	+2.6	+1.7	NS	..
Wldw p	WOR	17.10	17.95	−0.15	−2.1	−3.8	+8.7	C
WldwB	WOR	16.92	16.92	−0.15	−2.7	−4.4	NS	..
Gabelli Funds:								
ABC p	GRO	10.39	10.60	...	+3.6	+3.4	NS	..
Asset p	GRO	23.54	23.54	+0.09	+1.0	+0.1	+9.9	C
CnvSc	S&B	11.37	NL	+0.01	+0.4	−0.3	+9.1	B
EqInc p	EQI	11.70	12.25	+0.02	+3.2	+1.3	NS	..
GlConv	S&B	10.57	NL	−0.03	NS	NS	NS	..
GlIntCP	WOR	10.44	NL	...	NS	NS	NS	..
GlTel p	WOR	10.34	NL	−0.01	+1.4	+1.4	NS	..
Gold	SEC	11.66	NL	−0.03	NS			
Gwth								

JP InvGrBd
JPM Instl F
Bond
Diversifd
EmgMkEq
IntlEqty
SelEqty
ST Bon
Small
Jacks
Gr

On the other hand, if you bought high and sold low, your return could be a loss, despite earning the same $356 in dividends.

In any case, you have to figure total return for yourself. That number doesn't appear in the daily stock exchange columns.

RETURN ON MUTUAL FUNDS

When a mutual fund's earnings are reinvested, its total return is the percentage of gain (+) or loss (–) on the fund over a specific period of time.

The Mutual Fund Quotations column in The Wall Street Journal gives the total return for every mutual fund on a year-to-date (YTD) basis daily, plus details on other time periods throughout the week. In this example, for instance, Gabelli Asset Fund has a year-to-date return of 1.0%, a weaker record over the last 39 weeks (.1%) and a stronger return over five years (9.9%).

STOCK EXCHANGE CO

lose	Net Chg		52 Weeks Hi	Lo	Stock	Sym	Div	Yld %	PE	Vol 100s	Hi	Lo	Clo
19⅝	+ ¼		15⅛	9⅞	MunivestMI	MVM	.84e	8.2	...	287	10¼	10⅛	
8⅛	+ ⅛	▼	15⅛	9¾	MunivestNJ	MVJ	.85e	8.7	...	370	10⅛	9⅝	
17⅜	– ¼		15	10⅛	MunivestNY	MVY	.90e	8.7	...	197	10½		
23⅛	– ¼		15½	10½	MunivestPA	MVP	.92e	8.4	...	110			

was. But the three-year return could be less than 7% **compounded** if an initial bad year offset a final good one.

Investment purpose

If you have money in real estate, zero-coupon bonds, limited partnerships, and other investments that are hard to put a current value on or difficult to **liquidate** by turning them into cash, you can't figure return the same way or make a meaningful comparison. But many of these investments have tax advantages than aren't reflected in return and are the real motive for buying them in the first place.

APPLES AND ORANGES

While comparison can be hard, it's certainly not impossible if you're thinking in terms of stocks, bonds, and mutual funds. For example, if you want to compare a stock investment to a bond investment, you have to find the **annual return** on each one, or what you've made each year, as a percentage of your investment. For example, if you compare a bond yielding 8% to a stock with a dividend yield of 4% but a total return of 12.8%, you determine that the stock performance is stronger.

The comparison between stocks and bonds (or between stock mutual funds and bond mutual funds) is more telling when you compare stocks to riskier bonds and other high-yielding investments. The likelihood that the riskier bond will continue to pay well over the long haul—the time frame of investing for retirement—is small. Plus, you face at least as great a risk of losing your principal with these bonds as you do with stocks, and in some cases significantly more risk.

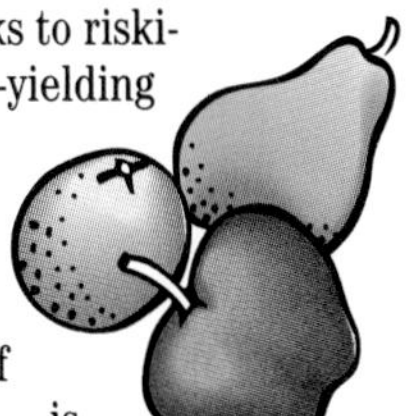

However, given the different goals of your investments, the most meaningful comparisons are those that compare similar investments, or investments with similar goals, like growth or income production.

Deferred Annuities

Annuities are appealing because they grow tax-deferred.

A deferred annuity is a contract you make with an insurance company. You invest money, either as a lump sum or over a period of years, building up a pool of income you can tap after you retire. The insurance company administers the contract, makes the investments, and pays out your benefit when you begin to collect. Because annuities are retirement plans, your investment grows tax-deferred, increasing the rate at which your earnings accumulate.

An annuity is a contract you make with an insurance company.

THE INVESTOR

66 I agree to invest a set amount in the annuity, either in a lump sum or over a period of years. **99**

Your money grows tax-deferred.

FIXED OR VARIABLE

If you choose a deferred annuity, you'll have to choose between a fixed or a variable account. A **fixed annuity** is the more conservative choice. It promises a set rate of return, though the rate can be—and usually is—reset regularly over the years. In many cases, the initial rate, or the one you're quoted when you buy your annuity, is higher than the rate at which your investment will actually grow.

If the rates drop, the earnings that have been projected for your investment decline—sometimes quite dramatically. While most fixed annuities have a **floor**, or guarantee of a minimum rate, it can be as low as current bank savings rates. The difference is that bank deposits are much more liquid, so you get cash easily when you need it. That's not the case with annuities.

For example, a typical annuity investment might offer an initial rate of 8.5%,

but a floor of 4%. If the annuity were actually paying at the lower rate, your investment return might not be strong enough to offset the rate of inflation.

Unlike a fixed annuity, a **variable annuity** lets you choose how your money is invested. The investment selection— usually mutual funds—may often be limited, and the return is not guaranteed. But you can put your money into higher paying investments, and you can profit by putting what you know to work for your own benefit. In that way, you can compare a variable annuity with a 401(k). In each case, you're responsible for deciding how your retirement savings will be invested. A major difference, though, is that the money you invest in annuities has already been taxed. So, most experts agree that if you have the opportunity to use a salary-reduction plan, it's smart to fund that first.

COLLECTING ON YOUR ANNUITY

After the **accumulation** phase, when your investment grows, there comes a point when you start collecting—and paying the taxes you've deferred.

You can choose among receiving regular payouts based on your contract, using the money to buy an immediate annuity from another source, or taking a lump sum withdrawal.

If you're taking the regular payments, you owe tax on the earnings portion of each payout, a calculation that the company will provide. If you take a lump sum, though, you owe all the tax that's due up front. You don't have the choice of five-year forward averaging the way you do with a pension payout. And you can't roll the amount over into an IRA so you can continue to defer taxes.

You can usually take money out of your annuity sporadically. If you're over 59½, there's no penalty, but you will get stuck with an extra tax bill. That's because the IRS says that the entire withdrawal, in this case, is made up of earnings, not principal. It's also possible to begin regular withdrawals before you retire, taking up to 10% of the total value of your account each year. Then you owe tax only on the earnings portion.

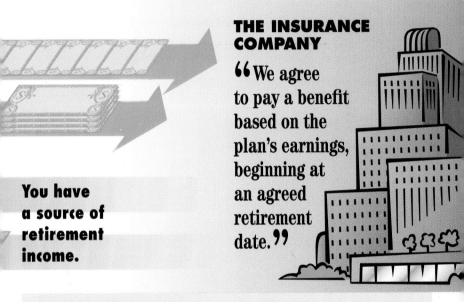

THE INSURANCE COMPANY

66 We agree to pay a benefit based on the plan's earnings, beginning at an agreed retirement date. 99

You have a source of retirement income.

DEFERRED ANNUITIES—CHARMS BUT WARTS

Deferred annuities, both fixed and variable, provide major investment benefits. For all their charms, however, deferred annuities also have some drawbacks.

ADVANTAGES

- Tax-deferred growth
- No limit on the amount you can contribute each year
- No mandatory withdrawals after you reach age 70½
- A wide choice of plans, letting you find one that suits your investing style and goals

A side benefit of annuity income is that it doesn't count as income when you're figuring out whether part of your Social Security is taxable. Unlike earnings on other investments—including tax-exempt municipal bonds—which you have to add when you figure your annual income, you can ignore what you get from an annuity. Whether that will always be true is hard to say—but it's a selling point now.

DRAWBACKS

- Amount you invest isn't tax-deductible
- Stiff penalties if you withdraw early, or in some cases, if you make a lump sum withdrawal at any point in the contract
- Minimized tax advantages for high-income tax payers because earnings are taxed as straight income, not at lower capital gains rate
- Potentially disappointing return on variable annuity investment
- Potentially large fees, which reduce investment growth, a particular problem with variable annuities

Immediate Annuities

If you buy an immediate annuity, you'll get a steady regular retirement income.

Immediate annuities fill a specific niche in retirement planning by providing a regular monthly income, the way a pension annuity does. But instead of building up your assets over time, you buy the annuity with one lump sum payment and usually start collecting right away.

Insurance companies sell the annuities, administer your contract, and invest your money. That's a major attraction for many people, who prefer not to be responsible for investment decisions or money management themselves.

Buy an Annuity

Get Paid Monthly

COMPARISON SHOPPING

The amount of your monthly annuity check is based on the size of your investment, your age, and what the insurance company estimates it will earn on the investment you're making. In fact, the monthly payout on the same

sized investment can vary enormously from company to company. So get several different proposals to be sure you end up with the best deal.

You should also look at the financial stability of the insurance company itself. Because you're making a lifetime deal, you want the company to be around to make your payments. Though a high rating from Best & Company or Standard and Poor's doesn't guarantee a company will stay solvent, a poor rating can spell trouble. Ask your agent, or check the financial press for ratings.

Also be wary of buying an annuity from anyone who wants you to act quickly. That's especially true if you're feeling the stress of making financial decisions or if you're looking for a way to invest a large sum of money, like an inheritance or a capital gain. The only one who benefits from speed is the person who sells the annuity.

MAKING CHOICES

If you do decide on an immediate annuity, you'll have to make some decisions about the terms of the annuity contract. Among other things, an annuity is **irrevocable**, which means you can't change your mind once you've made the purchase. Also, there's no lump-sum repayment provision. That's why it's especially important to understand some of the basics.

You also have to decide how much to invest. Experts advise no more than 25% of your nest egg.

ARE THEY SMART?

Whether immediate annuities are smart investments depends very much on your personal situation. Among the points to consider are where an immediate annuity fits in your overall retirement plan and if there are better choices for your investment dollars. It might make sense, for example, to roll your pension payout over into a tax-deferred IRA to continue postponing taxes and avoid an annuity's administrative costs.

Without question, one major advantage of an immediate annuity is the security of a guaranteed income. If returns on other investments dip—because interest rates are down or the stock market slumps— annuity payments remain steady. Since you've already paid taxes on the money you use to buy an annuity, typically more than half of the income is tax-free.

On the down side, if you buy an annuity when interest rates are down, your payments may not keep up with inflation. And while you aren't responsible for managing your portfolio, that also means you can't take advantage of changing market conditions to make better investments.

For a Certain Amount of Time

UNTIL YOU DIE

SINGLE LIFE ANNUITIES are paid each month for the duration of your lifetime. The advantage of single life is that your payment will be larger than with other options. But when you die, the payments stop. If you have a survivor who is dependent on your annuity income, that could be a problem.

It's also true that if you die within a short time of buying the annuity, you don't get your money's worth. For example, if you invested $50,000 in an annuity that paid you $450 a month, you'd have to live more than nine years to get back what you put in.

UNTIL YOU DIE **AND** **THE TIME IS UP**

LIFE OR PERIOD CERTAIN ANNUITIES are paid for your lifetime or for a fixed period of time. You get less each month than you would with a single life plan, but if you die before the fixed term ends, your beneficiary receives the payments instead. That way, you've protected your investment if you don't live long enough to get it back. Unlike life insurance, though, the amount due to your beneficiary is not paid as a lump sum, but in annuity payments of the same size that you were receiving.

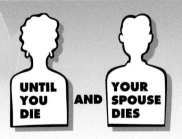

UNTIL YOU DIE **AND** **YOUR SPOUSE DIES**

JOINT AND SEVERAL ANNUITIES are paid over your lifetime **and** the lifetime of your beneficiary, usually your spouse. When things work right, the smaller monthly payments are offset by being paid out over a longer period of time.

The one drawback is if your beneficiary dies shortly after the annuity begins. Since you're getting a smaller payment, you'll have to live longer to recoup your investment.

BUILDING A LADDER

If you're ready to buy an annuity, but interest rates are low, you can divide the amount you've set aside for annuities and buy a series of smaller annuities over four or five years instead of one larger one.

The technique resembles laddering bond or CD investments (see page 99), and lets you hold back some of your money on the expectation of getting a higher rate down the road. It means cashing several monthly checks instead of one, but if your income is higher, it's probably worth it.

What's Your Estate?

An estate isn't just expensive property surrounded by a fence.

Your estate is everything you own in your own name, and your share of anything you own with other people. Your property can be **real**—meaning land and buildings—or **personal**, such as jewelry, a stamp collection, or a favorite table or chair. Money is property, too, as are stocks and bonds, a mutual fund account, or a life insurance policy.

The actual value of your estate is computed only after you die—when you're not around to figure it out. But realistically, you need

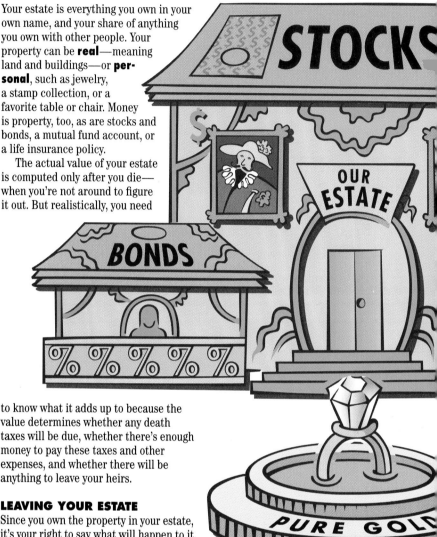

to know what it adds up to because the value determines whether any death taxes will be due, whether there's enough money to pay these taxes and other expenses, and whether there will be anything to leave your heirs.

LEAVING YOUR ESTATE

Since you own the property in your estate, it's your right to say what will happen to it. You might tell your spouse, your children, or your lawyer what you want to happen, but unless it's written down, there's no assurance your wishes will be respected.

There are several ways to make clear what you want to happen to your estate.

- You can write a **will** to specify who gets what after you die.

- You can create one or more **trusts** to pass property, or income from that property, to others.

- You can name **beneficiaries** on pension funds, insurance policies, and other investments so they will receive the payouts directly.

- You can own property **jointly** with other people, so that it becomes theirs when you die.

Since wills and trusts are legal documents, you should consult your lawyer about them. Naming beneficiaries is simpler, usually requiring only your signature. And owning joint property such as homes and bank accounts—especially with your spouse—is fairly standard.

WHAT'S YOUR ESTATE WORTH?

Finding the value of an estate is a two-step process—adding up what it's worth and then subtracting the expenses of settling it and your non-taxable bequests. Usually, the valuation is figured as of the date of your death. The alternative is to value the estate six months after you

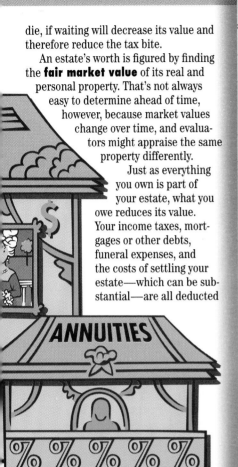

die, if waiting will decrease its value and therefore reduce the tax bite.

An estate's worth is figured by finding the **fair market value** of its real and personal property. That's not always easy to determine ahead of time, however, because market values change over time, and evaluators might appraise the same property differently.

Just as everything you own is part of your estate, what you owe reduces its value. Your income taxes, mortgages or other debts, funeral expenses, and the costs of settling your estate—which can be substantial—are all deducted from your estate's worth. So is the value of any property you transfer to a charity or to your surviving spouse. What's left is the value of your estate.

NOT IN YOUR ESTATE?

If you no longer own property, it's out of your estate. Something you give away belongs to the new owner. The same is true of something you sell.

You might owe gift or income taxes on the transfer, but its value isn't included in your estate. The larger your estate, the more important it is to reduce it as much as you can to reduce estate taxes.

SETTING A VALUE

One workable definition of *fair market value* is the amount someone would be willing to pay for your property, and that you'd be willing to accept—assuming that neither one of you is under any pressure to buy or sell, nor guilty of any misrepresentation.

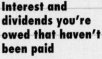

An Estate Inventory

If you own your home, have invested money, and are in a pension plan, the value of your estate is apt to be greater than you think. Here's a checklist of what might be included:

 Real estate

Securities (stocks, bonds, and mutual funds)

Interest and dividends you're owed that haven't been paid

 Bank accounts

All tangible personal property

Life insurance policies you own

 No-fault insurance payments due to you

 Annuities paid by contract or agreement

 Value of any qualified retirement plan, including IRAs

Claims paid for pain and suffering, even after your death (but not claims for wrongful death)

 Income tax refunds

Forgiven debts

 Dower and curtesy interests

 UGMA and UTMA custodial accounts for which you are the custodian, if you created the accounts

Closely held businesses

What's in a Name?

If your estate includes everything you own, you want to be pretty clear about what **own**ership means.

Most people think of real property when the subject of ownership comes up, but all kinds of property—bank accounts, stocks, mutual funds—can be owned in a variety of ways. The way you own your property determines the flexibility you have to sell it while you're alive, and also what happens to it after you die.

Basically, there are four ways to be a property owner:

- By yourself, as a **sole owner**

- As a **joint owner**

- In an arrangement called **tenants by the entirety**, and

- As **tenants in common.**

In addition, if you're married and live in a community property state, half of what you buy or earn during your marriage legally belongs to your spouse.

JT TN W/ROS

This cryptic acronym, which frequently appears on bank accounts and mutual fund statements, stands for **joint tenants with rights of survivorship**. It means that both owners have equal access to the property while they're alive, and the property belongs to the survivor when one of them dies. For example, if you and your mother have a joint checking account with survivorship rights and your mother dies, the money is yours.

ESTATE IMPLICATIONS

If you own property jointly with your spouse and you die first, only half the jointly held property is added to your estate. For example, if you and your husband own a $200,000 house jointly, and you die, only half the value, or $100,000, is counted in figuring the value of your estate.

If the joint owner is someone other than your spouse—such as your child or

CERTIFICATE OF TITLE

SOLE OWNERSHIP

- One person.
- No limits on right to sell or gift, or pass by will or trust.

CERTIFICATE OF TITLE

JOINT TENANTS, WITH RIGHTS OF SURVIVORSHIP

- Two (or, rarely, more) people, often but not always a married couple.
- Any owner can sell during his or her lifetime by agreement of all owners, and as long as all owners receive proportional share of profits. Property goes directly to surviving owner(s) when other owner dies, not through will or trust.

VOID IF ALTERED

CERTIFICATE OF TITLE

TENANTS BY THE ENTIRETY

- A married couple.
- Neither can sell without the other's permission. Surviving spouse becomes sole owner. In a divorce, former spouses become tenants in common.

CERTIFICATE OF TITLE

TENANTS IN COMMON

- Two or more people, each owning a share. The shares are usually equal.
- Each owner owns and can sell his or her share independently. Each share can be passed by will or trust. Other owner(s) has no legal interest or right to inherit.

VOID IF ALTERED

your parent—the rule is that the entire value of the property is added to the estate of the person with more money to begin with—which is more likely to be you rather than your child or elderly parent. If you owned a $200,000 house jointly with your daughter, for example, the entire $200,000 would be added to your estate at your death—even though

WHO'S COMPETENT ANYWAY?

Competence, like beauty, may be in the eye of the beholder, but when it comes to decisions about your estate, your competence may have to be legally determined. There's a generally recognized test that's often applied: do you have a general knowledge of your affairs and do you know "the natural objects of your bounty?" Those "objects" are generally understood to be the members of your family, especially your children, if you have any.

If, for example, you make a will that omits any mention of your children, they might be able to challenge the will in court, on the grounds that forgetting about them shows you weren't competent to decide where your money should go. But if you mention them by name in the will and leave them each a dollar, your competence is not as open to question because you are clearly indicating your intentions.

she would become sole owner of the house. The only way to avoid this situation, and the possibility of increased tax on your estate, is to be able to prove the amount that each of you contributed to accumulating the property.

POWER CONTROL

Being a property owner gives you the right to control what happens to that property, at least as long as you are healthy, solvent, and of sound mind. And, of course, it also helps if you're around to keep an eye on it. But what happens if you aren't able to exercise control for one reason or another?

One solution is to grant, or give, **power of attorney** to your spouse, sibling, adult child, or close friend—someone you trust to act wisely and in your best interest. This attorney-in-fact, or agent, has the legal right to make the decisions you would make if you were able, as well as the authority to buy and sell property and to write checks on your accounts.

A lawyer can draw up the power of attorney for you, specifying the authority you are granting, and excluding those things you still want to control. Many experts suggest that you, as **grantor**, or principal, update a power of attorney—or even write

a new one—every four or five years so it will be less vulnerable to legal challenges.

Since an ordinary power of attorney is revoked if you become physically or mentally disabled, you can take the additional step of granting **durable power of attorney**. Unlike a limited or ordinary agreement, durable power is not revoked if you become incompetent, so you're not left in the lurch when you need assistance most. But not all states allow it, so check with your legal advisor.

You can also establish a **springing power of attorney**, which takes effect only at the point that you're unable to act for yourself. In every case but the last, you can revoke the power at any time, or choose a different agent.

A LESSER POWER

Unlike someone with power of attorney, a **payee representative** can receive your income and pay your bills—but nothing more. You still control your other financial affairs. But this arrangement helps you keep your accounts in order if you can't do them yourself because you're ill, traveling, or just too busy.

Estate Taxes

There's no secret here: the government wants a share of your estate.

The advantages of a large estate—a comfortable life for yourself and gifts or inherited property for your beneficiaries—can be severely trimmed by taxes imposed on the transfer of your estate's assets. The rate ranges from 37% to 55% for **federal estate taxes**, plus whatever additional **inheritance taxes** individual states impose. Sometimes referred to as **death taxes**, estate and inheritance taxes seem destined for a long life of their own.

Estates under $600,000 given to anyone
PAY NO ESTATE TAX

Estates over $600,000 given to anyone but spouse
PAY ESTATE TAX

Estates over $600,000 given to spouse only
PAY NO ESTATE TAX

55% ESTATE TAX

HOW TO FIGURE ESTATE TAX

First, determine the value of the gross estate.

Then, subtract the estate's expenses and reductions to find the

TAXABLE ESTATE.

Next, figure the tax amount due on the value of the taxable estate.

Finally, subtract the unified credit and credit for state death taxes to find the

NET ESTATE TAXES.

THE UNIFIED TAX CREDIT

For estate tax purposes, taxable gifts you make during your lifetime (see page 142) and any property transferred after your death are taxed at the same rates. You—and every other American—currently have a **unified tax credit** of $192,800 toward the transfer of property in either of these ways. That's the equivalent of the federal tax on an estate valued at $600,000. What the credit means, in practical terms, is that estates amounting to less than $600,000—after deductions—can be transferred tax-free.

SAVING TAXES

The only way to minimize, and maybe even avoid, death taxes on estates larger than $600,000 is to have a carefully thought out estate plan that you—and your financial and legal advisers—put into place. (Before you assume that this $600,000 limit doesn't apply to you, add up the value of everything you own, including your life insurance, retirement plans, and real estate. The amount might surprise you.)

TAKING DIFFERENT BITES

Estate taxes are taxes on the value of the property in your estate, and they're usually paid by the estate. There's a federal estate tax and, in some states, a state estate tax.

Inheritance taxes are state taxes your heirs pay for the value of the property they receive from your estate. You can specify in your will that your estate should pay whatever inheritance taxes are due to save your heirs from having to sell the property they inherit in order to be able to pay the tax.

MAKING A PLAN

Your estate plan should let you take advantage of several of these money-saving options:

- If you're married, you can use the **marital deduction** to leave everything in your estate to your spouse, free of tax. As long as your spouse is a U.S. citizen, no estate taxes are due during his or her lifetime.

- You can reduce the size of your estate by making annual **tax-exempt gifts** of $10,000 per recipient. If you're married and your spouse agrees, you can make annual gifts of $20,000 per recipient.

- You can make annual tax-exempt **charitable gifts** equal to half your adjusted gross income.

- You can set up a **testamentary trust** in your will so that both you and your spouse can take advantage of the $600,000 exemption—for a total of $1.2 million—even if your spouse's entire estate was originally yours (see page 138).

PAYING ESTATE TAXES

If estate taxes are due, the estate itself must pay them within nine months of your death, in most cases. It's your job, though, to anticipate the tax bill and plan so that there's enough money to pay it. If the estate doesn't pay when the tax is due, your heirs may be liable for the taxes themselves. That might mean having to sell assets at a loss, or tapping their own savings to meet the obligation, which is probably not what you intended in making them your beneficiaries.

To be sure there's money available in your estate to pay the taxes, you can set up an **insurance trust** (see page 140), or leave instructions for **liquidating**, or turning into cash, specific assets, or selling your share of a business. The best method of coming up with the cash depends on your own financial situation. But don't assume that decisions that seem obvious to you will be just as clear to someone else. Spell out what you think should happen in a letter of instruction to your executor or your heirs.

EXTRA ESTATE TAXES

Your estate may also owe tax if you have a lot of money, known as **excess accumulations**, left in qualified retirement plans when you die. The tax, figured at 15%, must be paid even if no regular estate tax is due, although it can be postponed if your spouse does an IRA rollover (see page 56). What makes an accumulation excessive, accord-

RESIDENCE AND DOMICILE

Federal estate taxes are figured at the same rate no matter where you live in the U.S. But where you hang your hat can make a big difference when it comes to state death taxes. For starters, real estate and tangible personal property are taxable in the state where they're physically located whether you are a resident of that state or not. Intangible personal property—stocks, for example—are taxable in the state of your legal residence, or domicile. There can only be one of those, no matter how many residences you have.

If there's a question about your domicile, documents showing where you voted, maintained bank accounts, registered your car, or the residence you declared in your will can be used to prove which place you considered home. One thing you should check while you're able to is the consequences of owning property in different states. You might decide to make some changes to save taxes, or legal fees, or both.

ing to the government, depends on how old you are when you die and how much you have left in your various plans.

Here's how the excess amount is figured:

1 Your executor finds the current value of a hypothetical life annuity (based on the life expectancy for your age) that would pay you the greater of $150,000 a year, or $112,500 a year, indexed for inflation as of the year of your death. (In 1993, that indexed figure was $144,551.)

2 Your executor then subtracts the value of that annuity from the combined total of your qualified pension plans and tax-deferred investments (like IRAs, Keoghs, and annuities). If there's a larger balance in your accounts, you owe tax on the difference.

The way the formula is set up, the people whose estates end up owing the most in excess estate tax are those who have a short life expectancy and large tax-deferred accounts.

A SEPARATE IDENTITY

Because an estate has an identity separate from the person whose property it was and from that of the executor, it needs its own federal ID number and its own bank account. You can apply for the number from the IRS using Form SS-4.

Wills

Where there's a will, there's usually a way to protect your estate.

A will is a legal document that transfers your property after you die, and names the people who will settle your estate, care for your children who are minors, and administer any trusts the will establishes. With rare exceptions, a will has to be a formal, written document that meets the legal requirements of the state where it's **executed**, or prepared. In some circumstances, a hand-written will, known as a **holograph**, passes muster. In very rare cases—usually a deathbed situation—an oral will, known as a **nuncupative** will, may be considered valid.

But why take a chance? Making a will is one situation where doing the right thing is easy and relatively inexpensive.

WHAT'S THE WORRY?

If you die **intestate**, that is, without a will, you'll have lost control over what happens to your property. And your estate will probably end up paying a lot more to settle your affairs—meaning that less will be available for your heirs. Any estate, large or small, can be settled faster if you've made a will naming the people, charities, or other institutions you want to inherit your property.

If you're married and die intestate, your property will go to your spouse and any children you have. Each state has a specific formula for dividing the estate, some giving a greater percentage to the spouse and others favoring the children. If you've been married more than once, or have children from different marriages, the rules for dividing your property could produce results you wouldn't be happy about.

If you're not married, your relatives—the ones the court decides on—inherit. Chances are, what you intended to leave to friends or to charitable, religious, or

ESCHEATING ALWAYS SHOWS!

If you die without a will and have no relatives, your estate is **escheated,** or turned over, to the state where you live. That's probably how your friends will feel. 66% of all Americans die intestate, including many who leave a large estate and minor children. Another 9% of existing wills are invalid for one reason or another.

educational institutions will go instead to a distant relative, even one you weren't very fond of. The bottom line is that if you're unmarried, childless, and without property, you can justify waiting to make a will. Otherwise, you can't.

THE PROBATE QUESTION

Any property that is transferred by will is subject to **probate**, the legal process of proving, or verifying, your will through the courts. Because the process can be slow, costly, and sometimes perverse, probate has a bad reputation.

However, you can't avoid probate even if you don't make a will. The only thing you accomplish is to give the probate court—sometimes called surrogate's court or orphan's court—more authority over your affairs, since the court will appoint an administrator to handle your estate.

A clear, unambiguous will has the best chance of surviving the probate process

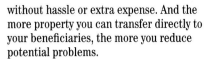
without hassle or extra expense. And the more property you can transfer directly to your beneficiaries, the more you reduce potential problems.

In recent years, some people have opted for a living trust to transfer the bulk of their property outside the probate process (see page 132). But you still need a will to leave property that isn't covered by the trust and to name an executor for your estate and a guardian for any minor children.

JOINTLY OWNED

You can't leave jointly owned property to someone other than your joint owner. If you have a joint bank account with one of your children and own your house jointly with another, that property is theirs when you die—whether or not the properties are of equal value. If your will states that your children should share your estate equally, but all your property is jointly held, your wishes can't be carried out. In fact, if one child generously equalizes her share of, say a $300,000 inheritance with her sibling, she'll be making a taxable gift of $150,000.

> **"To my children I leave…"**

> **"I name as my executor…"**

> **"To my loving husband I leave…"**

ANYTHING DOESN'T GO

You can divide your estate pretty much as you wish, though there are some things you can't do if you want your will to survive a court challenge.

WHAT YOU CAN DO

- ✔ You can limit the inheritance to one or more of your children, or in most states leave them nothing at all. But it's better to say so directly in the will. If you don't mention them, they might claim you simply forgot, or the laws in your state might say that children who aren't named in the will are entitled to a share of the estate, just as if you'd died intestate.

- ✔ You can specify whether your heirs' heirs inherit their share if the people you name die before you do.

- ✔ In some states, you can include an **in terrorem** clause that provides that anyone who contests your will loses whatever legacy you had provided for them. However, the court could rule there was a legitimate reason for challenging the will.

- ✔ You can add a legally executed **codicil**, or amendment, to your will to add, remove, or change beneficiaries or bequests.

WHAT YOU CAN'T DO

- ✘ No state lets you disinherit your spouse, as long as you're legally married. Most require you to leave a certain percentage of the total estate. In fact, a surviving spouse has the right to **elect against a will**. This means rejecting the terms and bequests of the will and taking instead the minimum percentage that state law sets as the spouse's share of the estate if there were no will.

- ✘ Louisiana won't let you disinherit your children. Several other states make it hard.

- ✘ You can't impose conditions on your heirs that are either illegal or against public policy. For example, if you tie an heir's right to an inheritance to a restriction on getting married or membership in a certain organization, your will might be successfully challenged.

- ✘ You can't write in changes or cross things out of the will after it has been signed and witnessed.

Cooking Up a Will

You can follow a number of different recipes to produce a valid will.

While wills are formal, ultimately public, documents, they're also very personal.

What they're doing, after all, is detailing the size and distribution of your estate.

YOU CAN MAKE A WILL THREE WAYS

OLD FASHIONED WILL

Simplified QUICK COOKING WILL

INSTANT WILL

JUST FILL OUT

Use a standard, fill-in-the-blanks will form.

Use a step-by-step legal guide or computer program to draft your own.

Ask your lawyer to draft a will for you.

The advantages of a fill-in-the-blanks will are easy availability—you can get them in stationery stores—and economy. The major disadvantage is that they're inflexible and cover only the most generic situations, like leaving everything to your spouse. Is a fill-in-the-blanks will better than no will at all? Probably. But there's no substitute for sound legal advice.

WHAT'S BEST FOR YOU

Most experts agree that using a lawyer who specializes in wills and estates is smart, and probably essential, if your estate is at all complex, involves real estate, or includes any bequests that might be challenged in court. One disadvantage may be the price tag, since a complicated will may cost a thousand dollars or more to prepare.

If you use a guidebook or computer program like those published by Nolo Press to write your own will, you can spend less for a perfectly legal document. It may pay, though, to have a lawyer review your work so that your estate doesn't end up paying in court fees or avoidable estate taxes everything you saved by doing it yourself—and more.

MAKING IT OFFICIAL

The steps to making your will official are clearly spelled out in the law. Your **execution**, or signature, has to be **attested to**, or witnessed, by two or three people who must sign the will in your presence. The witnesses don't have to read the will itself, or know what's in it, but you must tell them it's your will you're asking them to witness.

In some states a witness may not inherit anything that's included in the will, and in others people mentioned in the will may not serve as a witness. Sometimes the witnesses must appear in court when a will is filed for probate, but in many states witnesses can instead sign a document stating, or affirming, their participation at the time of the will's execution.

You should sign only one copy of your will and file it with your attorney, at home, or in some other safe place that is easy to get at. (Safe deposit boxes are not a good idea, since they are frequently sealed when the owner dies, making their contents inaccessible.)

If your will can't be found, the court will presume it's been revoked. On the other hand, multiple signed copies of the will can cause delays, since in most cases, all of them must be accounted for before the will can be probated. Unsigned copies, or photocopies, on the other hand, are fine and can be useful for reference.

WILL POWER

You can change your will as often as you want. There's no last word until you die, which means you can change every detail from one year to the next, and back again, as long as you're willing to foot the bill. When you make a new will, though, you should say specifically that you are revoking any prior will. If you have the old one, or copies of it, you should destroy them. That way, there will be no question about your intentions.

If you're making only minor changes, however, you can add a codicil to your will. Like the will itself, a **codicil** is a legal document that details your wishes. It must meet specific standards in order to be valid, including the requirement for witnesses.

DIVIDING YOUR ASSETS

When you divide your property among your beneficiaries, it's important to structure your will so that your wishes can be respected.

last wil ənd tes′ tə mənt
The sometimes elaborate and seemingly repetitive language of wills is, in part, a continuing struggle to avoid ambiguity. More often than not, legal battles over wills have been the direct result of imprecise or unclear language. The solution, over the years, has been to go on adding words to cover all the possible circumstances. That's why you use your "last **will** and **testament** to **give, devise, and bequeath** all the rest, residue, **and remainder** of your estate," using twice as many words as seem necessary to do the job.

For example, suppose you leave stock to your son, but the stock has been sold? Or you leave one daughter $75,000 and everything else to another—and $75,000 is all that's left after your bills are paid?

To avoid the most common problems, experts suggest you leave all major bequests as a **percentage** of your total estate, instead of a dollar amount. You can also name contingent beneficiaries, if your first choices die before you do, can't be found, or don't want your money.

SIMULTANEOUS DEATH

Many married people leave their entire estates to their surviving spouse, and to other beneficiaries if the spouse has died first. What that doesn't resolve, however, is what happens if the couple dies at the same time, or within a very short period of each other. To cover that possibility, you can include a **simultaneous death clause** in your will to pass your property directly to your surviving heirs.

You can also require that any beneficiary survive you by a certain length of time—often 45 days—in order to inherit. This provision saves double taxes and court costs, and lets you decide who is next in line for your property.

Who's in a Will?

You're the star of your will, but there's a big supporting cast.

Your will contains a list of names, starting with your own. The other people and organizations you mention either receive property when you die or have specific jobs to do. While almost anyone would be delighted to be on the receiving list, you ought to be sure that the people you're asking to carry out your wishes are willing and able to play their parts.

CHOOSING AN EXECUTOR

While beneficiaries don't need any special skills to qualify for inclusion in your will, executors do. The job of collecting your assets, paying your bills, and resolving legal and tax issues can be complicated and time-consuming. That means you should get the consent of the person you want to fill the executor's role. You should also name an alternative executor, should your first choice be unable or unwilling to do the job when the time comes. Otherwise the choice will be left to the probate court.

A spouse, child, or close friend is frequently named executor, and can handle the task if he or she is comfortable managing legal and financial issues. It's an added advantage if he or she can work with a family lawyer. With complex estates, however, or wills which might provoke controversy, it's often best to name an executor with professional skills. One solution may be to name joint executors, a professional and a family member or friend.

CONFLICTS OF INTEREST

If you want your will to resolve—not create—controversy over your estate, you should consider potential conflicts of interest in naming your executor.

Problems arise most often when the executor's responsibility to act in the best interests of the beneficiaries competes with his or her own best interest. For example, if your executor was your business partner and your will specified that the business should buy out your share, how would the executor set the price?

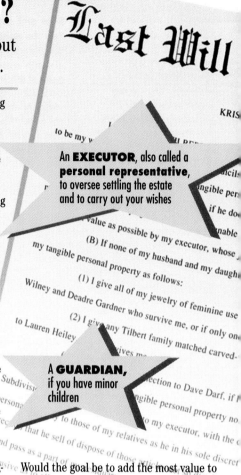

An **EXECUTOR**, also called a **personal representative**, to oversee settling the estate and to carry out your wishes

A **GUARDIAN**, if you have minor children

Would the goal be to add the most value to your estate or pay the least the business could get away with?

Similarly, you might create bad feelings, or even spark a contest to your will, by naming one of your children both executor and primary beneficiary of your estate. Though the conversation could be a painful one, many experts advise explaining the contents of your will to your family while you are able. That step could prevent trouble after you die.

PICKING A GUARDIAN

Children who are minors—those under 18 under the laws of most states and under 21 in the rest—need guardians if their parents die. A guardian has custody of the children and makes the decisions of daily life: where the children live, go to school, receive medical care, and spend their vacations, to mention a few. If you and your spouse each name a guardian—hopefully someone you agree on—in your will, your children should be provided for should something happen to both of you.

The primary factor for most people is naming a guardian who will raise your children as you would yourself. You choice might be a

ᴛ Testament

TILBERT

...unty of Duchess, State of N... declare this

...vive me, to s...
to be divi...
as to ...them in shares o...
...division shall be final.
...ves me, I direct my executor to distribute

...ment in equal shares to such...
survives me, all there...
...irs and...

...es me.
...se ef...ly disposed of by this
that he distribute the...
mines...
any p...
...under...
...udi...
...nd s...
...po...
...ys...

relative or a friend of yours, or even an older sibling of the children's, who will provide a good home. Someone they are already comfortable with is probably a good choice, though experts often advise against naming a grandparent because of the age factor.

Since raising children costs money, you should consider a potential guardian's financial situation as well as his or her personality before making a decision. Of course, if you leave a large estate or a lot of life insurance, the issue might be how well the guardian would manage the money. While you can name a different person to hold the purse strings—as **guardian of the property** or trustee of a trust created by your will—such an arrangement can cause complications unless the two are able to work comfortably together.

YOUR WILL ISN'T THE LAW

In some cases the probate court may overrule your choice of guardian and name another person. Relatives can also contest your will to have the guardian you name replaced by someone else, often them-selves. While there's no way to prevent either situation, the more logical your choice and the more direct you are with relatives who might poten-tially object, the greater the chance that your wishes will prevail.

The most difficult situations are often those that involve divorced parents, or parents who disagree about who should be named. The one thing you can be sure of in such cases is that the legal battle will be long, expensive, and probably damag-ing to the children.

NO BONDS ATTACHED

You can specify in your will that your executor and the guardian of your minor children serve **without bond**.

Bonding is a form of insurance against fraud, designed to protect the estate against a dishonest executor. Your estate pays the bond premiums, which can be expensive, and the insurance company can slow down the process by requiring every property transfer or financial transaction to be countersigned. One thought: if you're uncertain enough about your appointee's honesty to require a bond, you'd probably be better off choosing someone else.

If you die intestate, you don't have the option of expressing your position on bonding, and it will be required.

SPOUSAL PROTECTION

Financial protection for a surviving spouse is built into state laws, usually by insuring his or her right to some part of your estate—both in cases where you leave no will and where your will is at odds with the law. Though currently your surviving spouse has a right to a share— usually a third to a half of all the assets in your estate—making sure a widow or widow-er isn't left out in the cold is not a new idea. In the past, a surviving widow had **dower** rights and a surviving widower had **curtesy** rights, providing life interest, or the right to use and collect income from any real estate owned by his or her spouse during the marriage.

Beneficiaries

You have a free hand in naming beneficiaries, but you'll have to leave enough to go around.

Except for the requirement of providing for your spouse, if you have one, there are no rules about who your beneficiaries, or **heirs**, are. You can leave your property to family and friends, to organizations and institutions, even to your pets. By the same token, you can leave potential heirs little or nothing.

The only legacies that are turned down with any regularity are those in which property such as a house or a collection of something is given to a charitable organization without providing money for the property's upkeep. It's hard to imagine a Picasso would be rejected anywhere, but if you're making bequests that will end up costing the beneficiary money, you ought to get approval first.

NAMING YOUR BENEFICIARIES

In naming your beneficiaries, you should be as specific as possible, especially in cases where identities might be confused. Presumably you have only one cousin John. But if you leave him the bulk of your estate, you run fewer risks by identifying him more precisely. The same is true for colleges and universities, and for other institutions or organizations that may have similar names and may make a claim for your bequest by arguing that they have every reason to expect you to be generous. Conflicts not only create bad feelings. Any disputes that must be resolved in the courts cost money and time.

DISTRIBUTION PER STIRPES

If one child dies before you, your children's children split the share their parent would have received.

For example, if you left your entire estate equally to your two children, each of whom had two children, but one of your children died before you did, specifying the bequest as per stirpes or per capita would make a big difference to your surviving child. Under a per

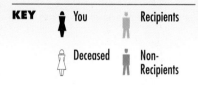

KEY		You		Recipients
		Deceased		Non-Recipients

OUTLIVING YOUR HEIRS

If you live a long life, you have to consider the possibility that the beneficiaries you name in your will may no longer be around when you die. Do you want the money you've set aside for an old friend to go to her husband if she dies before you do? If not, you can specify that your bequest is valid only if your friend survives you. If she doesn't, the money goes back into the general estate.

MULTIPLE FAMILIES

If you've been married more than once and have children from different marriages, it's important to spell out your wishes in your will. For example, if both partners in a current marriage have children of their own, they may want to leave the bulk of their own estates ultimately to their own children. If that's not clear in each partner's will, however, there could be some legitimately unhappy children.

DISTRIBUTION PER CAPITA

If one child dies before you, each surviving issue gets an equal share.

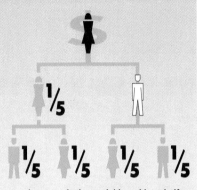

stirpes bequest, the living child would get half your estate and the two grandchildren whose parent had died would split the other half. Under a per capita bequest, however, the five (one child and four grandchildren) would get equal bequests of one fifth of your estate.

However, if you don't specify that your issue must survive you to get their share, then the heirs of your deceased children or grandchildren who may be of no relation to you—your deceased grandson's wife, for example—could claim a portion of your estate.

If the beneficiaries are your descendants, generally your children and grandchildren, known in the law as your **issue**, there is specific language you can use to designate the way your bequests will be made. If you leave an inheritance to your issue surviving you, **per stirpes**, then your children's children divide the share their parent would have received. If you leave the inheritance **per capita**, then each surviving issue gets an equal share.

KEEPING UP-TO-DATE

It's important to check your will on a regular schedule—every few years, for example—to be sure it still makes the provisions you want. If there's a major change in your financial circumstances or your family structure, you should revise your will immediately. A new spouse or a new child, for example, must be taken into account. Otherwise, some sections of the outdated document, and maybe the whole thing, can be thrown out and the estate settled as if you had died interstate.

SPECIAL SITUATIONS

If you're not married, but want to leave your estate to a long-time companion, it's especially important that you have a will that makes your bequest clear. Inheritance laws don't recognize common-law marriages or any non-marital relationships, however permanent they may seem to you. That's true even in states where you can register as domestic partners or qualify for benefits like health insurance coverage for your partner.

You can simplify the situation by avoiding the probate process, either by owning property jointly, or by naming your partner as beneficiary on pension plans and insurance policies. Those assets become your partner's directly. And, you can consider creating a living trust naming your partner as beneficiary. Trusts are more difficult to contest than wills, something that may be important if your family is not happy about your domestic situation.

IT'S ALL OVER

A divorce decree revokes your will, so you'll want to draw up a new one immediately, especially if there are custody issues or you remarry.

Acting as Executor

People often get a double look at this role—
acting the part and choosing the actor.

Since every will needs an executor, you may end up serving in that role as well as choosing someone to play it for you. Most people name a family member or close friend as executor or co-executor (with a lawyer or other professional), even when the estate is fairly complex.

Cost is one factor: it is usually cheaper to pay a lawyer an hourly rate to handle legal and other complex jobs than to act as sole executor. The personal touch is another. It's often easier for beneficiaries to relate to someone they know—though it may not always be easier on the executor if the will has unpopular or unexpected provisions to administer.

TESTATOR NAMES AN EXECUTOR

PROVIDING INFORMATION

A will does not ordinarily provide lists of bank and brokerage accounts, the location of your safe deposit box and its key, the details of your life insurance policies and pension plans, an inventory of valuable property, or business deals and outstanding debts. But you should provide them for your executor in a letter of instruction.

It's often true, too, that the knowledge you've accumulated—about how to liquidate a stamp collection or whether to pay off a mortgage, for example—may be as important to your heirs as the material goods you leave them. While it may seem morbid to write down that kind of information, it's a wise move.

ONLY IN THE MOVIES

You probably have a pretty clear picture of what happens when a will is read. You all gather around the lawyer, everyone listening eagerly for his or her name—and the good (or bad) news. Except it only happens that way in the movies. You're much more apt to get a letter in the mail if you're named as a beneficiary in a will.

WHO CAN SERVE?

Almost anyone can serve as an executor, as long as you're no longer a minor. Some states require that you be U.S. citizen. In addition, some states also require that you be a state resident to serve as executor unless you're a close relative. But, in others, like New York, noncitizens can serve, and even nonresident noncitizens, if they serve as co-executor with a resident. In a curious pairing of conditions, though, you're disqualified from serving as an executor if you've ever been convicted of a serious crime or if you're a judge. In any case, an executor must be confirmed by the probate court.

PAYING FOR THE JOB

Executors are entitled to a fee for doing the job—usually between 2% and 5% of the value of the estate—that is paid out of the estate's assets. Some people accept the payment, others don't. The decision is theirs, and is often based on the nature of their relationship with you and the complexity of the job. Professional executors almost always take the fee, so one way to save money is to appoint a family member (who probably won't take a fee) and have that person hire a lawyer to handle the more complex questions.

One case in which a family member who is also a beneficiary might take a fee for serving as executor is when estate taxes are due. The tax on the executor's added income would probably be less than the estate tax, and since the fees also reduce the estate, that might save some tax as well.

THE FINAL TAX BILL

As executor of an estate, one of your jobs is to be sure that all taxes are paid—a potentially mind-numbing responsibility. Here's what's due:

$ **Federal estate and gift taxes above the unified tax credit of $192,800**

> $ **State death taxes, which may be owed by the estate or by individual heirs**
>
> $ **State gift taxes (in seven states)**
>
> $ **Generation-skipping taxes, on transfers or trusts of more than $1 million that name grandchildren or great-grandchildren as primary beneficiaries**

$ **Income taxes on the earnings of the estate's assets**

$ **Excise taxes of 15% on excess pension and other qualified retirement plans (see page 121).**

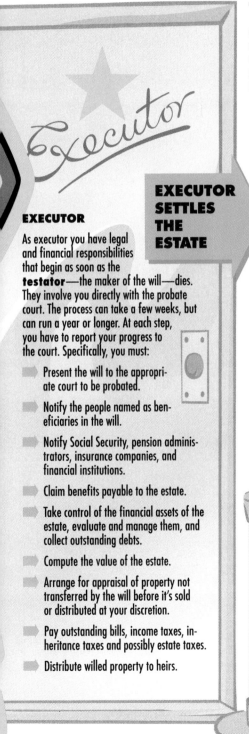

EXECUTOR

As executor you have legal and financial responsibilities that begin as soon as the **testator**—the maker of the will—dies. They involve you directly with the probate court. The process can take a few weeks, but can run a year or longer. At each step, you have to report your progress to the court. Specifically, you must:

▸ Present the will to the appropriate court to be probated.

▸ Notify the people named as beneficiaries in the will.

▸ Notify Social Security, pension administrators, insurance companies, and financial institutions.

▸ Claim benefits payable to the estate.

▸ Take control of the financial assets of the estate, evaluate and manage them, and collect outstanding debts.

▸ Compute the value of the estate.

▸ Arrange for appraisal of property not transferred by the will before it's sold or distributed at your discretion.

▸ Pay outstanding bills, income taxes, inheritance taxes and possibly estate taxes.

▸ Distribute willed property to heirs.

EXECUTOR SETTLES THE ESTATE

GET IN LINE

The law establishes the order in which an estate's assets are paid. Court fees, funeral expenses, and other costs of administering the estate—including executor's fees—come first, followed by taxes, medical expenses, debts, and rent or wages owed by the person who made the will. Then the other claims—including the legacies—are paid, from the most specific to the most general, or **residuary**, legacies. In general, bequests to spouses take precedence over bequests to other people.

A Matter of Trust

Once you create a trust, it takes on a life of its own.

Like a will, a **trust** is a written document that transfers property. But while a will is a statement of what you want to happen to your possessions after you die, a trust is a multipurpose tool that you can establish at any time to:

- **Manage your property**
- **Distribute assets to your beneficiaries**
- **Avoid probate, and**
- **Save on taxes.**

Since no single trust can accomplish everything you may want to achieve, you can establish different trusts to serve different functions or benefit different people or organizations. It's also true that restrictions on the trusts vary. To reduce your taxes, for example, you have to put your property into a permanent and unchangeable trust. But trusts you established solely to manage your assets can be changed as your circumstances change.

MONEY MATTERS

Creating a trust isn't cheap. There's a legal fee—sometimes substantial—for establishing it, and a fee when you transfer ownership of the property to the trustee. The trustee is also entitled to a fee for following your wishes, filing tax returns, and overseeing the investments. Most experts agree that trusts have limited value if you're talking about property worth less than $50,000–$75,000. Some bank trust departments, for example, set a minimum figure—usually in that range—before they'll talk to you about a trust.

HOW TRUSTS WORK

The Donor

- Sets up the trust
- Names the beneficiaries
- Names the trustees
- Transfers property to the trust

The Beneficiaries

Receive the benefits of the trust, according to its terms

THREE TYPES OF TRUSTS

Though there are many different types of trusts, each designed to achieve a certain goal, all trusts are created in one of three ways.

Testamentary	Living, or inter vivos	Pour-over
A testamentary trust is created by your will, funded by your estate, and administered by a trustee named in your will. Its primary goals are saving estate taxes and appointing someone to manage the assets included in the trust.	Living, or inter vivos, trusts are set up while you're alive. You can serve as the trustee yourself—though you usually name someone to succeed you when you die or if you're unable to serve. Its primary goals are asset management and transferring property outside the probate process. There may or may not be tax advantages.	A pour-over trust is created while you are alive, but is funded after you die. Its primary purpose is to receive one-time payouts like life insurance or pension benefits or the residue of your estate—that is, any property you haven't transferred specifically to someone by gift, trust, or will. There may or may not be tax advantages.

TRUST ALTERNATIVES

If you want some of the advantages but not the expense of a trust, you can designate bank and brokerage accounts, as well as U.S. Savings Bonds, **in trust for** a beneficiary. At your death, the money goes directly to your designee, outside the probate process. (It's similar to naming beneficiaries of insurance policies and employee-benefit plans, see page 116.)

One limitation, of course, is that you can't control what your beneficiary does with the money the way you can with a trust agreement. And, though you avoid probate, the amount in these trusts is part of your estate and may be subject to estate and inheritance tax.

The Trust

- **Earns income**
- **Pays taxes**
- **Distributes benefits**

The Trustees

- **Control the property in the trust**
- **Manage the trust's investments**
- **Oversee payments**

BENEFITS OF CREATING A TRUST

- **Taking advantage of the federal $600,000 estate tax exemption**
- **Providing income to one person during his or her lifetime and, eventually, what is left to others**
- **Protecting assets rather than leaving them outright to heirs**
- **Using professional investment management**
- **Postponing estate taxes on property transfers**

CREATING A TRUST

As the person creating a trust—known as a **settlor**, **donor** or **grantor**—you decide the terms of the trust, name the beneficiaries, decide which property will be included, and choose the trustee, or trustees, who will control it. You can also specify how the trust's assets will be paid to your beneficiaries, and how long the trust will last.

You specify what happens to the property you transfer to a trust by establishing the ground rules for how the assets will end up in your beneficiaries' hands. For example, you can set up a trust so that all the property goes directly to one person when you die. Or the terms of the trust might say that assets should be used for major investments like houses or business opportunities, or to pay for college tuitions.

All that information is contained in the trust document, which should be drawn up by a lawyer. You don't want to run the risk of writing your own. Since the main purpose in creating a trust in the first place is to accomplish a specific goal, it should be structured to satisfy federal and state requirements.

A FIDUCIARY RELATIONSHIP

If you have a fiduciary relationship with someone, your part of the bargain is to act for the benefit of the other person. In a trust, it's the trustee who is the fiduciary, acting on behalf of the beneficiary.

A SEPARATE IDENTITY

Since a trust has a separate financial existence, it needs a federal ID number—the equivalent of a social security number—and its own bank account.

Revocable Living Trusts

What's alive, in a living trust, is the person who creates it.

When you create a living trust, you must decide if it is **revocable** or **irrevocable**. If the trust is revocable, you can modify it as you wish: you can change the beneficiaries, replace the trustee, or end the trust altogether. If the trust is irrevocable, you can make no changes of any kind.

With either type of living trust you can transfer property to your beneficiaries outside the probate process, a plus for estate planning. But otherwise the two types of trusts are quite different. You choose the one that best accomplishes what you want the trust to do.

A REVOCABLE CHOICE

With a revocable trust, you can transfer as much property as you want to the trust—everything you own, for example—without owing any gift tax. That's because the property remains in your estate. When you die, the property in the trust can go directly to your beneficiary, or beneficiaries, if that's the way you set the trust up. Or, if you prefer, the trustee can continue to manage and distribute the property in the way you specify in the trust agreement.

Avoiding probate is especially valuable when you are leaving property to minors, or when you own real estate in more than one state. In those cases, going through probate can add time and expense. When property is left to minors, for example, the probate court can require continuing monitoring of the assets. And for each state where you have property, you add another probate court for your executor to deal with. If the property is passed by trust, none of that happens.

A living trust can also strengthen your intended beneficiary's claim to disputed property, since it is harder to contest a trust than a will. And since living trusts are not public information, as probate documents are, you can usually count on privacy in your bequests.

My latest revised alteration to the amendments of my Revocable

LIVING TRUST

Alterations to my amended Revocable LIVING TRUST

My amended Revocable LIVING TRUST

BENEFITTING YOURSELF

While the primary reason for setting up a trust is usually to benefit others, living trusts can provide advantages to the people who set one up.

While it's not a pleasant thought, people are sometimes unable to handle their affairs because of accident, illness, or age. If you've established a living trust, your trustee can protect you and your property from those who might take advantage of you, and at the same time manage your investments and pay your taxes on the trust's earnings.

Unlike someone with durable power of attorney, who can act for you only while you're alive, a trustee of a living trust can continue to manage the property in the trust after you die and for as long as the agreement remains in force. And you can simplify the process of transferring authority to your trustee by agreeing that your doctors—not the courts—can decide when you're no longer competent to act for yourself.

THREE'S A CROWD

The terms of a revocable trust permit its participants to play multiple roles.

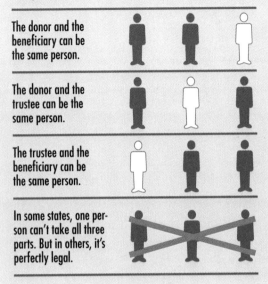

The donor and the beneficiary can be the same person.

The donor and the trustee can be the same person.

The trustee and the beneficiary can be the same person.

In some states, one person can't take all three parts. But in others, it's perfectly legal.

TRUST LIMITS

Revocable living trusts do have some limitations. Though they transfer the bulk of your property directly, they don't eliminate the need for a will to cover the balance of your estate after you die. And in some states your creditors may have longer to press their claims against trust property than against probate property.

But, most importantly, revocable trusts make no pretense of being tax shelters. They don't reduce the income tax you owe during your lifetime, or any estate or inheritance taxes that may be due after you die. The logic is that since you control the trust, it exists for your benefit and is therefore subject to tax.

ACTING AS TRUSTEE

As trustee, your primary job is to administer the trust in the best interest of the beneficiaries and in keeping with the wishes of the grantor. A specific problem arises if those two goals are in conflict, or if the best interests of one beneficiary are at odds with the best interests of another—say the person receiving the income from a trust and the person named to ultimately receive the principal.

As a trustee, your responsibilities are to:

- Manage trust assets to grow and produce income. That may require close supervision and ongoing decisions about what to buy and sell, and certainly means keeping accurate records.

- Get the trust a tax ID number and insure that trust taxes are paid.

- Distribute assets following the terms of the trust. The more discretion the trust provides about the payout terms, the more responsibility you have.

- Oversee the final distribution of assets to the beneficiaries, if you're still serving as trustee when the trust ends.

If you become trustee of a revocable trust because the person who set it up is no longer capable of making decisions, you may also, as a practical matter, be acting as guardian or conservator, handling living and health care arrangements as well as finances.

A LONG HISTORY

From their beginnings in England in the 12th century, property trusts have been used to protect ownership rights—including some the courts didn't recognize. For example, when a married woman couldn't own property in her own name, she could benefit from a trust established by her family.

Irrevocable Living Trusts

Irrevocable trusts are written in stone—or its modern equivalent.

Once property is put in an irrevocable trust, it's there for good. The same is true of beneficiaries. You can't add one, or take one away. And the only way to change a trustee is for that person to agree to resign or to die. So why would anyone agree to such an inflexible arrangement? The answer, in short, is tax savings.

Irrevocable trusts can provide significant tax savings because the property you transfer to the trust is no longer yours. The trust itself—not you—pays income taxes on what the assets earn. When you die, the trust property is not part of your estate and is not subject to death taxes. What's more, through the terms of the trust, you can exert continuing control over the way that your property is distributed to your heirs.

GIVING UP CONTROL
To reduce your estate for tax purposes, though, the assets you give away or put in trust must belong permanently and unconditionally to the recipient. From the government's point of view, you no longer control the property if someone else has the legal right to decide what to do with it, or if it's part of a trust that you can't change your mind about.

TAXING ISSUES
Recent changes in tax law, however, have diluted the income tax advantages of transferring property to an irrevocable trust. Now less of a trust's income is taxed at the lowest rate and most is subject to the the highest rate (currently 39.6%), as this chart from The Wall Street Journal shows. In some cases, that could even mean that trust income is being taxed at a higher rate than you're paying as an individual—an unkind irony.

THOU SHALT NOT

Control the Property

Change the Beneficiary

Alter the Trustees

and verily

THOU SHALT SAVE ON TAXES

TRUST

One way a trust can reduce its income tax is by distributing the earnings to the beneficiaries, so the money is spread around to be taxed at lower rates. But that solution may be at odds with your other goals for the trust, such as asset growth to provide greater income in the future, or limiting the current disposable income of your beneficiaries.

The Squeeze on Trusts

Tax rates on trust income not only are higher under the 1993 Tax Act, but also kick in at much lower income levels, creating a double whammy for many trusts.

TAX RATE	1992	1993
15%	Up to $3,750	Up to $1,500
28%	Over $3,750 to $11,250	Over $1,500 to $3,500
31%	Over $11,250	Over $3,500 to $5,500
36%	—	Over $5,500 to $7,500
39.6%	—	Over $7,500

allow distributions "for the benefit of the
beneficiary," says M

TRUSTS AND TAXES

When you set up a trust and transfer assets to it, you have to consider the tax consequences. You can give the trust up to $600,000—the unified credit amount—without owing federal gift taxes. But if you transfer more than that, the tax will be due, at the same rates as estate taxes.

Some states have gift taxes, too, and impose them on smaller gifts than the federal government does. So you might owe state taxes, but not federal ones. Often the biggest benefit from setting up an irrevocable trust is that any appreciation of the trust's assets, after the date of the gift, doesn't increase the value of your estate.

PLANNING AHEAD

Despite the shrinking income tax savings and the potential drawback of parting with your property while you're still alive, an irrevocable living trust is an ideal way to pass property to your heirs. That's because the one change you can make to an irrevocable trust is to add assets to it. If you make annual tax-exempt gifts, you're reducing your estate while protecting the property until your beneficiary is wise enough to use the assets in ways you would approve. But you must be certain the trust is set up with **Crummey** power, to meet tax-exempt requirements.

One smart idea is to put into a trust either assets which will increase in value, or the cash to buy those assets. If you put $10,000 worth of shares of a growth stock into a trust called a **qualified minor's trust**, for your daughter, for example, you're within the annual tax-free gift limit. When the trust terminates and the property becomes hers outright, it will be worth whatever the current value of the stock is—presumably more than its original price. By using the trust, you've not only saved gift taxes on the current gift, but also on the **appreciated value** of the stock. You've also reduced income and estate taxes because the property doesn't belong to you after you put it in the trust.

A CRUMMEY CHOICE

You can add up to $10,000 in cash or other assets to an irrevocable trust every year without owing gift tax, thanks to D. Clifford Crummey who won a court case against the IRS in 1968. The conditions? The beneficiary must have the right to withdraw the gift within a fixed time limit, and has to be notified of that right. And, of course, the money or other assets must be there to take out.

SKIP LIGHTLY

If you create a trust to benefit your grandchildren or their children, or anyone two or more generations younger than you are, it's known as a **generation-skipping trust**.

As long as the assets in the trust are $1 million or less ($2 million if a husband and wife each create a trust) the transfer is exempt from the Generation-Skipping Tax, or GST. If the assets are more, they're taxed using a complex formula based on the maximum federal estate tax rate of 55%, on top of whatever estate or gift taxes are due at the time the trust is created. Obviously, these trusts are not for everybody, but they can be a valuable estate planning tool.

WATCH OUT!

If you establish a trust to pay for your grandchild's—or any child's—college expenses, the annual amount counts as income to the child's parents in some states. The logic is that it's the parents' responsibility to provide for their children's education.

SPENDTHRIFT CLAUSES

If you're creating a trust because you're nervous about a beneficiary's ability to handle money, most states let you put on the brakes with a safety device known as a **spendthrift clause**. That way, borrowing against principal and any future income is limited, and the funds are protected from creditors— at least until the money is actually paid. So even if you can't control the spending speed, you can limit the refueling rate.

Testamentary Taxsavers

Creating a trust in your will lets you do good to others and well by your estate.

Like any other trust, a testamentary trust protects your assets while providing for your heirs. Unlike a living trust, where you part with your property while you're still alive, a testamentary trust is created by your will after you die. You choose the beneficiaries and set the terms that the trustee follows in paying out the assets. You can establish how long the trust will last and who gets what's left.

THE ESTATE ADVANTAGE

Of course, you can always leave up to $600,000 directly to your heirs without using a trust, or give them property worth that much when you are alive. The unified credit would still apply.

There are several advantages to using a trust, however. One is that you can establish how the assets are to be paid out to your heirs. And if you select a trustee who is good with money, the assets should continue to grow and produce even more income.

Finally, you can structure a **by-pass trust** so that someone—usually your spouse—benefits from the trust during his or her lifetime while the principal is held in trust for your other beneficiaries. Your spouse or other designee gets the income from the trust, and can be given the power to withdraw up to 5% of the assets, or $5,000 a year, whichever is greater.

If this first beneficiary doesn't need the money, it can be left to grow undisturbed. And if the trust's value has doubled or tripled by the time your spouse dies, there's still no estate tax due because the value of the trust, for tax purposes, was set at the time you died.

BETTER LATE...

Your heirs can sometimes do estate planning after your death by *disclaiming*, or renouncing, your bequest. Your spouse, for example, could disclaim the right to inherit a share of your estate to take advantage of your unified credit by allowing your children to inherit directly.

SAVING TAXES

A testamentary trust can limit the taxes on the estate of a married couple by allowing each partner to take advantage of the $600,000 federal estate tax exemption. Trusts that are set up to take advantage of this tax-saving feature are variously known as **family, bypass, credit shelter**, or **exemption equivalent** trusts.

Remember, though, the only property that can be put into a testamentary trust is property you own outright. Some legal

With a Will Only

HUSBAND

You can leave an estate worth up to $600,000 free of federal tax to anyone you choose. If you're married, and leave your entire estate to your spouse tax-free, it becomes part of his or her estate.

LEAVE ESTATE TO WIFE

WIFE

Your spouse can leave an estate of only $600,000 tax-free, even if your combined estates are worth more than that.

LEAVE COMBINED ESTATE TO HEIRS

HEIRS

ESTATE OWES TAX ON AMOUNT OVER $600,000

A SPRINKLING TRUST

If you establish a trust with a number of beneficiaries—your children or grandchildren for instance—you can give your trustee sprinkling powers. That way, if one beneficiary needs more income than the others, or if an uneven distribution would save on taxes, the trustee can sprinkle the benefits around rather than following a stricter formula.

experts advise, therefore, that couples whose accumulated wealth is greater than $600,000 split some of their jointly held assets. That way, each of them is able to fund a testamentary trust to take full advantage of the tax credit. In splitting joint assets, however, it may be wiser to divide investment assets—like stocks or bonds—rather than give up joint ownership of your home.

MARITAL TRUST

Even though you can leave your entire estate to your spouse tax-free, you might want to establish a **marital trust** to oversee the estate's management or the way it is distributed after your spouse's death. As long as your spouse has the right to the income from your estate for life, the marital deduction will still apply, and no estate tax will be due, no matter how large the estate.

Since the remaining value of assets in the marital trust is added to your spouse's estate when he or she dies, there's no tax advantage to your eventual heirs with this type of trust. But there can be both immediate and long-term benefits if your spouse is inexperienced or uneasy about managing money, or if you're concerned about who will ultimately benefit from your estate.

One kind of marital trust gives your spouse the right to distribute the property you leave in trust as he or she chooses. In legal language, that's known as a **general power of appointment**. The chief benefit of such a trust, from your perspective, is the financial management your trustee will provide.

With a **qualified terminable interest property trust, or QTIP**, however, you choose the ultimate beneficiaries of the trust—those who will get the income or principal of the trust after your spouse's death. If you want to insure that your assets will go to your children from a previous marriage, for example, this type of trust lets you do it.

With a Testamentary Trust

HUSBAND

WIFE

However, if you've created a testamentary trust funded with up to $600,000 of your assets, that is not part of your spouse's estate. It goes to your heirs free of estate tax.

LEAVE $600,000 IN TESTAMENTARY TRUST

LEAVE $600,000 IN TESTAMENTARY TRUST

In Trust

HEIRS

Then, when your spouse dies another $600,000, or a total of $1.2 million, can go to your heirs untaxed. Since there's no way to be sure which spouse will die first, the wills of both spouses should provide for a testamentary trust.

HEIRS GET $1.2 MILLION FREE OF ESTATE TAX

THE ONLY CATCH IS...

If you've made any taxable gifts, that is, gifts larger than $10,000 in any tax year. If you have, the tax due on those gifts is subtracted from the unified credit amount, reducing what you can leave free of tax when you die. To take a simple example, if you've given your daughter real estate worth $200,000, you can leave only $400,000 at your death exempt from estate tax.

The Universe of Trusts

The outer limits of the trust universe haven't been reached yet—and they may never be.

If you've got assets to protect or give away, you can probably create a trust to do the job. And in some cases, there are extra benefits—like charitable deductions on your income tax—in the bargain. Getting it right can be tricky, though. In some cases, for example, if you die within three years of transferring assets to a trust, the property is counted in your estate anyway. That's just one example of rules and regulations that govern the universe of trusts.

IT'S BETTER TO GIVE...
AND RECEIVE

If you create a living trust to give money to a charitable institution, there are some added benefits. That's because the trust not only reduces your estate and ultimately your estate taxes—but also lets you take a charitable deduction to reduce your income taxes in the year you establish the trust. Perhaps best of all, you can either get the income earned by the assets in the trust, or get the trust balance back after a specific period of time, with no capital gains tax paid on the assets that are sold.

A **charitable remainder trust** is designed to pay you or someone you choose current income, either for a set period of time up to 20 years, or for life. When the beneficiaries die, what's left in the trust—the remainder—goes to the charity. If the trustee sells the appreciated or non-income-producing assets once they are in the trust and replaces them with income-producing investments, the amount you or your beneficiary receive as income can increase as well.

The size of the charitable deduction you can take when you fund this type of charitable trust is figured using government valuation rules, and may not be the same as fair market value. You should consult your tax advisor or the IRS.

With a **charitable lead trust**, a charity gets annual income generated by the assets for a number of years specified in the trust agreement. When the trust ends your heirs get back what's left. The advantage is that the gift to your heirs is valued at a reduced gift tax cost, based on IRS tables, since your heirs won't benefit from it until sometime in the future. The discounted present value applies, no matter how much the principal appreciates during the life of the trust.

LIFE INSURANCE TRUSTS

While the whole issue of how much life insurance you need is complicated and controversial, it pays to be aware of how a large life insurance payout can affect the size of your estate—and the resulting estate taxes. While your heirs don't pay income tax on the insurance they receive when you die, if the death benefit pushes your estate over $600,000, estate taxes will kick in. You can usually avoid this situation by excluding the insurance from your estate.

One way to do this is to have another person own the insurance policy on your life. If you die, the insurance goes to the owner. Another solution is to have the policy owned by an insurance trust, so that the payout goes to the trust. Though there are some tricky legal issues to work out, you can pay the premiums and trustee's fees yourself with yearly gifts to the trust. You can also specify the ultimate beneficiaries of the trust, and any conditions that the trustee must follow.

A third alternative is a **second-to-die insurance policy**, which covers both spouses but pays nothing until the second one dies. The payout can then be used to pay any estate taxes that are due. However, unless you and your spouse have a combined estate worth substantially more than the $1.2 million—the amount the two of you together can leave tax-free—this option may not be worth the cost of the insurance.

Each of these strategies has advantages and limitations—and yards of red tape. Consult your tax adviser before you decide to use any one of them and to determine which is best for you.

A VANISHING TRUST

Before the tax law changed in 1993, you could establish an irrevocable trust to receive your assets, and then qualify for Medicaid assistance. People did this if they needed long-term care and didn't want to deplete their life savings. The only hitch was that the trust had to be in place at least 30 months before you applied for Medicaid assistance.

The new law extends the 30-month requirement and pegs your eligibility for Medicaid to the total value of property you transfer to the trust, not simply to when the assets are transferred. The consequence, for many people, is that Medicaid trusts are no longer a workable option.

TRUST OF THE HOUR

Though you wouldn't think so, there are fads in trusts just as there are fads in other things. New ways to protect assets from taxes keep springing up, like the recently popular **personal residence trusts**, which allow you to transfer your home to someone else, often a family member, to reduce your estate, while allowing you to retain the right to live there for a fixed period of time. The bottom line for any trust is weighing the advantages—mostly financial—against the hassles and set-up costs. Sad but true, the more perfect the idea sounds, the more likely it is to have hidden or not-so-hidden drawbacks, usually involving property that goes back into your estate so that you lose the entire advantage of setting up the trust in the first place.

BLIND TRUSTS

Instead of protecting your assets for your heirs, blind trusts are designed to protect your reputation for integrity, especially if you hold public office. When you set up a blind trust, you transfer complete control of your assets to a trustee. Equally as important, you're kept in the dark about what happens to them: what's bought or sold, what's making money or losing it.

The point of all this? The decisions you make as an elected or appointed official aren't tainted by the suspicion that you're acting in your own financial interest.

Gifts

From a tax perspective, there's more to giving gifts than meets the eye.

If the key to minimizing estate taxes is to reduce your estate, then giving gifts will get the job done. Before you start spreading money around, though, it pays to consider the benefits and the limitations of generosity.

You can give anyone you choose a tax-free gift of cash or other property valued at up to $10,000 each year for as many years as you like. While such gifts aren't tax-deductible, you pay no tax when the gift is made and neither does the recipient. If your spouse joins in the gift, together you can give each person up to $20,000 a year, even if all the money comes from one of you. You have to file a federal gift tax return, though, which the joining spouse signs.

Gifts over $10,000 are taxable. If you make one, you must file a gift tax return, IRS Form 709, with your income tax. When you figure out the tax you owe, you must take into account all the taxable gifts you have ever made, including those before 1976, when the rules changed.

The amount of tax due counts against your **unified gift and estate tax credit** of $192,800 (the equivalent of the tax on a $600,000 estate). Anything you accumulate in gift tax reduces the size of the estate you can leave tax-free at your death. And the rate at which the gift tax is figured is the same as the rate on the estate taxes. The good news, though, is that you don't actually owe any of the tax you may accumulate until you've used up all the credit.

GIFTS TO MINORS

If you want to make gifts to children but not just give them the cash, you can set up custodial accounts using either **The Uniform Gifts to Minors Act (UGMA)** or **The Uniform Transfer to Minors Act (UTMA)**, to protect the accumulating assets. There's no charge for setting up or administering the account, and you can build it regularly without owing gift taxes as long as you add no more than $10,000 a year. (The $10,000 is a combined total, though, of all gifts to the same person, including those under UGMA or UTMA.)

One advantage of UTMAs is that you can include assets that don't produce regular earnings (like real estate and paintings) in addition to cash and securities (stocks, bonds, and mutual funds).

THEY CAN TAKE IT WITH THEM

If you can live with the idea that the child will take control of the assets in a UGMA or UTMA account at age 18 or age 21, depending on state law, it's a simple way to pass along your assets. While you're not required to liquidate the account and hand over cash to the child on the date of majority (age 18 or 21), bear in mind that on that date the child has the right to the money and can demand it.

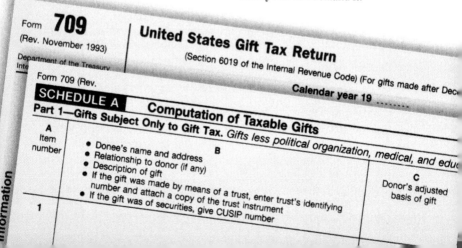

Form **709**
(Rev. November 1993)

Department of the Treasury
Inte

United States Gift Tax Return

(Section 6019 of the Internal Revenue Code) (For gifts made after Dec

Form 709 (Rev.

Calendar year 19 ....

SCHEDULE A **Computation of Taxable Gifts**

Part 1—Gifts Subject Only to Gift Tax. Gifts less political organization, medical, and edu

A Item number	B • Donee's name and address • Relationship to donor (if any) • Description of gift • If the gift was made by means of a trust, enter trust's identifying number and attach a copy of the trust instrument • If the gift was of securities, give CUSIP number	C Donor's adjusted basis of gift
1		

SPECIAL CONSIDERATION

There are some other things to think about with UGMAs and UTMAs that might influence the way you make your gifts:

1 First, any assets a young person has in his or her name own name can reduce college financial aid. That's because a student is expected to contribute a greater percentage of savings to pay college costs than a parent is.

2 Second, if you name yourself the custodian of the account and you die while the child is still a minor, the value of the account is included in **your** estate—completely defeating the purpose for which it was established. You can get around this problem by naming another adult as custodian.

3 Third, since children under 14 pay tax on earnings at their parents' rate, you might consider giving growth rather than income investments to minimize the tax bite.

GIFTS TO OTHERS

The $10,000 annual tax-exempt limit applies to gifts you make to people of all ages, not just minors. For gift tax purposes, the value of the gift, its **cost basis**, is its value at the time it is given—not what it was when you acquired it. If the item is worth more when you give it than it's been worth in the past, you don't have to pay capital gains, on the increased value. However, if the person receiving the gift sells it, she will owe capital gains based on your original cost, which might result in a sizeable tax bill.

SPECIAL GIFTS

If you want to pay for someone's educational expenses, you can make a tax-exempt gift to the college or university equal to the cost of tuition. The understanding is that the student's bill will be considered paid. You can't pay for room and board this way, but tuition is usually the bulk of the cost in any case. The same option exists for paying hospital bills. The process is known as a **qualified transfer**, and there don't seem to be any catches, at least not yet. Plus, these gifts do not limit your right to give up to $10,000 per year to the beneficiary of the transfer as a tax-exempt gift.

TAX-FREE GIFTS

If your spouse is a U.S. citizen, you may give him or her as much as you want, as often as you want, without owing gift taxes. But the picture changes when your spouse is the citizen of another country. Then, there's a $100,000 annual limit on tax-exempt gifts and, without special planning involving the use of a **qualified domestic trust (QDOT)**, no **marital deduction.** (That is, you can't leave your spouse your entire estate outright free of federal tax.)

Tax-exempt gifts to charities, like gifts to your spouse, aren't capped at $10,000, but they are limited to a percentage of your adjusted gross income. Check with your tax adviser or the IRS for the rules that apply to various kinds of gifts.

, 1991)

exclusions—see inst

D
Date
of gift

And More Gifts

It's hard-headed, not hard-hearted, to think about what your gifts will cost you and your estate.

When you're considering making a gift, you probably ought to consider the tax consequences of the way you give it. For example, if the choice is between giving property you own, or selling the property and making a cash gift, the identity of the recipient makes a big difference.

And if the choice is between making a gift or leaving the same property as a legacy in your will, you need to think about **cost basis**, the value assigned to the property that the recipient gets. It could make a major tax difference if he or she sells the property.

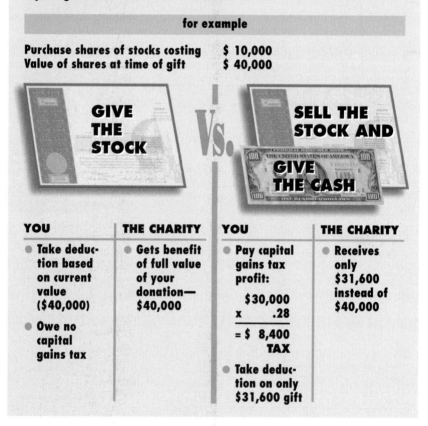

MAKING THE MOST OF A DEAL

When you make a charitable gift, you can take a tax deduction for the value of the property. In most cases, it makes the most sense to contribute appreciated assets—those that have increased in value since you bought them—because you can deduct the current value and avoid capital gains on the increase in value.

for example

Purchase shares of stocks costing $ 10,000
Value of shares at time of gift $ 40,000

GIVE THE STOCK **vs.** SELL THE STOCK AND GIVE THE CASH

YOU	THE CHARITY	YOU	THE CHARITY
• Take deduction based on current value ($40,000)	• Gets benefit of full value of your donation—$40,000	• Pay capital gains tax profit: $30,000 x .28 = $ 8,400 TAX	• Receives only $31,600 instead of $40,000
• Owe no capital gains tax		• Take deduction on only $31,600 gift	

GIFTS TO TRUSTS

Money you put into a trust is considered a gift in some circumstances, but not others. In general, the difference hinges on whether or not the trust is revocable or irrevocable, and who the beneficiary is.

Revocable trusts don't result in gift taxes because the transfer of property is considered incomplete. That's because you can change your mind about what's in the trust and who benefits.

But if the trust is irrevocable, gift taxes are due if the beneficiary is anyone but yourself or your spouse. In fact, if you're the beneficiary of an irrevocable trust during your lifetime, the property you put into the trust is considered a gift to your surviving beneficiaries. You figure the value based on U.S. Treasury department tables that are included with the rules on gift taxes.

Give It or Leave It

If you're undecided whether to make gifts now or leave property as a legacy in your will, you can balance a variety of pluses and minuses for each option.

GIFTS

Advantages	Disadvantages
● If you spread gifts over the years you can provide generously for your beneficiaries and reduce your estate at the same time.	● Once a gift is given, you don't have access to it even if you need it.
● Your gift may be worth more to the beneficiary since it's not subject to estate and inheritance taxes.	● You can't control how gifts are used.
● You can help meet financial needs when they occur.	● Your heir may end up owing capital gains tax if the asset is sold—but the silver lining is that capital gains taxes are lower than estate taxes.

LEGACIES BY WILL

Advantages	Disadvantages
● You keep your assets as long as you need them.	● Wills can be contested.
● You can change your mind about items left in your will until the last minute.	● Estate taxes may reduce the size of your legacy.
● For your heir, the cost basis of the asset—the starting point for figuring capital gains—is the value at the date of your death. That could save capital gains taxes.	● Your heir may owe inheritance taxes.

FAMILY LIMITED PARTNERSHIPS

Another approach to using gifts to pass valuable property to your children and grandchildren is to create a **family limited partnership**. The parents, or senior family members, serve as general partners and maintain control over the assets in the partnership, usually real estate or a family business. The junior members of the family are limited partners, with no current authority but a growing share of the partnership assets.

Each year, each general partner can give each limited partner a $10,000 share in the assets as a tax-free gift. However, because the general partners are allowed to transfer assets at a discount to face value, each gift can actually be worth up to 30% more, or closer to $14,000 than $10,000. The discount is legitimate if there's a valid business purpose for the partnership, according to an IRS ruling in 1993. Over ten years, for example, you could enrich each limited partner by $140,000, instead of $100,000.

If you use a family limited partnership as part of a long-term estate plan, and you don't make too many questionable decisions—like overdoing the discount or creating partnerships without valid business reasons—you should be able to keep the family property intact while reducing eventual estate taxes.

CAN YOU REMEMBER THIS?

If you received a gift before 1921 and are getting around to selling it or giving it away, the IRS says you should use its fair market value **at the time of the gift** to figure your profit or loss. They don't provide advice on how you determine that value. Nor do they let you adjust the pre-1921 value for inflation.

Protecting Health and Wealth

Health insurance protects you from the rising costs of medical care—for a price.

It's expensive—sometimes very expensive—to get sick. A typical hospital stay cost $5,046 a day in 1994, and a visit to the doctor averaged $100. And that's without tests and medication. Those numbers illustrate why health insurance is so important to a sound financial future: without it, every penny you've saved could be eaten up by a serious illness.

STAYING INSURED

If your employer provides health insurance, most of the legwork is handled for you. Generally, you choose from a limited number of plans, and your **premium**, or cost, is deducted from your salary. But if you arrange for coverage yourself, you face the double responsibility of finding the best plan you can afford and keeping up the payments. If you pay late, or miss a payment, your insurance might be cancelled. Not only would you have to start your search again, but you might be left without coverage when you need it.

It's also important *not* to let your insurance lapse when you change jobs or retire. You may be able to keep your old insurance on a temporary basis, either until you're eligible for coverage at your new job or old enough to qualify for Medicare—health care insurance the government provides for people over 65.

WHAT INSURANCE COVERS

Most health care insurance covers hospital care and medical treatment, including visits to doctors, medical tests, and similar expenses. There's always a **deductible**—a dollar amount you have to pay before the insurance kicks in. Generally speaking, there's one deductible level for an individual—$300 is typical—and a somewhat higher one if the policy covers an entire family.

ONE WAY TO SAVE MONEY

In most cases, the higher the deductible, the less expensive the insurance. If you have a choice, you might opt for the highest deductible you think you'll be able to afford. That way, you can use the insurance as protection against major expenses rather than as a way to pay for everyday health care. Check, though, to be sure that your deductible is applied against *all* the medical expenses you have in a year, not against each individual expense.

Once you've spent more than the deductible amount, the insurance company begins to pay. A typical arrangement is for the insurer to cover most of your hospital costs and 80% of your medical bills, while you're responsible for the other 20%. That 20% is referred to as a **co-payment**, a euphemism for your share of the bill.

THE 80% SOLUTION

The critical question about 80% coverage is 80% of *what.* If it's 80% of the bill you submit, you're fine. But if it's 80% of the fee the company allows for a particular type of treatment, you may find yourself paying a big share of the bill despite your insurance. The amount allowed by the insurance company may be out of line with current charges, or unrealistically low for the particular part of the country you live in—like a $36 insurance payment on a $150 bill.

Sometimes insurance plans provide better coverage if you use doctors and labs that have agreed to accept what the insurer pays. When you use those **participating providers**, you simply pay a small fee—often $10—at the time of the visit and the company takes care of the rest of the bill.

HMOs, which generally require you to use doctors in their networks, don't require co-payments of any kind.

Group vs. Individual Plans

Many people get health insurance through their employer, as part of a group insurance policy negotiated with an insurance company or health care organization. Employers who provide health insurance currently pay, on average, between half and two-thirds of the cost, but that percentage is plummeting. More and more workers are asked to pick up the lion's share of insurance costs. If your job doesn't provide coverage, your alternatives are buying an **individual policy** or joining a managed health care plan.

GROUP PLANS

ADVANTAGES

- Plan is generally cheaper than comparable coverage for an individual

- Plan may allow you to choose from a range of coverage options known as a **flexible benefit plan**: the list may include dental coverage, prescription drugs, life insurance, and other health services as well as basic hospital and medical plans

- You're automatically eligible for coverage and can't be dropped or charged more if you get sick

DISADVANTAGES

- Insurance payments may be much lower than actual expenses

- The group can drop the plan or substitute a less generous one

- The cost of your insurance may increase dramatically

- You may have to use participating doctors to receive full coverage

- You have few legal protections since plans aren't regulated by state laws

INDIVIDUAL PLANS

ADVANTAGES

- Price increases are monitored by state insurance regulators

- If your policy is guaranteed renewable, your coverage can't be dropped even if you get sick

- You don't pay for coverage you don't need just because it's part of the group plan

DISADVANTAGES

- The premiums are generally expensive, sometimes prohibitively so

- The screening process is often highly selective, making it difficult to get insurance if you have any medical problems

- The policy can limit maximum benefits, so that people with serious health problems run out of coverage

Examining the Details

All health insurance policies set conditions for what and whom they'll cover. Bigger risks mean higher costs.

Though the idea of health care insurance is fairly simple, understanding how it works can be a real challenge. That's because complex rules and regulations have been developed for defining what's covered, and for actually paying the bills. While these mechanisms have been created, in part, as a way of preventing fraud, they also serve as a buffer to protect the insurance companies' bottom lines.

PRE-EXISTING CONDITIONS

When you apply for coverage, you have to identify any previous or existing health problems. Your new insurer can limit coverage for those conditions, either for a specified period of time—typically six months—or for as long as the policy is in effect. If you're not honest, the company has the right to cancel your policy when the truth is discovered—and will probably do so, leaving you without insurance.

However, if you have existing medical problems you're not aware of, because they haven't been diagnosed or treated, your coverage should be safe. You may have to respond to the company's inquiries, though, or even provide supporting evidence.

It often seems that the people who need care the most have the hardest time finding coverage. But restrictions on coverage for pre-existing conditions can affect anybody who changes insurance carriers.

WHAT'S A GUARANTEE WORTH

All new insurance policies are **guaranteed renewable**. That means a policy can't be cancelled as long as you pay your premiums on time. The price of the coverage may go up, however, if the prices are raised for everybody with a similar policy. Less desirable, though, are older **conditionally renewable** policies, which can be cancelled if you make too many claims. Best of all, but hardest to find, are **uncancellable policies**, which guarantee both coverage and rates.

OPEN ENROLLMENT

Some insurers, especially non-profit Blue Cross and Blue Shield plans, have annual **open enrollment periods**, during which insured people can switch carriers, and people without insurance can apply. All applicants qualify for coverage during this period, even if they might be turned down the rest of the year. The insurer, however, may charge some applicants higher rates if they're in poor general health or have a serious illness.

OPEN ENROLLMENT

IT'S ALL IN THE RECORDS

Insurance companies have access to a lot of information about your medical history and the applications you've made to other insurers through their Medical Information Bureau (MIB). This industry-funded organization is headquartered in Boston, and maintains files on 11 to 12 million people.

In theory, at least, you should be told if information in the bureau has disqualified you for insurance or preferred rates. But that doesn't always happen. If you want to check what's in your file, you have a right to the non-medical information for free. And your doctor or other medical professional can get the medical records.

If there are mistakes, or if you feel that information is missing, you can correct your file by writing or calling the bureau. Be sure to check back later, though, to insure that the corrections have been made. The address is Medical Information Bureau, P.O. Box 105, Essex Station, Boston MA 02112, and the phone number is 617-426-3660.

INDEMNITY PLANS

Most health care policies provide **payment for service**. That means the amount the insurer pays is based on the cost of the service, such as a doctor's visit or hospital stay. **Indemnity plans**, on the other hand, guarantee that they'll pay a specific amount per claim—$100 for every day you're in the hospital, for example. In general, they're not a smart use of your insurance dollar, even though the coverage is cheap. That's because the amount they pay often covers only a fraction of the actual cost of any care you receive, and the conditions under which they will pay are usually more restrictive than they seem when the policy is sold.

TOUGH TO GET COVERAGE

Sometimes it can be difficult, or even impossible, to get health insurance. Here are some of the reasons:

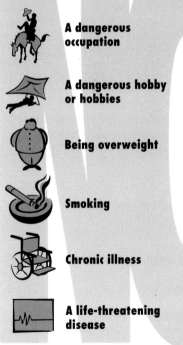

A dangerous occupation

A dangerous hobby or hobbies

Being overweight

Smoking

Chronic illness

A life-threatening disease

UNDERWRITING

When an insurance company evaluates you as a potential client, trying to decide if you're going to end up costing them money, the process is known as **underwriting**. If they decide the risk is too great, they can turn you down, offer more expensive coverage, or limit the coverage for certain illnesses or other medical problems.

Are You Covered?

Changes in your life usually mean changes in your insurance. Keeping adequate coverage at all times is essential.

When you retire before age 65, change jobs, or get married or divorced, you may face a change in insurance coverage. While occasionally you might have the luxury of choosing between two policies, you're much more likely to find yourself uninsured. However, if you've had coverage either as an employee or the dependent of an employee, you may be able to buy insurance from the same company at close to group rates.

COORDINATION OF BENEFITS

If you and your spouse are covered by separate health insurance plans through your jobs, you and your dependents are generally in good shape.

If the insurance isn't costing you anything, or if the charges are reasonable for what you get, you can keep both policies and get even better coverage, using a technique known as **coordination of benefits**. That means, for example, if you incur a medical cost, you submit a claim to your own insurance company first. You then submit a report of your insurance settlement to your spouse's insurer. When the system works right, you can recover a larger proportion

of any medical expense, though never more than your actual cost.

There's also an advantage to having two plans if each provides superior coverage in one or two areas, like hospitalization, prescription plans, or mental health. Keeping both plans allows you to take advantage of what's best in each.

If one of your policies is significantly better than the other, either because it costs a lot less or provides more generous payments, or both, you can decline coverage on the inferior plan. Some employers are willing to pay you a bonus for refusing health insurance— so it could be worth your while, especially if you can be covered by the better plan.

COMPARING POLICIES

It pays to compare the coverage provided by different plans. Sometimes it's worth it to pay for both, if it means you're better protected.

Your policy	Benefits	Your Spouses's Policy
✓	Hospitalization	✓
	Prescriptions	✓
✓	Checkups	
✓	Eyeglasses	

for example

Expenses	Your Policy	Your Spouses's Policy
Doctor visit	80%	0%
Dental visit	0%	80%
Eye glasses	80%	20%
Prescriptions	50%	40%

WHICH PLAN PAYS?

When a dependent is eligible for coverage on both parents' plans, which one pays? Usually it's the plan of the parent whose birthday comes first in the calendar year—January taking precedence over May or July over October, for example. The year of birth isn't a factor. But what if the parents' birthdays fall on the same day? In at least one case we know, the father's insurance was considered the **primary,** or first-paying carrier, and the mother's, **secondary.**

MINE ?

YOURS ?

COBRA INSURANCE

Since the Consolidated Omnibus Budget Reconciliation Act of 1985—fortunately simplified to COBRA—you have the right to continue your group insurance for 18 months after you leave a job, whether you quit, are laid off, or retire, and for 29 months if you're disabled. Though the details vary from state to state, the general rule is that you can buy coverage for 102% of your employer's cost.

Your employer can't deny you COBRA coverage, except by ending health insurance for all employees. However, there are no limits on how much the costs can go up each year—and with a COBRA plan you're paying the entire freight yourself. While it's not cheap, COBRA coverage is almost always less expensive than individual coverage. (Companies with fewer than 20 employees and church groups don't have to participate.)

Your dependents are eligible for three years of COBRA coverage under the same terms you are—102% of your employer's cost—when they no longer qualify for coverage under your plan. That might happen if you die, if you and your spouse are legally separated or divorced, or if your children are no longer full-time students after they reach age 19.

COBRA also provides you and your former dependents the option of buying a **conversion policy**, that is an individual policy with the same company that provided your group plan. However, you usually get fewer benefits than through the group plan, and at a much higher cost. But if you can't get insurance on your own, or through a high-risk pool in your state, the conversion policy may be your only alternative.

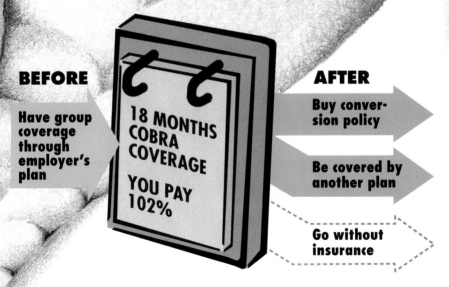

BEFORE

Have group coverage through employer's plan

18 MONTHS COBRA COVERAGE

YOU PAY 102%

AFTER

Buy conversion policy

Be covered by another plan

Go without insurance

BLUE CROSS

Blue Cross is the oldest health care insurer in the U.S. When it was founded in Texas in 1929, it provided 21 days of hospitalization for a group of school teachers who paid 50¢ a piece each month for the coverage. Blue Shield—coverage for medical expenses—was added in 1939. By 1994, Blue Cross and Blue Shield had 65.5 million subscribers across the county.

HMOs

Managed care is increasingly the preferred solution to health coverage problems.

Managed care means providing access to health care while keeping a sharp eye on costs. For some, managed care is the way to solve the crisis of escalating health costs that result from **fee-for-service** medical care. For others, it symbolizes everything that's wrong with the health care system.

About one thing there is no debate: a leading force in the health care revolution of the last 25 years, **Health Maintenance Organizations (HMOs)** have dramatically altered the way medical treatment is provided and paid for. Instead of charging for each service or visit to a doctor or hospital, an HMO charges an annual fee that covers all the care you receive. As a HMO participant, you get all your care through the organization.

One big plus for prepaid care is that you never have to file insurance claims or wait to be reimbursed for money you've paid out for treatment. A second, and probably more important benefit, is that all the care you get is covered. You won't suddenly find yourself facing an enormous bill for medical care. And, since annual checkups and other kinds of preventive care are included, problems may be diagnosed more quickly. That can mean improving your chances for a full recovery.

A GROWING TREND

Some HMOs operate across the country, in dozens of cities and suburban areas. Kaiser Permanente, currently the largest, has 255 offices, 28 medical centers, and 6.6 million members. Others are located within a small geographic region, or have

How HMOs Work

PATIENTS PAY ONE ANNUAL FEE

NO FORMS

NO DOCTOR BILLS

NO HOSPITAL BILLS

only a few branches. In all, more than 50.5 million people, or 20% of the population, are currently members of an HMO.

Variations on the HMO theme have appeared more recently. **Preferred Provider Organizations (PPOs)**, for example, are networks of doctors that provide discounted care to members of a sponsoring organization, such as an employer or a union. If you use a participating doctor, you pay a small co-payment at the time of your visit: $10 or 10% of the bill are typical. Your share of the bill jumps dramatically, though, if you go to a doctor who isn't on the list.

> Kaiser Permanente, the first prepaid health care organization, began operating in 1933, and cost 5¢ a day.

THE HMO MANAGES AND PAYS

**Doctors Nursing Specialists
Care**

HMO DOCTORS SEE PATIENTS

HMO OPERATES HOSPITALS

THE HMO STRUCTURE

While there are several varieties of HMO, the typical one employs a staff of salaried doctors, nurses, therapists, and other medical personnel, covering a range of specialties. When you need treatment, either for a specific problem or for preventive care, you see the appropriate person on staff. If you need hospitalization or nursing home care, you're treated either in an HMO-operated facility or one that has ties to the organization.

In most cases, the HMO will not pay for the treatment you receive from non-affiliated doctors or hospitals, except in case of an emergency. They will, however, sometimes pay for you to get a second opinion from a non-staff person, or, in particular cases, pay for your treatment

by an acknowledged specialist who isn't on staff.

There are also some **open-ended HMOs** that will cover visits to the doctor of your choice. You'll probably have to pay an extra fee for this option, but you might welcome the flexibility if you want to use a particular practitioner.

BEFORE YOU JOIN

Managed care, whether through an HMO, a PPO or other group, is seen by many as the wave of the future. In some cases, employers offer managed care plans as your only health insurance choice. Other times you can choose between a managed care plan and a more traditional fee-for-service plan. In most cases, choosing managed care will cost you less.

If you can choose among various insurance plans, it pays to ask a few questions about the managed care option before you join. The questions become even more critical if you're footing the cost of the coverage yourself:

- **Can you choose the doctor you want to see, or are they assigned by availability?**
- **How long is the average wait for an appointment?**
- **Can you see doctors outside the network? How much will it cost?**
- **Are there limits on the length of hospital stays?**
- **Is there a cap on the total coverage the HMO will provide?**
- **Can you be dropped if you need lots of care or make lots of visits?**
- **Are prescriptions covered?**

THE OTHER SIDE

While there's little question about the benefits of HMOs, both for normally healthy people and for those with chronic problems, some aspects of their operation worry potential members and may even keep them away.

Some people feel that the care is impersonal and that it is difficult to establish a comfortable relationship with a regular doctor. There's also been criticism that doctors are offered incentives to limit or deny care and testing in order to keep costs down. In addition, there have been charges of limited choices of hospitals and doctors, long waits for appointments, and few available services.

One solution, of course, is to look for a well-funded and well-managed HMO. State insurance departments evaluate the organizations operating in their jurisdiction and can provide guidance and advice. So can consumer groups, professional organizations, and the Department of Health and Human Services.

Medicare

One bonus of turning 65 is that you're eligible for Medicare insurance coverage.

Medicare, the government program that provides medical insurance for people over 65, has made an enormous, positive difference in the health care of an entire generation of Americans. Like Social Security, it has become an institution, though it has its share of problems.

Since the first bills were paid—$4.6 billion in 1967—Medicare has exploded in size. A steadily aging population and increasing medical costs pushed payments in 1994 to $161 billion. Running the program costs, on average, about 2% of the total budget.

As the population ages, changes may be inevitable to keep the program alive. The two most frequently mentioned changes are raising the minimum qualifying age, and adjusting benefit payments based on financial need.

A DOUBLE DEFENSE
Medicare actually provides two insurance programs, one that you get automatically when you enroll, and another one that's optional.

HOSPITALIZATION

MEDICAL SERVICES

Medicare Part A provides hospitalization insurance to everyone who qualifies. You have to apply for the coverage, but approval is assured if you qualify for Social Security or are the dependent of someone who does (see page 76). If you're not eligible for this no-cost coverage, like some government workers and non-citizens, you have the option of buying it for an annual fee.

Medicare Part B is optional insurance that covers medical services, including doctor's visits, medical equipment, and medical tests, but not routine checkups, other types of preventive care, or prescription drugs. If you enroll, you pay a monthly fee, which covers about 25% of the total cost of the coverage. The government pays the rest with general tax revenues.

WHAT'S NOT COVERED
Medicare is very specific about what it does not cover:

Custodial care, which means help with daily living chores like eating, dressing, bathing or taking medicine.

Experimental drugs or procedures, including medicines or treatments not approved by the Food and Drug Administration (FDA)

Any treatment Medicare doesn't consider reasonable and necessary, whether a hospital or nursing home stay, visits to or from a doctor, or other treatment.

Treatment outside the U.S.

HANDLING THE CLAIMS

Though Medicare is a federal program run by the Health Care Financing Administration (HCFA), your claims aren't handled by a government agency. Instead, they go through the insurance company designated for your state or region. The insurers who process Part A claims are known as **intermediaries**, and those who handle Part B are known as **carriers**.

You can find the name, address and telephone number of the insurance company handling your area on the reports they send you each time you submit a claim. Part B carriers are also listed in **The Medicare Handbook**, which is updated each year and available through Social Security or HCFA.

PAYING FOR MEDICARE

Part A is funded by a payroll withholding tax of 1.45% on the salaries of all working people. Unlike the money that's withheld to fund other Social Security programs, like retirement and disability benefits, there's no cap on the salary that's taxed.

Your monthly premium for Part B coverage—$46.10 a month for 1995, or $553.20 a year—is deducted from your Social Security check, if you get one. Otherwise, you pay the premium directly. Your premium goes up each year at the same rate as the Social Security cost of living adjustment.

Medicare Part A is retroactive, so hospital stays after you turned 65 *might* be covered, even though you applied late. But Part B isn't retroactive at all. Doctors' visits or diagnostic tests aren't covered until your coverage takes effect.

Applying late for Part B has another penalty as well. If you delay more than a year from the time you're eligible, your premium goes up 10%. Every added year adds another 10%.

HOW TO ENROLL

If you start collecting Social Security before you turn 65, you'll get a Medicare enrollment card in the mail. And if you apply for Social Security to begin as you turn 65, you can apply for Medicare at the same time.

But if you're still working, or if you delay in applying for Social Security, you've got to apply for Medicare on your own. And you have to do it within a fairly strict seven-month timeline or risk delays in getting coverage.

The Seven-month Window

3 MONTHS BEFORE

THE MONTH OF YOUR 65TH BIRTHDAY

3 MONTHS AFTER

You can apply up to three months before your 65th birthday. If you do, your coverage begins as soon as you reach 65.

If you enroll in the month you turn 65, coverage begins on the first of the following month.

If you enroll within the next three months, there's a two-month wait. Medicare doesn't cover any of your Part B bills during that period.

If you miss that deadline...

If you miss the deadline, you have to wait until the next general enrollment period—January 1 to March 31 each year—to sign up.

General Enrollment

Jan 1–Mar 31

COVERAGE BEGINS

J F M A M J J A S O N D

For example, if your 65th birthday was in April, 1995 and you hadn't applied by the end of July, you couldn't enroll until January, 1996 and your coverage couldn't begin until July, 1996.

ALWAYS AN EXCEPTION

The rules are different, though, if you're still working at age 65 and have employer-provided insurance. Then you can delay applying for Part B coverage until you need it, and your premium won't be increased. You might find, however, that your employer encourages you to switch to Part B when you first become eligible. In fact, the company might even pick up the cost of the Part B premium, because it would cost less than covering you through the group policy.

What Medicare Covers

With Medicare, everything's spelled out in black and white—except the grey areas.

Medicare Part A
Part A coverage is measured in benefit periods.

SERVICES	BENEFIT
Hospitalization Semi-private room and board, general nursing and other hospital services and supplies	First 60 days
	61st to 90th day
	91st to 150th day†
	Beyond 150 days
Skilled Nursing Facility Care Semi-private room and board, general nursing, skilled nursing and rehabilitative services, and other services and supplies	First 20 days
	Additional 80 days
	Beyond 100 days
Home Health Care Part-time or intermittent skilled care, home health aide services, durable medical equipment and supplies and other services	Unlimited, as long as you meet Medicare conditions
Hospice Care Pain relief, symptom management, and support services for the terminally ill	For as long as doctor certifies need
Blood	Unlimited, if medically necessary

*Rates for 1995

Medicare Part B
Part B coverage works on an annual calendar.

SERVICES	BENEFIT
Medical Expenses Doctors' services, inpatient and outpatient medical and surgical services and supplies, physical and speech therapy, diagnostic services	Unlimited, if medically necessary
Clinical Laboratory Services Blood tests, urinalyses, and more	Unlimited, if medically necessary
Home Health Care Part-time or intermittent skilled care, home health aide services, durable medical equipment and supplies and other services	Unlimited, as long as you meet Medicare conditions
Outpatient Hospital Treatment Services for the diagnosis or treatment of illness or injury	Unlimited, if medically necessary
Blood	Unlimited, if medically necessary

*Rates for 1995

TIME FRAMES

Part B Medicare coverage works on an annual calendar: you pay a year's premium in monthly installments and you are responsible for the annual deductible. After that, Medicare covers its share of whatever approved claims you submit during the year.

Part A coverage is measured in benefit periods. The first one starts the first day you begin to get hospital care, and ends when you've been out of the hospital for 60 consecutive days. The next period begins the next time you enter a hospital, and ends the same way as well. Each time a new benefit period begins, you're

FILING "A" CLAIMS

When you've been in a Medicare-approved hospital or treatment center the claim system can work smoothly. The provider files a claim, gets a check from Medicare, and bills you for the 20% you owe. That's the end of it, as long as Medicare agrees that your treatment is appropriate and should be covered. After a claim is filed, you get a **Notice of Utilization**, which explains what Medicare has paid or not paid. If you have a question you can call the intermediary, or insurance company, whose name and address appear on the form.

In some cases, if Medicare refuses a claim but you had no way of knowing that your treatment wouldn't be covered, you are not legally responsible for paying the bill. That's known as a **limitation liability**.

MEDICARE PAYS*	YOU PAY
All but $716	$716
All but $179 a day	$179 a day
All but $358 a day	$358 a day
Nothing	All costs
100% of approved amount	Nothing
All but $89.50 a day	Up to $89.50 a day
Nothing	All costs
100% of approved amount; 80% of approved amount for durable medical equipment	Nothing for services; 20% of approved amount for durable medical equipment
All but limited costs for outpatient drugs and inpatient respite care	Limited costs for outpatient drugs and inpatient respite care
All but first 3 pints per calendar year	For first 3 pints

MEDICARE PAYS*	YOU PAY
80% of approved amount (after $100 deductible)	$100 deductible, plus 20% of approved amount and limited charges above approved amount
Generally 100% of approved amount	Nothing for services
100% of approved amount; 80% of approved amount for durable medical equipment	Nothing for services; 20% of approved amount for durable medical equipment
Medicare payment to hospital, based on hospital cost	20% of billed amount (after $100 deductible)
80% of approved amount (after $100 deductible and starting with 4th pint)	First 3 pints plus 20% of approved amount for additional pints (after $100 deductible)

FILING "B" CLAIMS

If you visit a participating doctor, the system works the same way as claims under Part A. Non-participating doctors must also file your Medicare claims for you, for free and within one year of the service. But you're billed for their service when you receive treatment, and it can be a long—sometimes very long—time before you receive a Medicare reimbursement check. If you disagree with your carrier's decision on what qualifies for coverage or the amount they will pay, you must choose between filing an appeal or absorbing the uncovered cost.

After your claim is filed, you'll get a response known as an **Explanation of Your Medicare Benefits (EOMB)**. If you question the decision Medicare has made, or the amount that's been approved, you can use the phone number or address on the form to contact the carrier, the insurance company that handles your Part B claims.

responsible for meeting the deductible, but there's no limit on the number of benefit periods you're covered for.

After you've met your Part A deductible, Medicare pays 100% of covered services for the first 60 days you're in the hospital.

† This 60-reserve-days benefit may be used only once in a lifetime.

The Medicare Dictionary

Confusing definitions can cloud Medicare's silver lining.

To understand how Medicare works—especially Part B coverage—you have to be familiar with the language of health insurance. Sometimes the words don't mean what you think they do.

ON ASSIGNMENT

Assignment means that a doctor, lab, or other provider accepts Medicare's approved charges on all eligible claims. The approved charges for these **Medicare participants** are higher than they are for those who don't accept assignment. About 67% of all doctors have signed full participation agreements, or accept assignment in certain cases. But you may have trouble finding one in your community, or one willing to take on new Medicare patients.

Doctors who accept assignment may charge you separately for services that aren't covered by Medicare. But they're not allowed to demand excess charges or any prepayment for services like annual checkups as a condition of accepting you as a patient.

FIGURING ALLOWABLE CHARGES

Since 1992, Medicare has set allowable fees for Medicare Part B based on the time and skill of providing specific services and the costs of practicing in a specific geographical area. Fees to specialists have generally been reduced and those to general practitioners increased.

Critics argue that, on average, about 60% of the charges Medicare allows are unrealistically low. These low allowable charges can cause hardship for people who struggle to pay their share of medical bills. And many doctors feel that they aren't getting enough to cover their costs.

The counter-argument is that Medicare can't afford to pay more, and that the current level of coverage allows people to get the medical treatment they need. It seems likely, though, that the current repayment system is one of the things about Medicare that will be revamped in the next few years, as the government continues to struggle with health care issues.

WHAT MEDICARE PAYS FOR PART B CLAIMS

Assuming you receive a total doctor's bill of $157

Approved, or allowable charges are what Medicare sets as the amount it will cover for a medical service. However, the amount is usually less than the bill you have paid. Here it's $137.14 of a $157 bill, or **total charge**.

A **deductible** is the amount you have to pay for approved medical bills before Medicare begins to pay its share. The Medicare deductible for Part B in 1994 was $100, and you pay it once a year, regardless of the number and type of services you receive. In this case, the deductible is subtracted from the approved charge. **YOU PAY**

Your 20%, or the **co-payment**, is the part of an allowable charge which you are responsible for paying yourself. Here it's $7.43, or 20% of the approved charge after subtracting the deductible. **YOU PAY**

Medicare pays 80% of the approved charge. In this case Medicare's share is $29.71.

MEDICARE PAYS

Excess charges are amounts above approved charges that a doctor, laboratory, or other medical provider charges. The practice is also known as **balance billing**. You are responsible for those excess charges, up to the payment limits the government sets. For example, in 1994 doctors could charge up to 115% of the allowable charge on most covered services. If you are billed for more than this **limiting charge**, you're not legally responsible for the amount over the limit. In this case though, the excess is within the 115% limit—by 71¢.

HERE'S THE RUB

Although the rules that limit permissible charges are clear, you can end up paying more. That's true in part because of how the system works: you pay first and are then reimbursed by Medicare. In most cases that's when you find out how much the allowable charge is. And it's your responsibility to try to get back the extra amount you paid, either directly from the doctor or with the insurance carrier's help. Medicare tells you how much the excess is, but so far it hasn't gone after doctors who overcharge.

You may also feel strongly enough about continuing your relationship with your doctor to pay the charges despite what you get back from Medicare.

MORE LANGUAGE

In Medicare's vocabulary, a decision is known as a **determination**. If you appeal, you get a **reconsideration determination**.

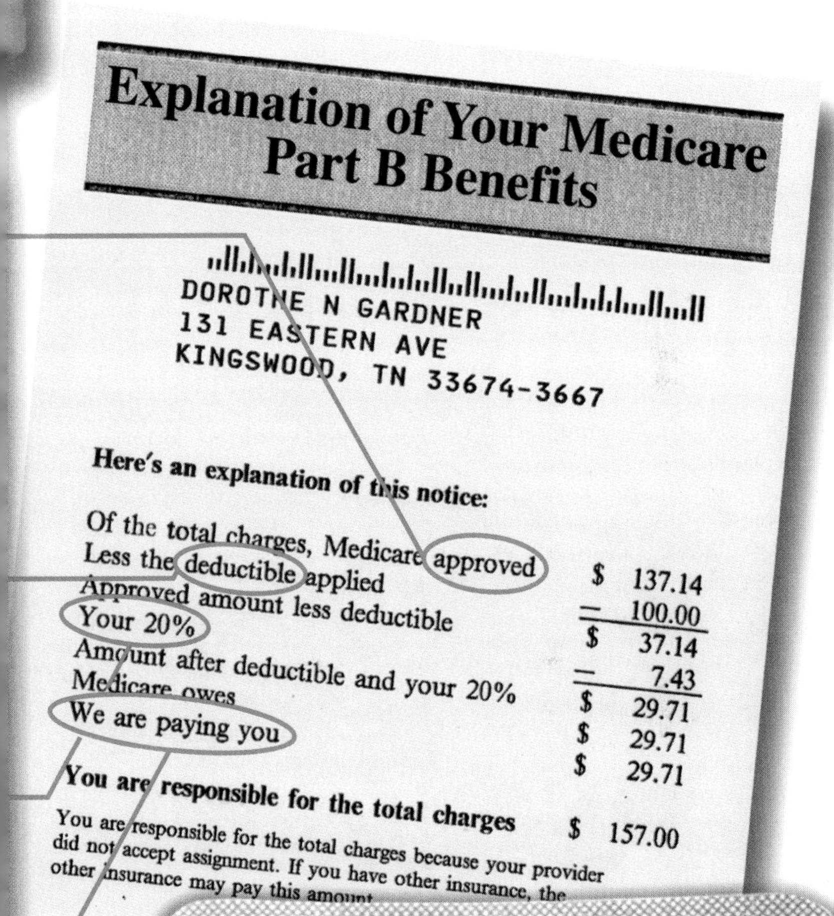

Explanation of Your Medicare Part B Benefits

DOROTHE N GARDNER
131 EASTERN AVE
KINGSWOOD, TN 33674-3667

Here's an explanation of this notice:

Of the total charges, Medicare approved	$ 137.14
Less the deductible applied	− 100.00
Approved amount less deductible	$ 37.14
Your 20%	− 7.43
Amount after deductible and your 20%	$ 29.71
Medicare owes	$ 29.71
We are paying you	$ 29.71

You are responsible for the total charges $ 157.00

You are responsible for the total charges because your provider did not accept assignment. If you have other insurance, the other insurance may pay this amount.

GENERAL

The flu s
remember

LOSING MEDICARE COVERAGE

In most cases, you don't have to worry about getting Medicare coverage, or about losing it. If you are eligible for Medicare Part A based on your work record, it's good for life. But if you're eligible based on your spouse's work record, you do lose your coverage if you divorce before you've been married for at least ten years.

The only way you can lose your Medicare Part B insurance is by cancelling your coverage or not paying your premium. If you're paying for Part A coverage yourself, you must also buy Part B—and if you cancel B, you lose A. Getting cancelled coverage renewed means waiting until the next general enrollment period and probably paying a higher premium.

The System at Work

The problem with Medicare is that it's tough to keep the lid on and the fire burning at the same time.

Controlling costs and controlling the quality of care sometimes get mixed together in Medicare's efforts to serve its constituents. While no public official seriously advocates ending the program, almost no one is content with the way it's working. In addition to what it costs, there's a major disagreement on the extent to which Medicare is managed—some would say dictated—by review boards, insurance companies, and government overseers.

On the plus side, Medicare maintains state-by-state counselling and assistance programs that answer questions, explain benefits and limitations, and help with bills and claims.

R E V I E W
GOVERNMENT
INSURANCE

A JURY OF THEIR PEERS

Peer Review Organizations (PROs) in each state review the quality and type of care that's provided to Medicare patients in hospitals, outpatient clinics, and some HMOs. These groups of doctors and other health care workers, who are paid by the federal government to participate on the boards, approve or deny payment for various services, and serve as the review panel for beneficiary complaints about the quality of care.

PRICE-FIXING

Medicare sets the price it will pay a participating hospital for your care during a specific stay, and by law the hospital must accept that payment, whatever it costs to treat you. While this **prospective payment system (PPS)** should not affect the length of your stay or the level of care you get, some critics charge that certain hospitals tailor your care to the amount they know they will receive when you check out.

THE FIRST CARD

Harry S. Truman carried Medicare identity card #1. As President, he led the fight for government health insurance to complement the protection Social Security provided for older people. Getting it passed took almost 20 years.

THE ODDS ARE...

The government estimates that 89% of all Medicare Part B claims are reduced or denied. But when those claims are appealed, the initial decision is overturned, at least in part, 76% of the time. The most telling statistic, though, is that only 2% to 3% of all Medicare beneficiaries do appeal, despite the fact that the odds are very clearly in their favor. Since there's nothing to lose but time, and maybe your patience, it may be that the complexity of the process, or the seeming futility of appealing to the people who turned you down in the first place, explains why so few people exercise their right.

LEGAL PROTECTIONS

In addition to the internal appeals process in place with Medicare, you have access to federal courts. You can also sue private insurers. Remember, though, that these actions mean you'll have to use—and pay—a lawyer. And they often take several years to resolve. On the other hand, the insurance company is hoping you'll run out of energy or money, and drop the case.

The law generally protects you against a policy's unclear language, especially if you could reasonably have interpreted what it says to mean you were covered. And you have a good chance of winning if the only problem with your claim is that you filed late.

BOARDS

OVERSEERS

COMPANIES

APPEALING DECISIONS

Once you get an official response from your Medicare insurance intermediary or carrier—a Notice of Utilization or Explanation of Benefits—you can file an appeal. Generally speaking, all appeals begin by asking the initial decision maker to reconsider. Instructions on the steps you should follow are included with the notice. Or you can get help through your Social Security office, which will file an appeal for you.

If you're appealing a decision denying in-hospital treatment or hospital admission, you appeal to the Peer Review Organization (PRO) in your state. You have up to 60 days from the day you get the official notification that you've been turned down.

If the situation is more urgent, and you want the PRO to reverse a hospital's decision not to admit you, you can request a speedy review if you file within three days. If you aren't satisfied with what the PRO decides on review, you may be able to take your case to Federal Court, though you'll need to use an attorney at that point.

Part A appeals, for nursing home, home care and hospice claims, go to the Medicare intermediary (insurance company) for your state. Here, too, you have 60 days to ask for a review and the right to carry your appeal to higher levels.

You appeal Part B decisions within six months to the Medicare carrier (insurance company) that processed your claim initially. If they reject your appeal, you have the right to take the case to a hearing officer and ultimately to an Administrative Law Judge or Federal Court, depending on the dollar amount under dispute.

Bridging the Gap

You need supplemental insurance to bridge the gaps in your Medicare coverage.

There is a way to stop a flood of hospital and medical expenses from wiping you out financially. What 80% of all Medicare recipients do is buy supplemental protection, either through **Medigap** insurance or participation in a managed care plan.

Unless you're eligible for Medicaid (see page 172), there's probably little question about whether you need Medigap coverage or not. *You do.* But to get the best protection, you have to be clear about what Medicare covers, and you have to make some assessments of your own health care needs.

The ABCs

The major provisions of each option are spelled out in the chart below. Every insurer must

NOT ONE PLAN, BUT TEN

Medigap insurance isn't a one-size-fits-all solution. There are actually ten different standard plans, labeled A through J, that are sold as Medicare supplements.

Since each state decides how many of the different plans can be sold to its residents, you may not be able to choose from the full range. But where they're sold, all A plans are alike in the coverage they provide. So are all Bs, Cs, and so on, right down the line. That includes the way the policy looks, the words it uses, and what those words mean. The only differences are the cost of the coverage among insurers and the efficiency with which they resolve claims.

BASIC BENEFITS
Part A Hospital (Days 61–90)
Lifetime Reserve Days (91–150)
365 Life Hospital Days—100%
Parts A and B Blood
Part B Coinsurance—20%

OPTIONAL BENEFITS*
Skilled Nursing Facility Coinsurance (Days 21–100)
Part A Deductible
Part B Deductible
Part B Excess Charges
Foreign Travel Emergency
At-home Recovery
Prescription Drugs
Preventive Medical Care

*Most benefits have payment ceilings.

THE TIME TO BUY

The time to buy Medigap insurance is within the first six months after you begin coverage under Medicare Part B. During that period, insurance companies *must* sell you the policy you want. That's particularly important if you have any health problems that put you into a high-risk category—including being overweight.

If you have a known health problem, or **pre-existing condition**, the insurer can refuse to cover treatment for that ailment for the first six months. But if you miss the initial six-month application period, the company can turn you down for coverage altogether.

If you need an added incentive to buy Medigap insurance as soon as you're eligible, keep in mind that insurers also have the right to charge higher premiums to people who delay applying.

of Medigap Plans

show you a comparison like this as part of the sales pitch and give you a copy of the prices for each plan. Agents who don't provide this information are breaking the law.

Plan A	Plan B	Plan C	Plan D	Plan E	Plan F	Plan G	Plan H	Plan I	Plan J
All Medigap plans provide the same basic coverage, picking up your share of approved amounts for doctors' services, long hospital stays, and the first three pints of blood.									

Plan A	Plan B	Plan C	Plan D	Plan E	Plan F	Plan G	Plan H	Plan I	Plan J
		✓	✓	✓	✓	✓	✓	✓	✓
	✓	✓	✓	✓	✓	✓	✓	✓	✓
		✓			✓				
					100%	80%		100%	100%
	✓	✓	✓	✓	✓	✓	✓	✓	✓
			✓			✓		✓	✓
							✓	✓	✓
					✓				
									✓

THE CORE

Plan A is the **core package**, or basic coverage, and it's available everywhere. In fact, any company that sells Medigap insurance must offer Plan A. It covers Medicare Part A coinsurance for hospitalizations longer than 60 days, Part B coinsurance, and the first three pints of blood you need under either Medicare A or B in any year, unless they're covered by the federal government through some other plan. (Coinsurance is another word for co-payment.)

Shopping for Protection

Since comparison shopping for supplemental plans has been streamlined, there's no excuse for cutting corners.

Medigap plans are designed to supplement and complement the government's insurance plans and make choosing among them easy. However, some may offer extras that the legislation creating the plans allows but does not require.

So you have the curious task of deciding among standardized plans that may not be absolutely standard. In addition, a zealous agent may want to sell you one plan rather than another, and may slant the information that's provided.

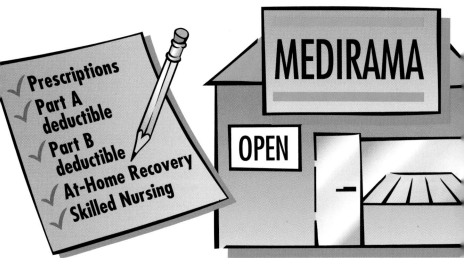

Buy What You Need

First, ask yourself what coverage you need. For example, though you might be tempted by a policy that covers excess doctor charges, it's smart to compare the added cost of that coverage with the benefits you'll get. Since doctors' charges above the allowed limit are now illegal, you may spend more for the coverage than you'll ever collect in benefits.

Or, if you're spending less than the typical $500 a year for prescription drugs, coverage that adds hundreds of dollars to your premium, requires a 50% co-payment for each prescription, and sets benefit limits may not make sense.

CINDERELLA PLANS
Most employee health plans turn into Medigap plans after you retire, rather than continuing to provide the kind of coverage you had while you were working. That means you don't have to buy your own Medigap insurance, but you do have to enroll in Medicare B to get basic coverage. Other employers tell you to find your own Medigap plan, and provide money to pay the premium.

Comparison Shop

Next, request prices on three or four different plans, including the one your employer offers. It pays to check out one from a big group like AARP (American Association of Retired Persons) or your union or professional association, one from the Blue Cross/Blue Shield or other not-for-profit insurer in your state, and an individual plan suggested by your insurance agent.

Generally speaking, buying Medigap insurance through a group is cheaper than buying as an individual, especially if your employer pays a big chunk of the cost. But you have to be careful. For example, individual policies you buy from your employer's group insurer often cost more than the group plan and provide inferior coverage.

ALTERNATIVES TO MEDIGAP

Strictly defined, Medigap coverage is standardized insurance that supplements Medicare benefits. But there are a number of alternatives to Medigap insurance that provide similar health care protection.

- Medicare SELECT, available through 1994 on a trial basis in 15 states, provides Medigap coverage but restricts policyholders to using specific doctors and hospitals. If you get medical treatment elsewhere, the plan may not pay some or all of your expenses. Some insurers and HMOs offer the policies, generally at lower rates than conventional Medigap policies.

- Three states, Minnesota, Massachusetts, and Wisconsin, have their own benefit plans regulated by each state's insurance department.

- Some HMOs and other managed health care plans (see page 152) sell Medigap-type plans in addition to their regular plan, to serve people who aren't full HMO members.

- You may also purchase long-term care insurance (see page 168) either through your employer's plan or from another insurer.

Avoid Duplication

Avoid buying insurance that duplicates or overlaps coverage you already have. If you have an older policy and can switch, you're better off with one policy that includes all the coverage you want rather than keeping track of two or more plans that combined provide full coverage but duplicate the basics.

Cheap Now? Still Cheap Later?

Look ahead. Cheap today is not necessarily cheap tomorrow. Though all insurance plans sold currently must be **guaranteed renewable** if you make your payments on time, there is no restriction on price increases. Some companies quote artificially low initial prices to get your business, and then raise prices substantially over time.

GETTING HELP

You can get free advice on your insurance options and answers to your Medigap questions through your state's insurance counselling office. You can find their number in your telephone book or in the HCFA's **Guide to Health Insurance for People with Medicare**, which is available from your local Social Security office.

You might also check with the agency in your state that coordinates information and services for older residents, such as the Offices or Departments of Aging, Elder Affairs, or Adult Services. The numbers are available in the **Guide to Health Insurance**, in the telephone book, and from advocacy groups like the United Seniors Health Cooperative. Remember that each state's insurance rules are a little different, so if you move after you retire, you may need to revise your coverage.

Putting Medigap to Work

You can help Medigap work for you by following some basic record-keeping and filing rules.

The whole point of Medigap insurance, of course, is for your policy to pay your medical expenses. When things work right, that's what happens—with a minimum of paperwork and within a reasonable amount of time.

But, quality of service, as well as the cost of coverage, are also important.

And while it's harder to check insurers' reputations for settling claims than it is to compare their prices, you can get information on the performance of different insurers from your state's offices of insurance, advocacy groups like AARP, and articles in The Wall Street Journal.

SIMPLE AS ONE, TWO, THREE

Keep accurate records

File all forms, or make sure they're filed for you

KEEPING RECORDS

Things go wrong with Medigap claims, just as they do in all dealings with health insurers. That means it's critical to keep accurate records of all your payments, reports, claims, and other communications from the time you visit a doctor or hospital until everything is resolved to your satisfaction.

If your claim gets lost or if you want to appeal any decisions, you must have copies of all the paperwork. If you get a bill in duplicate or triplicate, you can send one in and keep the rest. But never submit your only copy. Make a photocopy, or two, file them in an accessible place, and keep checking the status of your claims.

It's often difficult, if not impossible, to get replacement copies of the information you need.

FILING CLAIMS

After you've had medical treatment and received the Explanation of Medical Benefits (EOMB) from your Medicare B carrier, or the Notice of Utilization from your Medicare A intermediary, you send a copy—plus a copy of the the the doctor's treatment statement or comparable document—to your Medigap insurer to request payment. Even when your doctor accepts payment directly from Medicare, you follow this process to collect the 20% co-payment you've made.

While the process itself is relatively simple, it's sometimes slow because nothing starts until your doctor files the claim. In a typical case, the repayment process takes about a month.

The delay matters less if you haven't had to pay for your share of the medical care at the time it was given. Then any delay in filing affects only the doctor's cash flow. But if you have to pay for your visit on the spot, as is usually the case, you're out the money until your claim is settled.

PLAYING BY THE RULES

One thing you never want to do is get caught without adequate medical insurance because you missed some detail or deadline. Here's a checklist of potential problems to avoid:

☑ If you change your coverage, never drop your old policy until your new one becomes effective. You might end up without insurance

Don't get caught without adequate insurance

☑ If your spouse's health plan covers you, or the other way around, be sure you know what will happen when one of you turns 65, retires, or both. Since Medicare and Medigap policies cover individuals, but not their spouses, one of you could be left without coverage.

☑ Employer sponsored plans aren't regulated and don't necessarily offer the same coverage as a Medigap plan. They may pay for more services, or fewer.

☑ Ask if prices are based on **community rates** or **attained age**. With the former, all policy holders pay the same price, but with attained age pricing, you pay more for coverage as you get older. That could mean you wouldn't be able to afford the cost of coverage when you needed it most.

☑ No plans are government sponsored; any insurer making that claim may be misleading you in other ways as well.

LOSS RATIOS

Another way that the government tries to protect people who buy Medigap insurance is to police each insurance company's **loss ratio**. That's the annual amount paid out in claims divided by the premiums collected. For example, insurers who paid out 50¢ for every $1 collected would have a 1 to 2, or 50%, loss ratio. And they'd be in trouble, because the law says that any company selling individual policies must pay out 65¢ per $1 and anyone selling group policies must pay out 75¢. Otherwise, the insurer has to pay a refund or give a credit to its clients.

GETTING HELP

There are times when it's Medicare's obligation to file your claim directly with your Medigap carrier, by putting your Medigap policy number on the Medicare claim form. That happens when:

- **Your doctor or other health care provider accepts payment directly from Medicare, and**

- **You have a Medigap policy, and**

- **You say that you want to have your insurer pay the benefit directly to the provider rather than to you.**

If your insurer offers **automatic claims handling**, you should probably take advantage of it. The company gets copies of the reporting forms directly from Medicare and pays you their share of the bill. You don't have to deal with the paperwork yourself.

WHAT YOU DON'T KNOW

The old adage is wrong. When it comes to health care, what you don't know can hurt you, financially at least. Here's one example. The law says that a nursing home can not demand, or even request, a deposit—the equivalent of prepayment—as a condition of being admitted. It doesn't matter what they call the money—security deposit, co-payment, whatever. They aren't supposed to do it.

In fact, however, requests—even demands—for payments are frequently made, in amounts ranging from a few hundred dollars to $2,500 or more. If you're not sure of the law, if you're under a lot of stress, or if you're afraid that if you refuse the home will not accept the patient, you may pay the illegal charge.

Long-term Care Insurance

The jury is still out on the merits of buying insurance to cover long-term care.

The longer you live, the greater the risk that you'll need long-term health care, either at home or in a nursing home.

That kind of care can be an expensive proposition, often costing $100 a day or more. Unless you're getting hospice care because you're terminally ill, or qualify for Medicaid, those bills are usually your responsibility. One solution may be to shift the financial burden to an insurance company that will cover long-term care.

TWO PERSPECTIVES

There are two schools of thought on long-term care insurance. Advocates praise it as the wave of the future, an extension of the protection that Medigap insurance now provides. Though the coverage can be costly, it can more than pay for itself if you need it. For example, it might cost you $20,000 for insurance over ten years, but a year in a nursing home could easily run to $40,000 or more.

Critics attack the policies for their expense, their payout restrictions and their coverage limitations. Not all policies, for example, cover degenerative conditions like Alzheimer's, although people suffering from it are very likely to need extended care. And if you've ever been treated for a medical problem that may recur or can be linked to future illness, you probably won't be able to buy coverage even if you want it.

As this fast-growing segment of the insurance industry matures, the policies are also improving. And, in all likelihood, increasing regulation will also weed out some of the worst problems. So this may be one area where delay pays, especially if you're in generally good health.

THE LONG-TERM MARKET

Sales of long-term care policies now top $1 billion a year, though they've been on the market only about 15 years. That astounding growth aside, only 1% of the population is covered for long-term care, and only 5% of those who are 65 or older.

THE TIME TO BUY

If you decide that long-term care insurance makes sense for you, the next question is when you should buy it. Unfortunately, there's no right answer. As with other kinds of insurance, the older you are when you buy a policy, the more you pay—about twice as much at age 60 as at age 50, and nearly ten times as much at age 75. Most plans won't sell you a policy after you reach age 80, though you can continue to be covered under one you bought earlier.

Since the rates are set when you buy, under many plans you'll spend less for 30 years of coverage starting at age 50 than you would for 20 years of coverage starting at 60, or for 10 years of coverage starting at 70. However, that's before you add in the inflation protection you'd have to pay for if you bought a plan early on.

Experts generally agree that the best time frame for buying a policy is between 60 and 65—before it gets astronomically expensive, but somewhat closer to the time when you're more likely to need the protection it provides.

Like other kinds of insurance, long-term care protection

you can buy through your employer will probably be cheaper and often better than any coverage you can buy on your own.

THE INFLATION ISSUE

One of the most troublesome unknowns in health care is what it will cost tomorrow, next year and 20 years from now. Judging from the past, the outlook isn't very encouraging, since health care costs have increased much faster than the rate of inflation. Anticipating costs is especially important with a long-term care policy, since you're buying coverage for the future.

Unless an insurance company promises to pay whatever your health care costs will

be—and no long-term policy now on the market does that—the only way to ensure that your coverage will be adequate is to get inflation protection. That can be provided in two ways, either with built-in benefit increases pegged to the real cost of care, or by allowing you to buy supplemental insurance in the future to compensate for increased costs.

Although the built-in increases can raise the cost of your insurance significantly, perhaps as much as 25% to 50%, it's better protection for you in the long run, in part because you know the cost of the coverage up front. However, most plans that provide inflation protection offer the second option, making no promises about what the added insurance will cost you. Chances are it will be a lot, especially if you're relatively young when you buy the initial policy.

TRY SELF-INSURANCE

Some experts suggest that self-insurance might make more sense than paying for long-term care insurance. They maintain that if you started investing the money that you would pay in premiums early enough, you would build a significant protective cushion that could be used for other things if it turned out you never needed long-term care.

The Limits of Coverage

Long-term care policies have their limitations. Knowing them now saves problems later.

In deciding whether or not to buy long-term care insurance, you should investigate not only the quality of the coverage, but the quality of the company providing it.

It's frustrating to try to collect on an insurance policy only to discover that something you thought was covered actually isn't. And it's devastating to find out after years of paying your premiums that your insurer isn't around to make good on your claims.

! BUYER BEWARE

Don't let an agent who's trying to sell you a policy convince you that you can be less than candid in answering questions about your medical history. And be sure that the agent writes down everything you report. If your claim is denied or your policy revoked at some future date, the agent (with a handsome commission) isn't responsible. You are.

COVERAGE TRAPS

Since long-term care plans aren't regulated the way Medigap plans are, it's up to you to find out what's covered. Here are some of the questions you ought to ask:

- Does the policy cover only nursing home care, only home care, or both? Generally, the more comprehensive the coverage, the better.

- Are you covered if you move into a nursing home directly from your own home rather than from a hospital? Not all moves to a nursing home are medically necessary. Be sure they're covered.

- Does the policy cover custodial care, or help with tasks like eating and bathing, as well as skilled nursing care? If not, it may be replicating your Medicare coverage rather than supplementing it.

- Does it cover disabling diseases like Alzheimer's as well as medical problems? It should. That may well be the protection you need.

- Does the coverage provide inflation protection? Twenty years from now, the $80 a day some plans agree to pay won't begin to cover your bills.

- Is there an exclusion period— a period of no coverage—for pre-existing conditions? If so, it shouldn't be longer than six months.

- What is the waiting period? If you buy a policy that doesn't begin to pay until you've been in a nursing home for an extended period, it will cost you less. You're gambling the potential for higher out-of-pocket expenses against the hope you won't need long-term care.

THE DAILY BENEFIT

One choice you'll have to make is how much protection to buy. You do that by choosing the dollar amount per day that your insurance will pay during the period you're receiving care. Usually you can choose among two or three levels, typically $80, $100, and $120. Obviously, the greater the coverage, the higher the monthly cost to you.

No plan will pay more than your actual expense, no matter what level of coverage you're paying for. And what you can't figure, of course, is what the actual expenses will be at that time in the future when you begin to collect. You may be able to get some guidance from your employer's personnel office, or from your state's insurance office. But, finally, what you'll have to do is balance what you think you'll need with what you are willing (or can afford) to pay for the insurance.

POST-CLAIMS UNDERWRITING

Sometimes an insurer will sell you a policy, but revoke it after you file a claim. This after-the-fact rejection is known as **post-claims underwriting**.

Companies have, on average, a two-year period from the date your policy was issued to contest your eligibility and cancel your coverage. That right hinges on whether or not you were honest in what you told them when you applied. For example, if you file a claim after a hip operation, but haven't mentioned a skiing accident in which you injured it, they can cancel your policy.

Neglecting to tell the whole story is grounds enough for cancelling your policy during the right-to-cancel period. And if the company can prove fraud—a deliberate omission or misstatement—they can cancel at any time.

One clue that might alert you to a company that does a lot of post-claims underwriting—and does it successfully—

is how easy it is to get a policy. An agent who can promise you speedy coverage may well work for a firm that counts on weeding you out in the future.

CONSUMER PROTECTIONS

You should be sure that any policy you are considering provides for a **waiver of premium**. The waiver means that you can stop paying your premiums during a period in which the company is paying you benefits. However, even with a waiver there may be a waiting period when you're both paying and receiving.

If you buy a policy through your employer, check to see if it has a **non-forfeiture clause**, which means that you don't lose the equity you've built up in your policy if you stop paying the premium, or die without ever making a claim. This protection could mean you were eligible for partial coverage or that you or your heirs get some of your money back. It may be harder to find this protection in an individual policy.

DEFINING WHAT'S NECESSARY

Long-term care insurers are notoriously nitpicky about what qualifies for coverage and which nursing homes or other places are eligible facilities. The real problem is that many of the decisions are subjective, because the definitions in the policy are vague—like what constitutes a medically necessary treatment. Or, worse, a company may attempt to reduce loss by making the claims experience very unpleasant. Often the only way to fight back is to take the case to court, but that's expensive and time-consuming.

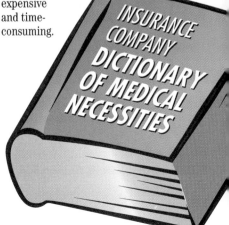

Medicaid

Medicaid pays just slightly less that 50% of all nursing home costs nationwide.

Like other government programs designed to provide medical care for older Americans, Medicaid is a lifesaver. But it is enormously expensive and extremely controversial.

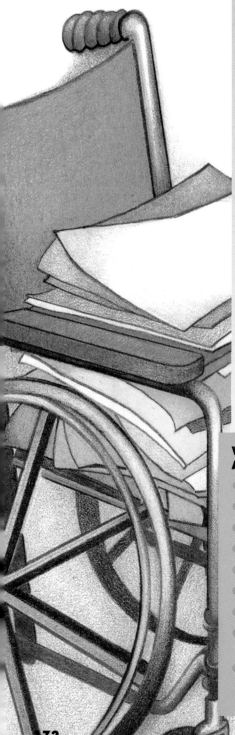

WHO IS IT INTENDED FOR?

Medicaid, a federally-sponsored, state-run insurance program that provides health care for low-income people with few assets, takes over when people are unable to pay their nursing home bills.

WHEN YOU NEED HELP

If you need **skilled nursing care** in an approved nursing home following a hospital stay, Medicare will cover the entire bill for 20 days, and part of it for another 80. Beyond that, there's no coverage from either Medicare or your Medigap policy. If you don't need skilled care, or if you go into a nursing home directly from your own home, neither Medicare nor Medigap covers any of the cost. It's the patients themselves who are responsible for paying the nursing home, or turning to Medicaid for assistance.

Since some facilities aren't eager to accept Medicaid patients, being able to pay for your care initially can mean you'll be able to get into a better-run establishment. Once you're in, they can't evict you when Medicaid takes over payment. But you have to be careful, though, to choose a place that meets Medicaid's standards, or what's generally known as an **eligible facility**. Otherwise, Medicaid won't pay.

WHAT TO LOOK FOR IN ADULT DAY CARE

- Written policies on fees and emergency procedures
- Written, up-to-date plan of care for each participant
- Planned menus and meals for special diets
- Daily, planned communication with care-givers
- Referrals provided to other needed services
- Active, involved staff trained in CPR and first aid
- Warm inviting atmosphere
- Adequate space, furniture, and equipment, indoors and out
- A variety of appealing activities

GETTING IT BACK

Your state government has the right to try to collect the money it spent for your care from you or from your estate after you die. For example, that might mean your home would have to be sold if it were no longer your or your spouse's primary residence.

Another joint owner, even a child, might be considered ineligible to keep it. No one knows how vigorously various state governments will go after your resources, even the ones you've given away. Your best bet is to get solid advice before you move ahead with a spend-down plan.

WHO USES IT?

Each state establishes its own criteria that people must meet to qualify for Medicaid assistance.

WHO QUALIFIES?

In most cases, you can hold onto a small amount of what you've saved or invested over the years, plus your home and personal possessions. If you're married, your spouse can keep some of your joint resources so that he or she isn't impoverished by your health needs.

That amount is set by each state and differs widely from state to state.

When you've **spent down** your assets by paying long- term care bills, Medicaid picks up the tab. You turn over all your income, like Social Security or pension checks, directly to the nursing home (except a small amount for personal expenses). Medicaid pays the balance directly to the home.

Neither your children or other relatives are responsible for paying nursing home bills if you qualify in your own right for Medicaid assistance.

MEDICAID AT HOME

If you're eligible, and you don't need medical care, Medicaid may pay the costs of attending a adult day care center, including the cost of transportation, so that you can continue to live at home. You may also be eligible to have a home-care worker visit you to help with the details of daily living, like bathing, taking medication, or receiving therapy.

If Medicaid pays for day care rather than for nursing home care—at less than half the annual cost—you're also entitled to keep more of your Social Security income. As long as your assets—like banks accounts—are small enough to qualify for assistance, you can keep income up to the official poverty level, about $7,000 in 1994. The amount is adjusted annually for inflation.

WHO CAN'T USE IT?

It's increasingly difficult for middle-income people to qualify for Medicaid before using up their assets on nursing home costs.

SPENDING DOWN ARTIFICIALLY

People who anticipate lengthy nursing home stays because they have Alzheimer's or some physically debilitating disease can take some steps to speed up their qualification for Medicaid. The motive, almost always, is to preserve some of their financial assets for their children or other heirs, rather than spending all of their money on nursing home care.

For example, you can use your money to buy a home, which you're allowed to keep if it's your primary residence. Or you can transfer property to friends or relatives, either directly or by setting up an irrevocable trust (see page 141). However, recent changes in the law have tightened up on these transfers, in part by extending what's known as the **look-back period**—the amount of time that must elapse between the date of the gift or establishment of the trust and the date you become eligible for Medicaid. In 1994, the look-back period was 36 months.

44% of all Americans age 65 and older spend some time in a nursing home.

Finding Information

Asking the right questions in the right places can save you time and money, and help you avoid costly mistakes.

You can save yourself aggravation—and worse—by learning from other people's experiences. Whether your question is how to get the best prices on prescription drugs, or what your legal options are if you're the victim of age discrimination, you can usually find an answer. There are federal and local government agencies, plus hundreds of private organizations, operating primarily for the benefit of older Americans. Every state, for example, has an office or department of aging and another for insurance. You can find those addresses and telephone on the following pages. In addition, Social Security provides information and assistance on a variety of issues. You can contact your local office, or call 800-772-1213.

The following list just scratches the surface, but it can give you an idea of the kinds of organizations you can contact, and the range of information available for advice and information. In some cases, membership in an organization provides ongoing advantages and services.

American Association of Homes and Services for the Aging
901 E St., NW, Suite 500
Washington, DC 20004
202-783-2242

Organization of nursing homes, continuing care facilities, community service organizations and independent housing. Provides information on retirement housing.

American Association of Retired Persons
(AARP)
601 E St., NW
Washington, DC 20049
800-424-3410, or 202-434-2277

Nonprofit group providing an extensive array of services and programs for members; also sells insurance, investments, prescription drugs.

Administration on Aging
330 Independence Ave., SW
Washington, DC 20201
202-619-0724

Federal agency, part of Department of Health and Human Services.

Children of Aging Parents
1609 Woodbourne Rd., Suite 302A
Levittown, PA 19057-1511
215-345-5104

Acts as a clearinghouse for information about caring for the elderly and provides contacts for support groups for adult children.

Choices in Dying
200 Varick St.
New York, NY 10014
212-366-5540

Provides information on living wills, health care proxies and other issues.

Equal Employment Opportunity Commission
1801 L St., NW
Washington, DC 20507
202-663-4264

Grey Panthers
2025 Pennsylvania Ave., NW, Suite 821
Washington, DC 20006
202-466-3132

Activist organization addresses issues of health care, age discrimination and problems of the disabled.

Legal Counsel for the Elderly
601 E St., NW, Bldg. A, Floor 4
Washington, DC 20049
202-234-0970

AARP-sponsored support center provides free advice and information on legal issues, plus annual publications.

Legal Services for the Elderly

130 West 42nd St., 17th floor
New York, NY 10036
212-391-0120

An advisory center for lawyers specializing in senior citizens' legal problems; also produces a number of related publications.

National Academy of Elder Law Attorneys

1604 North Country Club Rd.
Tucson, AZ 85716
602-881-4005

Lawyers' association provides referrals for help with estate planning, Medicaid planning and other legal matters.

National Alliance of Senior Citizens

1700 18th St., Suite 401
Washington, DC 20009
202-986-0117

Nonprofit lobbying group concerned with pension, health care and Social Security issues. Provides a wide range of services to members.

National Association of Area Agencies on Aging

1112 16th St., NW, Suite 100
Washington, DC 20036
800-677-1116

"Eldercare Locator" provides information on services for the elderly available in your area.

National Association of Professional Geriatric Managers

1604 North Country Club Rd.
Tucson, AZ 85716
602-881-8008

Provides information on private care managers in all parts of the country.

National Council on the Aging

409 Third St., SW, Suite 200
Washington, DC 20024
202-479-1200

Nonprofit organization provides an information and consultation center, sponsors conferences and publishes a range of materials.

National Council of Senior Citizens

1331 F St., NW
Washington, DC 20004
202-347-8800

Nonprofit lobbying group provides a job-assistance program, plus a benefits package for members.

National Senior Citizens Law Center

1815 H St., NW, Suite 700
Washington, DC 20006
202-887-5280

Public interest law firm specializes in senior citizens' legal problems, including disputes with Social Security.

Older Women's League

666 11th St., NW, Suite 700
Washington, DC 20001
202-783-6686

Advocacy organization focusing on job discrimination, housing, health care, Social Security and other issues affecting women.

Pension Rights Center

918 16th St., Suite 704
Washington, DC 20006
202-296-3776

Provides advice, information and publications on pensions and pension-related issues.

Right Choice, Inc.

151 Woodland Rd., Suite 4
South Hamilton, MA 01982
800-872-2294

Provides an analysis of how your cash flow would be affected by moving from your present home to another location.

United Seniors Health Cooperative

1331 H St., NW, Suite 500
Washington, DC 20005
202-393-6222

Provides an analysis of Medigap policies to help you make the best choice.

Directory of State Agencies

You can get information—and help—from state agencies and departments.

Insurance Counseling	Insurance Department	Agency on Aging
ALABAMA 800-243-5463	Insurance Department Consumer Service Division 135 South Union St. P.O. Box 303351 Montgomery, AL 36130-3351 205-269-3550	Commission on Aging 770 Washington Ave., Suite 470 Montgomery, AL 36130 P.O. Box 301851 800-243-5463 205-242-5743
ALASKA 800-478-6065 907-562-7249	Division of Insurance 800 E. Dimond, Suite 560 Anchorage, AK 99515 907-349-1230	Older Alaskans Commission P.O. Box 110209 Juneau, AK 99811-0209 907-465-3250
ARIZONA 800-432-4040	Insurance Department Consumer Affairs Division 2910 N. 44th St. Phoenix, AZ 85018 602-912-8440	Dept. of Economic Security Aging & Adult Administration 1789 W. Jefferson St. Phoenix, AZ 85007 602-542-4446
ARKANSAS 800-852-5494 501-686-2940	Insurance Department Seniors Insurance Network 1123 S. University Ave. 400 University Tower Bldg. Little Rock, AR 72204-1699 800-852-5494 501-686-2940	Division of Aging and Adult Services 1417 Donaghey Plaza South P.O. Box 1437/Slot 1412 Little Rock, AR 72203-1437 501-682-2441
CALIFORNIA 800-927-4357 916-323-7315	Insurance Department Consumer Services Div. Ronald Reagan Building 300 S. Spring St. Los Angeles, CA 90013 213-346-6500	Department of Aging 1600 K St. Sacramento, CA 95814 916-322-3887
COLORADO 303-894-7499, ext. 356	Insurance Division 1560 Broadway Suite 850 Denver, CO 80202 303-894-7499, ext. 356	Aging and Adult Services Department of Social Services 1575 Sherman St., 4th Fl. Denver, CO 80203-1714 303-866-3851
CONNECTICUT 800-443-9946	Insurance Department P.O. Box 816 Hartford, CT 06142-0816 203-297-3802	Elderly Services Division 175 Main St. Hartford, CT 06106 800-443-9946 203-566-7772
DELAWARE 800-336-9500	Insurance Department Rodney Building 841 Silver Lake Blvd. Dover, DE 19901 800-282-8611 302-739-4251	Division of Aging Dept. of Health & Social Services 1901 N. DuPont Highway 2nd Fl. Annex Admin. Bldg. New Castle, DE 19720 302-577-4791

Insurance Counseling	Insurance Department	Agency on Aging
DISTRICT OF COLUMBIA 202-994-7463	Insurance Department 613 G St., NW Room 638 P.O. Box 37200 Washington, DC 20001-7200 202-727-8009	Office on Aging 441 4th St., NW 9th Floor Washington, D.C. 20001 202-724-5626 202-724-5622
FLORIDA 904-922-2073	Department of Insurance 200 E. Gaines St. Tallahassee, FL 32399-0300 904-922-3100	Department of Elder Affairs 1317 Winewood Blvd. Building 1, Room 317 Tallahassee, FL 32399-0700 904-922-5297
GEORGIA 800-669-8387	Insurance Department 2 Martin L. King, Jr., Dr. 716 West Tower Atlanta, GA 30334 404-656-2056	Division of Aging Services Dept. of Human Resources 2 Peachtree St., NW, Rm 18.403 Atlanta, GA 30303 404-657-5258
HAWAII 808-586-0100	Department of Commerce and Consumer Affairs Insurance Division P.O. Box 3614 Honolulu, HI 96811 808-586-2790	Executive Office on Aging 335 Merchant St. Room 241 Honolulu, HI 96813 808-586-0100
IDAHO 800-247-4422	Insurance Department Public Service Department 700 W. State St., 3rd Fl. Boise, ID 83720 208-334-4350	Office on Aging Statehouse, Room 108 Boise, ID 83720 208-334-3833
ILLINOIS 800-252-8966	Insurance Department 320 W. Washington St. 4th Floor Springfield, IL 62767 217-782-4515	Department on Aging 421 E. Capitol Ave. Springfield, IL 62701 217-785-3356
INDIANA 800-452-4800	Insurance Department 311 W. Washington St. Suite 300 Indianapolis, IN 46204 800-622-4461 317-232-2395	Division of Aging & Home Services 402 W. Washington St. P.O. Box 7083 Indianapolis, IN 46207-7083 800-545-7763 317-232-7020
IOWA 515-281-5705	Insurance Division Lucas State Office Bldg. E. 12th & Grand Sts. 6th Floor Des Moines, IA 50319 515-281-5705	Department of Elder Affairs Jewett Bldg., Suite 236 914 Grand Ave. Des Moines, IA 50309 515-281-5187

Insurance Counseling	Insurance Department	Agency on Aging
KANSAS 800-432-3535	Insurance Department 420 S.W. 9th St. Topeka, KS 66612 800-432-2484 913-296-3071	Department on Aging 150-S. Docking State Office Building 915 S.W. Harrison Topeka, KS 66612-1500 913-296-4986
KENTUCKY 800-372-2991	Insurance Department 229 W. Main St. P.O. Box 517 Frankfort, KY 40602 502-564-3630	Division of Aging Services Cabinet for Human Resources 275 E. Main St., 5th Floor, West Frankfort, KY 40621 502-564-6930
LOUISIANA 800-259-5301 504-342-5301	Senior Health Insurance Information Program (SHIIP) Insurance Department P.O. Box 94214 Baton Rouge, LA 70804-9214 800-259-5301 504-342-5301	Governor's Office of Elderly Affairs 4550 N. Blvd. P.O. Box 80374 Baton Rouge, LA 70896-0374 504-925-1700
MAINE 800-750-5353 207-624-5335	Bureau of Insurance Consumer Division State House, Station 34 Augusta, ME 04333 207-582-8707	Bureau of Elder and Adult Services State House, Station 11 Augusta, ME 04333 207-624-5335
MARYLAND 800-243-3425	Insurance Administration Complaints and Investigation Unit – Life & Health 501 St. Paul Place Baltimore, MD 21202-2272 410-333-2793 410-333-2770	Office on Aging 301 W. Preston St. Room 1004 Baltimore, MD 21201 410-225-1102
MASSACHUSETTS 800-882-2003 617-727-7750	Insurance Division Consumer Services Section 470 Atlantic Ave. Boston, MA 02210-2223 617-521-7777	Executive Office of Elder Affairs 1 Ashburton Place, 5th Floor Boston, MA 02108 800-882-2003 617-727-7750
MICHIGAN 517-373-8230	Insurance Bureau P.O. Box 30220 Lansing, Ml 48909 517-373-0240 (General Assistance) 517-335-1702 (Senior Issues)	Office of Services to the Aging 611 W. Ottawa St. P.O. Box 30026 Lansing, MI 48909 517-373-8230
MINNESOTA 800-882-6262	Insurance Department Department of Commerce 133 E. 7th St. St. Paul, MN 55101-2362 612-296-4026	Board on Aging Human Services Building 4th Floor 444 Lafayette Rd. St. Paul, MN 55155-3843 612-296-2770

Insurance Counseling	Insurance Department	Agency on Aging
MISSISSIPPI 800-948-3090	Insurance Department Consumer Assistance Division P.O. Box 79 Jackson, MS 39205 601-359-3569	Div. of Aging & Adult Services 750 N. State St. Jackson, MS 39202 800-948-3090 601-359-4929
MISSOURI 800-390-3330	Department of Insurance Consumer Services Section P.O. Box 690 Jefferson City, MO 65102-0690 800-726-7390 314-751-2640	Division of Aging Department of Social Services P.O. Box 1337 615 Howerton Court Jefferson City, MO 65102-1337 314-751-3082
MONTANA 800-332-2272	Insurance Department 126 N. Sanders Mitchell Bldg., Rm. 270 P.O. Box 4009 Helena, MT 59601 406-444-2040	Office on Aging 48 N. Last Chance Gulch P.O. Box 8005 Helena, MT 59620 800-332-2272 406-444-5900
NEBRASKA 402-471-4506	Insurance Department Terminal Building 941 "O" St., Suite 400 Lincoln, NE 68508 402-471-2201	Department on Aging State Office Building 301 Centennial Mall South Lincoln, NE 68509-5044 402-471-2306
NEVADA 800-307-4444 702-367-1218	Dept. of Business & Industry Division of Insurance 1665 Hot Springs Rd., Ste. 152 Carson City, NV 89710 800-992-0900 702-687-4270	Dept. of Human Resources Division for Aging Services 340 N. 11th St., Suite 114 Las Vegas, NV 89101 702-486-3545
NEW HAMPSHIRE 603-271-4642	Insurance Department Life and Health Division 169 Manchester St. Concord, NH 03301 800-852-3416 603-271-2261	Department of Health & Human Services Div. of Elderly & Adult Services State Office Park South 115 Pleasant St. Annex Building No. 1 Concord, NH 03301 603-271-4680
NEW JERSEY 800-792-8820	Insurance Department 20 West State St. Roebling Building CN 325 Trenton, NJ 08625 609-292-5363	Dept. of Community Affairs Division on Aging S. Broad and Front Sts. CN 807 Trenton, NJ 08625-0807 800-792-8820 609-984-3951
NEW MEXICO 800-432-2080	Insurance Department P.O. Drawer 1269 Santa Fe, NM 87504-1269 505-827-4500	State Agency on Aging La Villa Rivera Bldg. 224 E. Palace Ave. Santa Fe, NM 87501 800-432-2080 505-827-7640

Insurance Counseling	Insurance Department	Agency on Aging
NEW YORK 800-333-4114	Insurance Department 160 West Broadway New York, NY 10013 212-602-0203 Outside of New York City 800-342-3736	State Office for the Aging 2 Empire State Plaza Albany, NY 12223-0001 800-342-9871 518-474-5731
NORTH CAROLINA 800-443-9354	Insurance Department Seniors' Health Insurance Information Program (SHIIP) P.O. Box 26387 Raleigh, NC 27611 800-662-7777 (Consumer Services) 919-733-0111 (SHIIP)	Division of Aging 693 Palmer Drive Caller Box 29531 Raleigh, NC 27626-0531 919-733-3983
NORTH DAKOTA 800-247-0560	Insurance Department Capitol Bldg., 5th Fl. 600 E. Blvd. Bismarck, ND 58505-0320 800-247-0560 701-224-2440	Department of Human Services Aging Services Division P.O. Box 7070 Bismarck, ND 58507-7070 701-224-2577
OHIO 800-686-1578	Insurance Department Consumer Services Division 2100 Stella Court Columbus, OH 43266-0566 800-686-1526 614-644-2673	Department of Aging 50 W. Broad St. 9th Floor Columbus, OH 43266-0501 800-282-1206 614-466-1221
OKLAHOMA 405-521-6628	Insurance Department P.O Box 53408 Oklahoma City, OK 73152-3408 405-521-6628	Department of Human Services Aging Services Division 312 NE 28th St. Oklahoma City, OK 73125 405-521-2327
OREGON 800-722-4134	Department of Consumer & Business Services Senior Health Insurance Benefits Assistance 470 Labor & Industries Bldg. Salem, OR 97310 800-722-4134 503-378-4484	Dept. of Human Resources Senior & Disabled Services Div. 500 Summer St., NE, 2nd Floor Salem, OR 97310-1015 800-232-8096 503-378-4728
PENNSYLVANIA 717-783-8975	Insurance Department Consumer Services Bureau 1321 Strawberry Square Harrisburg, PA 17120 717-787-2317	Department of Aging 400 Market St. State Office Building Harrisburg, PA 17101 717-783-1550
PUERTO RICO 809-721-5710	Office of the Commissioner of Insurance P.O. Box 8330 San Juan, PR 00910-8330 809-722-8686	Governor's Office of Elderly Affairs Gericulture Commission Box 11398 Santurce, PR 00910 809-722-2429

Insurance Counseling	Insurance Department	Agency on Aging
RHODE ISLAND 800-322-2880	Insurance Division 233 Richmond St., Suite 233 Providence, RI 02903-4233 401-277-2223	Department of Elderly Affairs 160 Pine St. Providence, RI 02903 401-277-2858
SOUTH CAROLINA 800-868-9095	Department of Insurance Consumer Services Section P.O. Box 100105 Columbia, SC 29202-3105 800-768-3467 803-737-6180	Division on Aging 202 Arbor Lake Drive Suite 301 Columbia, SC 29223-4554 803-737-7500
SOUTH DAKOTA 605-773-3656	Insurance Department 500 E. Capitol Ave. Pierre, SD 57501-5070 605-773-3563	Office of Adult Services and Aging 700 Governors Drive Pierre, SD 57501-2291 605-773-3656
TENNESSEE 800-525-2816	Dept. of Commerce & Insurance Insurance Assistance Office 4th Floor 500 James Robertson Pkwy. Nashville, TN 37243 800-525-2816 615-741-4955	Commission on Aging 706 Church St. Suite 201 Nashville, TN 37243-0860 615-741-2056
TEXAS 800-252-3439	Department of Insurance Complaints Resolution, MC 111-lA 333 Guadalupe St. P.O. Box 149091 Austin, TX 78714-9091 800-252-3439 512-463-6515	Department on Aging P.O. Box 12786 (78711) 1949 IH 35 South Austin, TX 78741 800-252-9240 512-444-2727
UTAH 801-538-3910	Insurance Department Consumer Services 3110 State Office Bldg. Salt Lake City, UT 84114-1201 800-439-3805 801-538-3805	Division of Aging and Adult Services 120 North 200 West P.O. Box 45500 Salt Lake City, UT 84145-0500 801-538-3910
VERMONT 800-642-5119	Dept. of Banking & Insurance Consumer Complaint Division 89 Main St., Drawer 20 Montpelier, VT 05620-3101 802-828-3301	Dept. Of Aging & Disabilities Waterbury Complex 103 S. Main St. Waterbury, VT 05671-2301 802-241-2400
VIRGINIA 800-552-4464	Bureau of Insurance Consumer Services Division 1300 E. Main St. P.O. Box 1157 Richmond, VA 23209 800-552-7945 804-371-9741	Department for the Aging 700 Centre, 10th Floor 700 E. Franklin St. Richmond, VA 23219-2327 800-552-4464 804-225-2271

Insurance Counseling	Insurance Department	Agency on Aging
WASHINGTON 800-397-4422	Insurance Department Insurance Bldg. P.O. Box 40255 Olympia, WA 98504-0255 800-562-6900 206-753-7300	Aging & Adult Services Admin. Department of Social & Health Services P.O. Box 45050 Olympia, WA 98504-5050 206-586-3768
WEST VIRGINIA 304-558-3317	Insurance Department Consumer Service Division 2019 Washington St., E. Charleston, WV 25305 800-642-9004 800-435-7381 (hearing impaired) 304-558-3386	Commission on Aging State Capitol Complex Holly Grove 1900 Kanawha Blvd., East Charleston, WV 25305-0160 304-558-3317
WISCONSIN 800-242-1060	Insurance Department Complaints Department P.O. Box 7873 Madison, WI 53707 800-236-8517 608-266-0103	Board on Aging and Long Term Care 214 N. Hamilton St. Madison, WI 53703 800-242-1060 608-266-8944
WYOMING 800-438-5768	Insurance Department Herschler Building 122 W. 25th St. Cheyenne, WY 82002 800-438-5768 307-777-7401	Division on Aging Hathaway Building 2300 Capitol Ave., Room 139 Cheyenne, WY 82002 800-442-2766 307-777-7986

INDEX

401(k) Plans   14, 28, 30-35, 37, 43, 44, 47, 48, 53, 54, 56, 58, 101, 105, 112

403(b) Plans 28, 30, 31, 33, 34, 37, 54

457 Plans 28, 30, 31, 33

A

Annual Report of Earnings 82

Asset allocation..........................63, 104-107

B

Beneficiaries 73, 90, 116, 120, 121, 123, 125-140, 144, 145

   Distributions among.......................128, 129, 131, 135, 139

   Naming 64, 116, 125, 126, 128, 129, 133

   of insurance policies 116, 129, 133

   of IRAs 57, 64

   of wills and trusts...........116, 121, 123, 125, 127-140, 144, 145

Bismarck, Otto von 69

Blind trusts..141

Blue Cross/Blue Shield...................151, 164

Bonds and bond funds ....7, 34, 52, 73, 91, 93-96, 99-103, 105-109, 111, 113, ...115-117, 133

Bonding...127

C

Capital gains........14, 18, 20, 45, 52, 72, 73, 99, 113, 114, 140, 143-145

CDs...............................7, 52, 53, 94-97, 99, 100, 102, 103, 105-109

Charitable gifts 121, 140, 144

Choices in Dying 15

CMOs (Collateralized Mortgage Obligations) 103, 107,

COBRA insurance 151

Codicil...123, 125

Cohen, Ira..53

COLAs (cost of living adjustments)..............25, 26, 27, 49, 71, 73, 79, 89, 155

Cost basis............................20, 21, 143-145

Crummey, D. Clifford 137

Crummey power 137

D

Deferred annuities.............23, 41, 112, 113

   Fixed 41, 112, 113

   Variable 23, 41, 52, 53, 112, 113

Defined benefit plans 24-29, 31, 34, 39, 41, 43, 44, 47-49, 60, 62, 63

Defined contribution plans........24, 25, 28, 29, 31, 33, 34, 39, 49, 62

   Employee stock ownership plans 28

   Matching funds 28, 32, 33, 37, 58, 59

   Money purchase plans 28, 29, 62, 63

   Profit sharing plans 28, 29, 43, 46, 47, 62, 63

   Salary reduction plans 30-33, 37, 58, 59, 112

   Thrift or savings plans 28

Diversification................................100, 101

Dollar cost averaging...............................98

Durable power of attorney 15, 119, 135

E

Early retirement 7, 47

Employee Retirement Income Security Act (ERISA)....................................49, 53

Equity investments 31, 92, 94, 100, 101

Estate.........17, 18, 42, 57, 64, 116-145, 173

Estate taxes...................7, 10, 11, 116, 117, 119-121, 124, 131-133, 135-143, 145

   Excess accumulations 39, 121, 131

   Tax rates 120, 121, 137

Estimated taxes 12, 91

Executor(s) 121, 123, 126, 127, 130, 131, 134

F

Fair market value.............17, 117, 140, 145

Family limited partnerships 145

Federal Deposit Insurance Corporation (FDIC)..................................53, 103, 106

Federal Home Mortgage Association (FHMA) 19

Federal Housing Administration (FHA) 19

Federal Insurance Contribution Act (FICA) 68, 78

Fixed income investments 7, 31, 33-35, 95, 100, 107

Forward averaging....................14, 40, 41, 45, 46, 58, 61, 63, 113

Fuller, Ira...71

G

Government National Mortgage
Association (GNMA) 107
Guaranteed Investment Contracts
(GICs) 35
Guardian (s) 123, 126, 127, 135
  of the property...................................127

H

Health Care Financing Administration
(HCFA) 155, 165
Health care proxy 15
Health insurance.....8, 9, 11, 12, 13, 49, 68,
129, 146-153, 158, 160, 165-167
  Balanced billing 158
  Coordination of benefits 150
  Co-payment....................146, 147, 152,
158, 164, 166, 167
  Conversion policy............................151
  Deductible..................146, 156-158, 162
  Enrollment 149, 155, 159
  Flexible benefit plan 147
  Group plans 9, 147, 150,
151, 164, 167
  Indemnity plans..............................149
  Individual plans 146, 147,
151, 164, 167, 171
  Participating providers.........147, 152,
157, 158
  Pre-existing conditions...148, 163, 170
  Premium..................147, 148, 155, 156,
159, 163, 164, 169-171
  Renewable policies 147, 148, 165
Heirs 7, 11, 18, 116, 120, 121, 123,
125, 128, 130, 131, 133, 138, 139,
140, 171, 173
HMOs 147, 152, 153, 160, 165

I

Immediate annuities 113-115
Inflation 9, 10, 41, 44, 47, 48,
57, 71, 77-79, 92-95, 100-104,
106, 112, 115, 121, 145, 169, 170
Inheritance taxes...........120, 133, 135, 145
Integrated pension plans 24
Internal Revenue Service (IRS) 12, 21,
23, 33, 39, 43, 45, 55,
58-60, 63-68, 71, 91, 99

Intestate 122, 123, 127
Investment(s) 6, 7, 9-11, 13, 16,
22, 23, 25, 29-35, 37, 41, 43,
44, 46-54, 56, 57, 60-67, 72,
73, 75, 82, 91, 93-116, 121,
132, 133, 135, 139, 140, 143
  Risk..................................6, 7, 34, 35, 98,
102-104, 106, 107, 109, 111
  Strategy 10, 33, 52,
66, 67, 96-99, 106, 109
  Styles 98
IRA contributions 44, 48, 50, 51,
53-55, 57-59, 92
  Contribution limits ...50, 51, 58, 59, 61
  Non-deductible 53-55, 57
  Tax-deductible 50-52
IRA rollovers 38, 40, 44,
46, 47, 56, 57, 63, 121
IRA withdrawals.........................13, 15, 46,
52-57, 64-67, 91, 96
  Annuitized..65
  Early withdrawal penalties..... 41, 46,
54, 56, 57, 65, 96
  Required 13, 15, 41, 64, 65-67
  Taxes on 13, 44, 46, 52,
54-57, 64-67
IRAs
  Advantages and disadvantages 54,
55, 61, 64
  Fees...52, 57
  Rollover IRAs 38, 40, 44,
46, 47, 56, 57, 121
  Rules governing 50, 51,
55, 56, 58, 59, 64
  Segregated IRAs 45, 57

  Term certain withdrawals 66
IRS Forms and Publications
  Form 2119..21
  Forms 5500-C, EZ, R 63
  Publication 523...................................21
  Publication 524...................................13
  Publication 590............................64, 67

J

Joint and survivor annuity ...38, 41-43, 115
Joint tenants with rights of survival 118

K

Keogh, Eugene 61
Keogh Plans...............14, 39, 53, 54, 56, 58,
        60-63, 66, 69, 92, 93, 96, 121
Keogh trusts 61, 63

L

Laddering investments....................99, 115
Living wills 14, 15
Long-term care insurance..............168-171

M

Marital deduction 121, 139, 143
Medicaid 141, 162, 168, 172, 173
    Qualifying for 141, 168, 173
    Medicaid trusts 141, 173
Medical Information Bureau (MIB)....149
Medicare................11-13, 15, 71-73, 76, 77,
        89, 146, 154-167, 170, 172
    Appeals 157, 161, 166
    Approved charges 157, 158, 163
    Assignment..158
    Claims..................................13, 155-158,
        161, 166, 167
    Coverage 11, 146, 154-159, 170
    Enrollment 154, 155, 159
    Excess charges 158, 159, 162, 164
    Limitation liability 157
    Losing coverage 159
    Part A 154-157, 159, 161-163
    Part B...........................154-159, 161-163
    Paying for 71-73, 77, 154-156
    Prospective payment system 160
    Qualifying for 15, 76, 89,
        146, 154, 159
Medigap insurance 162-168, 170, 172
    Core package 163
    Alternatives to..................................165
    Loss ratios 167
    Filing claims...........................166, 167
Mutual funds 6, 7, 9, 33-35,
        52, 53, 56, 57, 67, 71, 92-94, 96,
        98-103, 105-107, 110-112, 116-118

N

Nolo press...124

O

Ownership, types of 118

P

Payee representative...............................119
Peer Review Organizations (PROs) 160
Pension Benefit Guaranty
    Corporation (PBGC) 41, 49
Pension Rights Center.............................49
Pensions...........6, 7, 9-11, 13-15, 22-49, 54,
        56-63, 66, 68, 69, 72, 73, 79, 82,
        89-96, 101, 113-117, 129, 132, 173
    Calculating size of 26, 44
    Collecting on 7, 24, 36, 38-49
    Contribution limits 22, 25,
        33, 37, 58-63
    Self-directed pensions 34, 35,
        58, 61, 63
    Supplemental plans (SERPs) 36, 37
    Underfunding 41, 48, 49
Pension annuities 38-44, 47, 49, 114
Pension maximization 41
Pension payouts 14, 22, 24,
        36, 37, 39, 40, 42-45, 49, 56,
        57, 62, 63, 66, 101, 116, 132
    Lump sum payments 39, 40, 42-45,
        49, 56, 57, 63
    Payout limits 22, 39, 66, 67
    Periodic payments 39, 40, 43
Period certain annuity 43, 115
Personal Benefit Statement...................77
Power of attorney.....................15, 119, 135
    Durable power 15, 119, 135
    Springing power..............................119
Probate 17, 122-127, 129-135
Property...................14-16, 18, 20, 21, 109,
        116-123, 125-141, 144, 145, 173
    Jointly held 103, 118, 123, 129, 139
    Personal 116, 117, 121, 173
    Real 16-21, 116-118, 120,
        121, 127, 134, 139, 145

Q

Qualified transfer...................................143

INDEX

R

Real rate of growth 94, 95
Retirement plans 10-13, 22-33,
    36, 37, 39, 44-47, 50, 51, 54,
    56-66, 68, 69, 90, 92, 93, 96, 101,
    105, 112, 113, 115, 117, 120, 121
  Contributions to 6, 22-25, 28-34,
    36, 37, 47, 50, 51, 53, 54, 57-63
  Early withdrawal penalties 10, 37,
    41, 45, 46, 54, 57, 96, 106
  Nonqualified plans 23, 36
  Qualified plans ...11, 13, 22, 23, 37, 39,
    56, 58-61, 63, 105, 117, 121
  Supplemental plans (SERPs) 36, 37
  Taxes on 6, 7, 11, 13, 22-24,
    30, 31, 33, 36, 37, 39, 41,
    44-47, 50, 53, 54-57, 60,
    63-67, 112, 113, 115, 121
  Withdrawals from 12-15, 38-41,
    44-46, 53, 54-57, 61, 63-67, 96, 113
Return 34, 35, 52, 57, 94,
    95, 98, 102, 105, 107-113
  Annual return 105, 110, 111
  Total return 110, 111
Reverse mortgages 18, 19
Risk ratio 102
Roosevelt, Franklin 68
Rule of 72 95

S

Sale-leaseback 17
SAR-SEPS 58, 59
Second-to-die insurance 140
SEPs 14, 39, 54, 58-61, 66, 69, 92, 93
Severance 47
Single life annuity 38, 41-43, 115
Social Security 6, 11, 13-15,
    24, 25, 68-91, 155
  Appeals 75, 88, 89
  Applying for 74, 79-81, 85, 86, 88
  Bend points 78
  Benefit limits 75, 81-83, 85, 87
  Collecting benefits 69, 73,
    76-85, 87, 89-91
  Disability benefits 70, 72, 73, 75,
    77, 85, 88, 89
  Employee contributions 68, 69,
    72, 90
  Employer contributions 69, 72, 73
  Family coverage 84-87
  Former families 85-87
  Medicare contributions 72, 155

Opening an account 71, 74
Primary insurance
  amount (PIA) 78, 81
Qualifying for coverage 76, 84,
    87, 89
Self-employed contributions 69, 73
Survivor benefits 68-70,
    72-74, 77, 84-89
Taxes on benefits 13, 70, 73, 90, 91
Using a representative 75
Social Security Act 68
Social Security
  Administration (SSA) 74, 75, 77-89
Social Security card 70, 71
Social Security forms
  SS-4 12
  SS-5 74
  SSA-7004-SM 77
  SSA-777 77
Social Security number 70, 71, 74, 133
Stocks and stock funds 6, 7, 28, 29,
    33-35, 39, 46, 47, 52, 67, 91-94,
    96, 98-103, 105-107, 110, 111,
    115-118, 121, 125, 137, 139, 144
Supplemental Security
  Income (SSI) 70, 75, 88, 89

T

Tax-deferred investment 11, 22, 23,
    30-37, 41, 44, 50, 52, 53,
    57-65, 112, 113, 115, 121
Tax-exempt gifts 121, 137, 142-145
Tax-exempt investments 52, 91, 99, 113
Tax exclusion (real estate) 14, 21
TIAA-CREF 33, 47
Top hat plans 37
Truman, Harry 160
Trust(s) 10, 11,
    36, 61, 63, 72, 73, 88, 116, 118,
    121, 123, 127, 129, 132-141, 173
  By-pass trusts 138
  Charitable 140
  Crummey trust 137
  Generation-skipping trusts 131, 137
  Irrevocable 134, 136, 137,
    141, 144, 173
  Life insurance 140
  Living, or inter vivos 123, 129, 132,
    134, 135, 140
  Marital 139
  Pour over 132
  QTIP 139
  Revocable 134, 135, 144

Spendthrift clause 137
Sprinkling 139
Testamentary 121, 132, 138, 139
Trust taxes 132, 133, 135-143
Trustee(s) 127, 132-136, 138-141

U

Underwriting 149
Post-claims underwriting 171
Unified tax credit 120, 131,
137-139, 142
Uniform Gifts to Minors
(UGMA) 117, 142, 143
Uniform Transfers to Minors
(UTMA) 117, 142, 143

V

Vested pension rights 27, 29, 47, 58
Veteran's Administration 9
Variable annuities.................23, 33, 41, 52,
53, 112, 113

W

Will(s) 11, 14, 15, 21, 116,
122-131, 132, 138, 144, 145
Electing against a will 123
Execution of 124
Executor 121, 123, 126,
127, 130, 131, 134
Holograph...122
Nuncupative......................................122
Per capita 129
Per stirpes 129
Simultaneous death 125
Withholding...........................12, 56, 57, 68,
71-73, 77, 155
Working after retirement 82, 83

X Y Z

Yield 93, 99, 103, 107-109, 111

Written by authors with 25 years of experience in the financial and communications fields, these visually appealing, user-friendly guides painlessly initiate you into the mysteries of money and investing. They point out the things you need to know to make smart financial decisions—and to avoid the pitfalls.

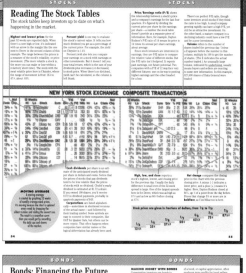

THE GUIDE THAT HELPS YOU UNDERSTAND TAXES, THE IRS, AND HOW THE TAX SYSTEMS WORKS— EVEN BEFORE YOU PICK UP YOUR RETURN.

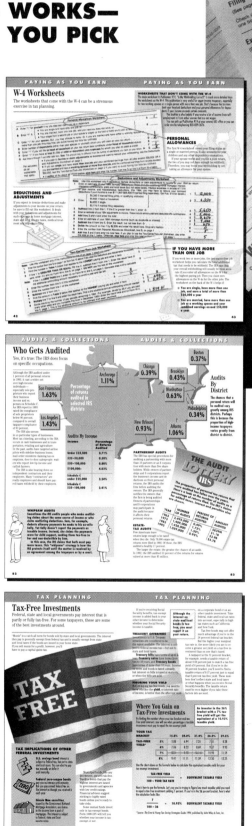

Written by authors with years of experience in tax journalism and tax form simplification, this visually appealing, user-friendly guide uncovers the mysteries surrounding taxes. You'll find clear, illustrated pages explaining the different types of taxes we pay, how to survive an audit, and how to plan for and reduce your taxes.

This Wall Street Journal guide tells you in plain, everyday English what you need to know about:

- The tax system

- The IRS and recent changes in the tax code

- Withholding and estimated taxes

- Your annual return and other forms

- What records to keep

- Audits, and how to prepare for them

- Tax planning for the short and long term

JUST $14.95.
AVAILABLE AT BOOKSTORES EVERYWHERE.

Or from:
Lightbulb Press
1185 Avenue of the Americas
New York, NY 10036

Phone   800-581-9884
              212-575-0513

Fax   212-575-2903